Nineteenth-Century Major Lives and Letters

Series Editor: Marilyn Gaull

This series presents original biographical, critical, and scholarly studies of literary works and public figures in Great Britain, North America, and continental Europe during the nineteenth century. The volumes in *Nineteenth-Century Major Lives and Letters* evoke the energies, achievements, contributions, cultural traditions, and individuals who reflected and generated them during the Romantic and Victorian period. The topics: critical, textual, and historical scholarship, literary and book history, biography, cultural and comparative studies, critical theory, art, architecture, science, politics, religion, music, language, philosophy, aesthetics, law, publication, translation, domestic and public life, popular culture, and anything that influenced, impinges upon, expresses or contributes to an understanding of the authors, works, and events of the nineteenth century. The authors consist of political figures, artists, scientists, and cultural icons including William Blake, Thomas Hardy, Charles Darwin, William Wordsworth, William Butler Yeats, Samuel Taylor, and their contemporaries.

The series editor is Marilyn Gaull, PhD (Indiana University), FEA. She has taught at William and Mary, Temple University, New York University, and is Research Professor at the Editorial Institute at Boston University. She is the founder and editor of *The Wordsworth Circle* and the author of *English Romanticism: The Human Context*, and editions, essays, and reviews in journals. She lectures internationally on British Romanticism, folklore, and narrative theory, intellectual history, publishing procedures, and history of science.

PUBLISHED BY PALGRAVE MACMILLAN:

Shelley's German Afterlives, by Susanne Schmid
Coleridge, the Bible, and Religion, by Jeffrey W. Barbeau
Romantic Literature, Race, and Colonial Encounter, by Peter J. Kitson
Byron, edited by Cheryl A. Wilson
Romantic Migrations, by Michael Wiley
The Long and Winding Road from Blake to the Beatles, by Matthew Schneider
British Periodicals and Romantic Identity, by Mark Schoenfield
Women Writers and Nineteenth-Century Medievalism, by Clare Broome Saunders
British Victorian Women's Periodicals, by Kathryn Ledbetter
Romantic Diasporas, by Toby R. Benis
Romantic Literary Families, by Scott Krawczyk
Victorian Christmas in Print, by Tara Moore
Culinary Aesthetics and Practices in Nineteenth-Century American Literature, edited by Monika Elbert and Marie Drews
Reading Popular Culture in Victorian Print, by Alberto Gabriele
Romanticism and the Object, edited by Larry H. Peer
Poetics en passant, by Anne Jamison
From Song to Print, by Terence Hoagwood
Gothic Romanticism, by Tom Duggett
Victorian Medicine and Social Reform, by Louise Penner
Populism, Gender, and Sympathy in the Romantic Novel, by James P. Carson
Byron and the Rhetoric of Italian Nationalism, by Arnold A. Schmidt
Poetry and Public Discourse in Nineteenth-Century America, by Shira Wolosky
The Discourses of Food in Nineteenth-Century British Fiction, by Annette Cozzi
Romanticism and Pleasure, edited by Thomas H. Schmid and Michelle Faubert

Royal Romances, by Kristin Flieger Samuelian
Trauma, Transcendence, and Trust, by Thomas J. Brennan, S.J.
The Business of Literary Circles in Nineteenth-Century America, by David Dowling
Popular Medievalism in Romantic-Era Britain, by Clare A. Simmons
Beyond Romantic Ecocriticism, by Ashton Nichols
The Poetry of Mary Robinson, by Daniel Robinson
Romanticism and the City, by Larry H. Peer
Coleridge and the Daemonic Imagination, by Gregory Leadbetter
Dante and Italy in British Romanticism, edited by Frederick Burwick and
  Paul Douglass
Romantic Dharma, by Mark Lussier
Jewish Representation in British Literature 1780–1840, by Michael Scrivener

FORTHCOMING TITLES:

Robert Southey, by Stuart Andrews
Playing to the Crowd, by Frederick Burwick
The Regions of Sara Coleridge's Thought, by Peter Swaab

DANTE AND ITALY IN
BRITISH ROMANTICISM

Edited by
Frederick Burwick
and
Paul Douglass

palgrave
macmillan

First published in 2011 by
PALGRAVE MACMILLAN®
in the United States—a division of St. Martin's Press LLC,
175 Fifth Avenue, New York, NY 10010.

Where this book is distributed in the UK, Europe and the rest of the world,
this is by Palgrave Macmillan, a division of Macmillan Publishers Limited,
registered in England, company number 785998, of Houndmills,
Basingstoke, Hampshire RG21 6XS.

Palgrave Macmillan is the global academic imprint of the above companies
and has companies and representatives throughout the world.

Palgrave® and Macmillan® are registered trademarks in the United States,
the United Kingdom, Europe and other countries.

ISBN: 978–0–230–11448–7

Library of Congress Cataloging-in-Publication Data

Burwick, Frederick.
    Dante and Italy in British Romanticism / Frederick Burwick, Paul
Douglass [editors].
        p. cm.—(Nineteenth-century major lives and letters)
        ISBN 978–0–230–11448–7 (hardback)
        1. Romanticism—Great Britain. 2. English literature—Italian influences.
3. Italian literature—Appreciation—Great Britain. 4. Dante Alighieri,
1265–1321—Influence. 5. Dante Alighieri, 1265–1321—Criticism and
interpretation. 6. Italy—In literature. I. Douglass, Paul, 1951– II. Title.

PR448.I73B87 2011
820.9'007—dc22   2011005261

A catalogue record of the book is available from the British Library.

Design by Newgen Imaging Systems (P) Ltd., Chennai, India.

First edition: September 2011

10 9 8 7 6 5 4 3 2 1

Transferred to Digital Printing in 2012

The Brightness of the World, O thou once free,
And always fair, rare Land of Courtesy!
O Florence! with the Tuscan Fields and Hills,
And famous Arno fed with all their Rills;
Thou brightest Star of Star-bright Italy!

— *Samuel Taylor Coleridge,*
The Garden of Boccaccio, *ll. 73–77*

The fifth canto of Dante pleases me more and more—it is that
one in which he meets with Paulo and Francesca—...I dreamt
of being in that region of Hell. The dream was one of the most
delightful enjoyments I ever had in my life...O that I could dream
it every night.

— *John Keats, Letter of April 16, 1819*

Yet, Italy! through every other land
Thy wrongs should ring, and shall, from side to side;
. . . . .
Europe, repentant of her parricide,
Shall yet redeem thee, and, all backward driven,
Roll the barbarian tide, and sue to be forgiven.

— *Lord Byron,* Childe Harold *4.47*

Also by Frederick Burwick and Paul Douglass:

A Selection of Hebrew Melodies, Ancient and Modern, by Isaac Nathan and Lord Byron, 1988.
The Crisis in Modernism: Bergson and the Vitalist Controversy, 1992.

Also by Frederick Burwick:

Romantic Drama: Acting and Reacting, 2009.
Mimesis and Its Romantic Reflections, 2001.
Thomas De Quincey: Knowledge and Power, 2001.
Poetic Madness and the Romantic Imagination, 1996.
Illusion and the Drama: Critical Theory of the Enlightenment and Romantic Era, 1991.
The Haunted Eye: Perception and the Grotesque in English and German Romanticism, 1987.
The Damnation of Newton: Goethe's Color Theory and Romantic Perception, 1986.

Also by Paul Douglass:

The Works of Lady Caroline Lamb, ed. with Leigh Wetherall Dickson, 2009.
The Whole Disgraceful Truth: Selected Letters of Lady Caroline Lamb, 2006.
Lady Caroline Lamb: A Biography, 2004.
Bergson, Eliot, and American Literature, 1986.

CONTENTS

Acknowledgments

The editors are very thankful for the support of the Romualdo del Bianco Foundation of Florence in providing the symposium venue that afforded the occasion for the sharing of scholarly work from which *Dante and Italy in British Romanticism* has been drawn. In particular, the editors wish to thank Paolo del Bianco, Carlotta del Bianco, and Simone Giometti, Secretary General of the Foundation. We admire the work of the Foundation deeply and encourage readers to learn more about its mission to encourage an exchange of knowledge among students, academicians and professionals from universities, libraries, museums, and other public and private cultural institutions and organizations worldwide. The editors express their gratitude to Silvia Benvenuto for preparing an excellent index for this volume.

The editors and contributors also owe a special thanks to Marilyn Gaull for her mentorship and support, and to the members of the editorial team at Palgrave Macmillan.

INTRODUCTION

Frederick Burwick and Paul Douglass

The Grand Tour, intended to provide an elegant polish to the education of young men of the landed gentry and nobility, typically took the wealthy traveler and his entourage through France to Venice, Florence, and Rome to wander amidst the ruins of classical antiquity and behold the great treasures of the Renaissance.[1] The nature of the traditional tour was altered by the French Revolution, not simply because the route to Italy was shifted through the Lowlands, the German provinces, and over the Swiss Alps, but also because travelers were more frequently accosted by banditti on the highways and by beggars and unscrupulous merchants in the cities (Chaney 209–212). In addition, the streets of London were soon crowded with Italian immigrants hawking the same wares that were displayed in the market places of Italy. As the Romantic era dawned, the Italian experience of the Grand Tour had been radically recontextualized by political and economic conditions affecting all of Europe. Italy took on new and altered meanings for the Romantics. This fact, though widely recognized, has not been rigorously assessed, especially in light of today's richly inclusive canon of Romantic-era literature. The essays in *Dante and Italy in British Romanticism* thus undertake a major task: a significant reevaluation of the role that Dante, Italian language, and Italian culture played in the formation of the Romantic movement. The reassessment comes from two angles. First, it recognizes those major revisions that have taken place in our understanding of what Romantic-era literature is and who wrote it. Second, it probes and extends readings of the Romantic writers in an ever-widening context of Italian cultural expression as it was disseminated, adulterated, valorized, and transformed by and in their works.

Although the Romantics, like their predecessors, celebrated Italian art and architecture, literature and music, there were also a few detractors and denouncers of contemporary Italy and Italians. William Hazlitt was among the more outspoken critics, a xenophobic observer of the Italians in London, and a malcontent spectator in the opera houses of Turin and Parma. Licentious and unwashed, Italians also "cheat, steal, rob (when they think it worth their while to do) with licensed impunity."[2] When Hazlitt himself embarked on the Grand Tour with the goal of seeing the great art works of the Italian Renaissance, he noted the absence of any models of feminine beauty.

> The women of Italy (so far as I have seen hitherto) are detestably ugly, They are not even dark and swarthy, but a mixture of brown and red, coarse, marked with the small pox, with pug features, awkward, ill-made, fierce, dirty, lazy, neither attempting, nor hoping to please.[3]

If there were such a thing as an Italian beauty, Hazlitt surmises, it must be such a rare treasure that it is kept concealed from the "common gaze." Eager to experience the much vaunted Italian opera, Hazlitt in Turin discovers instead, "the extravagance of incessant dumb-show . . . and heroines like furies in hysterics."

> Nothing at Bartholomew Fair was ever in worse taste, noisier, or finer. It was as if a whole people had buried their understandings, their imaginations, and their hearts in their senses; and as if the latter were so jaded and worn out, that they required to be inflamed, dazzled, and urged almost to a frenzy-fever, to feel any thing. The house was crowded to excess, and dark, all but the stage, which shed a dim, ghastly light on the gilt boxes and the audience. Milton might easily have taken his idea of Pandemonium from the inside of an Italian Theatre. (Hazlitt 10:196)

Although he blithely asserted that "the Neapolitan bandit takes the life of his victim with little remorse" (Hazlitt 12:171), he hastened to reassure his readers that at the time of his journey, 1824–1825, the dangers had much abated. The alarm was perpetuated primarily through echoes of old stories, but, in fact, the worst of the banditti had been captured and executed (Hazlitt 10:255). Hazlitt repeated the well-worn trope of Rome's lost glory, visible only amidst "the fragments of what has been." Refusing to indulge the pathos of the fall from former grandeur, he turned his attention to present-day street-hawkers trying to peddle counterfeit artifacts of the past (Hazlitt 10:258–259). Protesting the romantic excesses of literary description, Hazlitt wrote that in describing the Fall of Terni (*Childe Harold* 4.69–72), Lord Byron surrendered accuracy for the sake of poetic effect, pretending it to be "torturous, dark, and boiling like a witch's cauldron," while Hazlitt insisted that the waterfall is actually

> simple and majestic in its character, a clear mountain-stream that pours its uninterrupted, lengthened sheet of water over a precipice of eight hundred feet, in perpendicular descent, and gracefully winding its way to the channel beyond.

Conceding the power of Byron's verse, Hazlitt objected only that the description falsified the scene itself.

> If this noble and interesting object have a fault, it is that it is too slender, straight, and accompanied with too few wild or grotesque ornaments. It is the Doric, or at any rate the Ionic, among waterfalls. It was nothing of the texture of Lord Byron's terzains, twisted, zigzag, pent up and struggling for a vent, broken off at the end of a line, or point of a rock, diving under ground, or out of the reader's comprehension, and pieced on to another stanza or shelving rock. (Hazlitt 10:258)

Hazlitt's strategy of undermining the effulgence of Romantic representations of the Italian landscape, Italian peasants, Italian ruins is akin to the strains of anti-Romantic debunking that one finds in Heinrich Heine's *Harzreise* or, as Hazlitt acknowledges, Byron's *Don Juan*. But even in granting Hazlitt's reliance on a sardonic counterpoise, there remains in his polemic an unmistakable residue of abiding prejudice against Italian character and manners.

Aggravated by the influx of Italian immigrants in London, beginning in the 1820s in consequence of the Carbonari insurrections,[4] the discomfort with the crowded Italian presence was shared by many of Hazlitt's readers (Sponza 28–34). Their concerns were significantly different from the disparagement of the Italians that had prevailed in the previous century. Joseph Addison's *Remarks on Several Parts of Italy* (1705), Samuel Sharp's *Letters from Italy* (1766), and Tobias Smollett's *Travels through France and Italy* (1766), reported on the experiences of the Grand Tour by affirming British superiority to the degenerate state of modern Italy, where prevailing physical and moral decline was only accentuated by the ruins of its classical antiquity and the art treasures of the Medici dynasty. According to most eighteenth-century accounts, Roman Catholicism had enslaved the populace in superstitious ignorance and the rivalries among the provinces and left them vulnerable to occupation, so that the country regressed "into the barbarism of the middle ages" (Archenholtz 1:15). A radical change of attitude from Italophobia to Italophilia became evident in *The Arno Miscellany* (1784) and *The Florence Miscellany* (1786). Hester Lynch Piozzi, Robert Merry, William Parsons, and Bertie Greethead joined in their unabashed dilettantish celebration of sensibility and mannerist performance. These Della Cruscan poets fostered an awareness of Italy as the revitalizing retreat of artists and poets (Lessenich 161–163). On the Continent, Johann Wolfgang von Goethe became an advocate of the art-nurturing culture. Recording his travels to Italy in 1786–1787, Goethe waited thirty years before publishing his *Italian Journey* (*Italienische Reise*, 1816–1817).

For the most part, the essays in this volume are preoccupied with Italophilia. From the time of Chaucer's reading of Boccaccio, British culture responded continuously to persistent importations from Italy. In the seventeenth century Italians introduced the commedia dell'arte, which left its imprint in the form of harlequinades and Punch-and-Judy shows. In the eighteenth century Italians contributed to the advent of grand opera, virtuoso, and improvisational performance. In the nineteenth century Britain also became a place of refuge for Italians fleeing political turmoil. Among the enthusiastic mediators of Italian literature were William Wordsworth, Samuel Taylor Coleridge, Leigh Hunt, Lord Byron, Percy Bysshe Shelley, Mary Shelley, Felicia Hemans, and Germaine de Staël. Following the upheaval of the Carbonari rebellion and the Risorgimento, exiled nationalists settled in London's "Little Italy," where Foscolo and Mazzini pursued active journalistic careers. Italian opera, including the great soprano performers Angelica Catalani and Joséphine Grassini, attracted enthusiastic London audiences, as did the virtuoso violinist Luigi Paganini, and the *improvvisatore* Tommaso Sgricci.

Through the foundational work of David Sultana and the meticulous scholarship Edoardo Zuccato,[5] Coleridge's role as mediator of Italian art and literature is widely acknowledged. Edoardo Crisafulli, editor and commentator on Henry Francis Cary's translation of Dante's *Divine Comedy*, has also acknowledged Coleridge's generous support of Cary's work and personal involvement as translator.[6] Charles Lloyd, one-time ward under Coleridge's tutelage, satirized his mentor in the novel *Edmund Oliver* (1798) and spent his latter years in an insane asylum in France translating the plays of Alfieri. Dante excited the imagination of the artists, and Blake and Flaxman were among those who provided visual interpretations of the *Inferno*, *Purgatorio*, and *Paradiso*.

An oft-reiterated fiction prevails in literary criticism that the sensibility of the elder Romantics was "German," while only the younger Romantics might properly be said to possess an "Italian" sensibility.

In the opening chapter of this collection that fiction is effectively demolished. In "Wordsworth in Italy," Marilyn Gaull draws upon her thorough command of the poet's career and poetry to document the deep familiarity with Italian literature that remained an informing element in his writing throughout his career. She gives attention to Wordsworth's study of Italian under Agostino Isola, his early excursion into Italy over the Simplon Pass in 1794, his continental tour with his wife and sister in 1820, and his last Italian tour in 1837. The emphasis of her exposition throughout is Wordsworth's identification of Italian literature with its native culture and with the broader community of letters. Dante, together with Virgil, Cervantes, and Milton are absorbed into Wordsworth's own poetry not simply as imitation or appropriation but rather as a reassertion and reaffirmation of a vital poetic heritage.

Following Marilyn Gaull's account of Wordsworth's lifelong engagement of Italian letters as informed by his three Italian tours, the way is prepared for Bruce Graver to turn to Wordsworth's later tour of Italy in 1837 and its literary aftermath. Like Gaull, Graver, too, takes advantage of Duncan Wu's account of Wordsworth's reading of Dante and Italian literature in two meticulous and comprehensive books.[7] Graver begins his chapter, "Sitting in Dante's Throne: Wordsworth and Italian Nationalism," with the late sonnet, "At Florence." The sonnet describes the poet outside the Florentine Duomo as he "stood and gazed upon a marble stone, / The laurelled Dante's favourite seat." Overwhelmed by his conjuration of "the mighty Poet," Wordsworth says that it was "in reverence" that he "sate down, / And, for a moment, filled that empty Throne." As Graver notes, the sonnet addresses Dante not just as poet but also as patriot. Alert to Wordsworth's reiterations of the role of the poet in responding to the country's need, Graver discusses Wordsworth's understanding of Italian politics. Central to his analysis of the poems of the 1837 Italian tour is Wordsworth's representation of Dante as a national poet. More than merely "sitting in Dante's throne," Wordsworth attempts to assume Dante's voice in the Tour Memorials. As Graver observes, the endeavor is caught in the paradoxical circumstance of Wordsworth writing in English and as a foreign tourist.

In Chapter 3, "Byron between Ariosto and Tasso," Nicholas Halmi addresses the manner in which Byron, in creating *Don Juan*, attended to the *Orlando furioso*, "A new creation with [its] magic line," and to the *Gerusalemme liberata*, "unsurpass'd in modern song" (*Childe Harold's Pilgrimage* 4.40, 39). As Halmi observes, Byron refers repeatedly to the two poets and even adopts their stanzaic form. Also like these two predecessors, Byron maintains a cavalier insouciance rather than a soldierly obedience to the conventions of epic or heroic poetry. Halmi, however, does not build his case on such character-istics of form and genre. He presents evidence for a more pervasive attribute of narrative structure. Like Ariosto and Tasso, Byron too managed to engage the broad range of epic narrative by relying on the casual links of contingency rather than subservience to the strictures of a teleological narrative.

Continuing the focus on Byron, Peter Cochran turns from the epic narrative to the drama. Just as Halmi argued that Byron aligned himself with Ariosto and Tasso in a mode of epic poetry that repeat-edly distanced itself from the very conventions of the genre, Cochran argues that Byron found a kindred spirit in Alfieri in composing plays that resisted the expectations of stage performance. Cochran traces Byron's discontent with stage practice to his experience at Drury Lane. Attracted to the dramatic form, especially in its potential for character exposition, Byron nevertheless doubted the attentiveness of a London audience. Not until he arrived in Italy did Byron begin a serious commitment as a playwright. Starting with *Manfred*, Byron used the genre much as he had used the four Turkish tales and *Childe Harold* for the delineation of the dark, troubled character that has since been identified as the Byronic hero. He adhered to much the same model in *Cain*, but a difference becomes apparent in subse-quent plays. In 1819, Cochran explains, the plays of Alfieri begin to influence his sense of dramatic form, evident in *Marino Faliero* and *The Two Foscari*. Of Byron's eight plays, *Marino Faliero* was the only one performed during his lifetime. Questioning the nature of Byron's reception of Alfieri, Cochran suggests that Alfieri too, like many of Byron's other literary sources, was often mimicked for mere effect rather than as serious model.

Although Paul Douglass's essay, "Picturing Byron's Italy and Italians: William Finden's Illustrations of Byron's Life and Works," may seem to promise simply another chapter on Byron, the focus is rather on the posthumous reception of the poet and his subsequent influence on the tourist trade. As guidebooks for the hundreds of tourists, and many more armchair travelers, seeking to explore "Byron's Italy," William and Edward Finden, together with William Brockdon, produced attractive volumes illustrated with steel-plate engravings. These engravings, which played a large role in popular-izing Byron as an author, also perpetrated a reductive, sentimental, and simplified interpretation of his works. Douglass reveals how the *Landscape and Portrait Illustrations of the Life of Byron* undermined the energy of Byron's literary work and substituted a supercilious detachment from the landscapes and human scenes portrayed. Douglass demonstrates how the very selectivity of scenes from Byron's work avoids instances of struggle and violence, focusing instead on attractive females, picturesque ruins, and rustic tranquility, complemented by sometimes acerbic commentaries, composed by Brockedon, which distort, if they do not entirely falsify, Byron's (and Britain's) ambivalent relationship to Italian language and culture, the Carbonari, and the Risorgimento.

The next two chapters give scrutiny to Percy Bysshe Shelley in Italy. In Chapter 6, "Realms without a Name: Shelley and Italy's Intenser Day," Michael O'Neill explores how in Shelley's late responses to Dante, subtle effects of kinship and distance coexist. As Shelley suggests in *A Defence of Poetry*, Dante recognized an enduring dynamism in words that enabled them to kindle new inspirations, being "pregnant with a lightning which has yet found no conductor." O'Neill thus locates in Dante the source for Shelley's conviction that language could initiate a time-transcending causality and stimulate inspirations that may be at a far cultural and ideological remove from the original. O'Neill goes on to address Shelley's attempt to reassert that Dantesque causality of words in the material-bound causality of political events. At issue was whether the creative spirit existing in medieval or Renaissance Italy might be resuscitated in the present or future. That Venice had fallen to the Austrians, O'Neill argues, figured as a moment rather than as an end in Shelley's call for opposition to the ever-evolving tyrannies of social, political, and religious institutions.

In Chapter 7, "*Epipsychidion*, Dante, and the Renewable Life," Stuart Curran develops a provocative and engagingly revisionist approach to a major poem that has perennially been read as an allegory of love, predicated upon Percy Bysshe Shelley's relations with Emilia Viviani, whom he met while she was detained by her family in a convent near Pisa in 1820. Although Shelley gave ample cause for a reading of the poem as autobiographical, he also protested against that reductionism, which allowed undue attention to the self-pity that can be heard in some passages. In his alternative approach, Curran emphasizes how the poem distills some of Shelley's most sophisticated thinking on the subject of aesthetics. He brings together problems of language, expression, perception, and the visionary power that preoccupied him throughout his career. Instead of being preoccupied with the passion of the flesh and the wounds of mortal love, *Epipsychidion* grapples with the conflict between "two overshadowing minds, one life, one death," in order to establish the place of a divinely human creativity in the scheme of universal experience. In this, Curran argues, Shelley embraced the principle of the *Vita nuova*, the "renewing life"as it is inscribed moment-by-moment in Dante's great work.

In Chapter 8, "The Poetry of Philology: Burckhardt's *Civilization of the Renaissance in Italy* and Mary Shelley's *Valperga*," Tillotama Rajan draws upon Jacob Burckhardt's *The Civilization of the Renaissance in Italy* (1860) as a relevant critical tool for analyzing Mary Shelley's description of Italy in *Valperga*. Because Italy had no overarching system of government, Rajan declares in summarizing Burckhardt's argument, it was free to create different political forms through its multiplicity of competing despotisms and republics. Paradoxically, she goes on to assert, the very fragmentation of Italy allows for the birth of individualism, "personality," and political experimentation. Yet Italy by the same token could never consolidate itself as a nation and could not build on these experiments (Burckhardt, *Civilization* 69–71). For Burckhardt, then, the Italian Renaissance never achieved an "adequate embodiment of the Idea." Like Burckhardt, Shelley too researched her topic thoroughly, reading "a hundred old books" to write *Valperga*, intimating a method that is genealogical and anti-foundationalist rather than organized by a master-narrative. Like Burckhardt, Shelley was interested in the fragmented political geography of Italy at a time when Walter Scott was using the historical novel to institute and canonize the British nation-state. Like Burckhardt's *Civilization*, Shelley's novel is an encyclopedic bricolage of the political, the historical, and the aesthetic, temporarily focalized through the passions of three distinctive individuals (Euthanasia, Beatrice, and Castruccio), for whose emergence as individuals Italy's fragmentation serves as a condition of possibility. Italy, Rajan proposes, drew Shelley's attention because of its untimely position in history as the place of something that had not been adequately embodied. By the early nineteenth century that something had still not found a form, and its immaturity, prematurity, or belatedness questions the very idea of adequate embodiment implicit in theories of modernity. Shelley, writing well after the period now called "early modern" finds in Italy a space from which to think politics and history, as well as individuality, she uses philology and romance to unsettle the emergent linkage of history with modernity.

In Chapter 9, "Hemans's Record of Dante: "The Maremma" and the Intertextual Poetics of Plenitude," Diego Saglia notes "an entrenched resistance" in acknowledging the extent to which women writers were involved in the reception of Dante during the Romantic period. To be sure, a wide range of perspectives were offered by such women writers as Lady Morgan, Charlotte Eaton, Germaine de Staël, and Mary Shelley. While many of the women writers were attracted primarily to Petrarch, many also engaged extensively with Dante. Recommending Felicia Hemans's poem "The Maremma" (1820) as an example of effective engagement with Dantesque narrative, Saglia demonstrates how Hemans reinvents the tale of Pia de' Tolomei, adapting it to her own poetical idiom, but at the same time infusing it with Shakespearean overtones. In his concluding paragraphs, Saglia compares Hemans reworkings of Dante to those of Anna Seward and Mary Shelley. Concentrating specifically on their "national" approaches to the poet, Saglia emphasizes the contribution of these women writers to the Romantic reevaluation of the Italian bard and their relevance to discourses of cultural (and political) identity and agency.

Another important woman writer of the era, Germaine de Staël commanded a readership throughout Europe with such works as *Corinne, or Italy* (1807). That novel, as published by John Murray in London, was especially influential in Britain, the site of her heroine's destruction. In Chapter 10, Diane Hoeveler describes Staël's novel as an exploration of national character and historical destiny, as identified in the "Italy" part of the book's title. Staël's major accomplishment, however, was to invent not just a female character, but a female romanticism capable of rivaling in its performative potential the dominant male discourses of Romanticism. Given the facility, mobility, dexterity of mind and nature, Corinne's energy and endurance is nevertheless physically and emotionally limited. As Hoeveler observes, Corinne was perfectly familiar with the roles of masculine discourse, "Ossianism, Prometheanism, Faustianism, Rousseauvianism, or Wertherism." Through "Corinne's grandiose and heavily coded feminine performances" Staël may suggest to female readers a female repertory capable of promoting "a feminization of culture, history, and social institutions," but, as Hoeveler also notes, Corinne's fate reveals Staël's awareness "that her noble intentions were doomed." Having cast her protagonist as an *improvvisatrice*, Staël does not sustain the possibility that Corinne might provide nineteenth-century women writers with a model of spontaneity and liberation. Her very choice of performances predetermine an inevitable consequence. When Staël's *improvvisatrice* arrives in England, she is exposed to conventions and constraints that undermine and ultimately destroy her health and happiness.

Linking the fiction of improvisational performance in *Corinne* to the actual stage performance of the *improvvisitore*, Angela Esterhammer challenges the illusory boundaries between the two. In Chapter 11. "Coleridge, Sgricci, and the Shows of London: Improvising in Print and Performance," she finds a crucial mediation in Coleridge's "The Improvisatore," a poem written at the very time of the London performance by the most famous of *improvvisatori*, Tommaso Sgricci. The juxtaposition of these two events, performance and text, shows processes of embodied and written mediation to be distinct yet intertwined. Not only does the experience of real-life *improvvisatori* contrast with the fictional representations of *improvvisatrici* that were being offered to English readers at the same time, but it also gives rise to important reflections on mediation and mediality. In theatres and lecture halls, London audiences had opportunities to encounter poetry as an oral rather than a written medium, to discover how the conditions of immediacy and embodiment affect the composition and reception of literary works. Mediation becomes even more of an issue when print media attempt to reproduce improvisational performances and give them a more permanent form—for instance, when improvised poetry is published or when periodicals review ephemeral performances. The resulting reflections on mediality converge in Coleridge's intriguing text, "The Improvisatore."

In Chapter 12, "Masaniello on the London Stage," Frederick Burwick traces the many dramatic productions based on the career of Tommaso Aniello, the twenty-five-year-old Neapolitan fisherman, who 180 years earlier, in 1647, led the revolt against the rule of the Spanish Habsburgs in Naples. With interest in Italian politics reawakened in the 1820s by the failed Carbonari rebellion, eight different productions based on Masaniello and the revolt appeared in the theatres of London between 1825 and 1829. The earliest version, staged in 1649 in the immediate aftermath of the rebellion, was crafted for a London audience seeking clues to the volatile political circumstances. The mystery of those circumstances still intrigued the audiences of the late 1820s, who expected as well the keen impulse of revolutionary fervor charged with high degree of melodramatic pathos. The productions themselves were caught up in the London rivalries between the legitimate and the illegitimate theatres. George Soane's *Masaniello, The Fisherman of Naples* opened at Drury Lane on February 17, 1825, but lost the race to Henry M. Milner's *Masaniello, the Fisherman of Naples and Deliverer of his Country*, which opened ten days earlier at the Coburg on February 7, 1825. After Daniel-

François-Esprit Auber's opera, *La muette de Portici,* premiered with great success in Paris, there was again a scramble in London to adapt the libretto by Eugène Scribe for an English audience. When James Kenney's *Masaniello: A Grand Opera in Three Acts* opened at Drury Lane on May 4, 1829, once again Henry Milner was prepared on the very same night at the Royal Coburg to open his rival production, *Masaniello; or, The Dumb Girl of Portici, A musical drama, in three acts.* By no means compromised by musical adaption, the dramatization of Masaniello's fate still wielded its full political force and on occasion revealed its power to rouse the crowd to rebellion. In tracking subsequent productions, Burwick notes as well the ballet version by André-Jean-Jacques Deshayes, which adhered closely to Auber's opera, and the ballet by Jules Perrot, *Ondine, ou La naïade,* which offered a new plot and new music. These links lead to Turner's depiction *Undine giving the Ring to Masaniello* (1846), a fitting coda to the career of a "stage hero."

Although very few critics have bothered, a strong case can be made for the importance of Leigh Hunt's *Story of Rimini.* Jeffrey Cox undertakes a critical defense and justification of Hunt's work in Chapter 13, "Re-Visioning Rimini: Dante in the Cockney School." For one thing, Cox points out, it was highly influential when it first appeared: "We can find echoes of *Rimini* in such poems as Keats's "Isabella," Shelley's *Epipsychidion,* and the first canto of Byron's *Don Juan.*" It was Hunt, Cox insists, who "taught a generation of poets how to raid the Italian cultural archive in order to remake British poetry, how to use Italian classics to make Cockney poetry in the present." Hunt's accomplishment, he readily grants, would not have been possible without Cary's translation of *The Divine Comedy.* Following Cary's own commentary on his translation, Foscolo, Coleridge, and Samuel Rogers offered further critical assessment of Dante. The Paolo and Francesca episode from the *Inferno* became an oft-revisited topos for the second-generation Romantic. As the first chapters of this collection have shown, Wordsworth too was attentive to Dante, and he was not alone among the first-generation poets, for Blake in his illustrations to the *Divine Comedy* was a scrupulous interpreter of Dante's poetry. Cox also cites Coleridge's comments on Dante in *The Friend,* Shelley's turn to *La Vita Nuova* in *Epipsychidion,* Keats's use of Dante in "The Fall of Hyperion," and Byron in *The Prophecy of Dante.* Cox does not deny the charge that Hunt, along with most of his contemporaries, lacked "a sense of tragedy." Cox argues that Hunt may well have had a different goal, deliberately crafting a narrative "beyond tragedy." In rewriting Dante, Cox maintains, Hunt created in *Rimini* an "innovative, avant garde poetry that sought through the extravagance of its verse to image a world remade by love."

The final essay in this collection moves beyond attention to individual authors to a more comprehensive appraisal of one of the most profound and pervasive aspect of the experience of Italy—the Italian language. Timothy Webb opens Chapter 14, "Syllables of the Sweet South: Figuring the Sound of Italian in the Romantic Period," with reflections on Enlightment philology with its contrary impulses of a universal language, transcending nationalist identity, and its reinforcement of nationalist language through an intensified attention to nationalist character. Webb goes on to focus on the fascination with the sounds of the Italian language evident in the accounts of travelwriters and creative artists during the Romantic period. The characteristics of Italian were partly defined by way of comparison (for example, with English, German, French, and Spanish), but they were also regarded as giving expression to an identity that was quintessentially and recognizably "Italian." Sometimes this was connected not only with the intrinsic nature of the language but with the energy and dramatic force with which it was often enunciated: "gesture" is rarely far away from such characterizations. Many writers insisted on the softness of Italy and its femininity, characteristics that did not elude the notice of Germaine de Staël, especially in *Corinne*, and which, according to the narrator in Byron's *Beppo*, featured identifiably in its oral language where it could be distinguished clearly from the more guttural sounds and speech patterns of the north. Wordsworth, Coleridge, Byron, Percy and Mary Shelley, Staël, Leigh Hunt, and others who lived or travelled in Italy, recognized that a different soundscape distinguished Italy from England and France and gave expression to a culture also correspondingly distinct and different. The differences were further enhanced by the fact that "Italian" also varied from city to city. Coleridge in Sicily, Byron in Venice, Stendhal in Milan, Leigh Hunt in Tuscany, Mary Shelley in Rome, Leigh Hunt in Tuscany, Charles Burney in Florence, and Hester Piozzi returning to her native country, acknowledged the existence of dialect with a variety of responses. The very sound of Italian was often regarded as liberating and creative and most travelers acknowledged a language that was musical, resonant, and pleasingly expressive.

We acknowledged above that, for the most part, the essays in this volume deal with Italophilia, and that is understandable, for a love of Italian culture, language, and the sights, sounds, aromas, and sensual impressions of Italy, lies behind the Romantic response—though complicated sometimes by disappointment, anxiety, feelings of Imperial superiority, to be sure. Importations from Italy included Italians themselves, as well as robust representations of Italy's contemporary political and literary scene, and these receive extended treatment in the following pages. The effects of previous waves of influence have not been neglected, including that of grand opera on the Romantic response to Italy, a taste for which arrived also with Italian expatriates, and Mazzini and Foscolo are, therefore, merely representative of a large and noticeable Italian presence in the London of the Romantics. This collection of essays consolidates previous scholarship on the interpreters of Italy—from Coleridge, Wordsworth, Byron, and Hunt to Hemans and the Shelleys—and enlarges and extends that knowledge with groundbreaking work on the visual arts and the stage, including improvisation, painting, and theatrical productions based on Italian history. Shelley's deep and comprehending response to Dante finds echoes throughout the book, and so it is fitting that we end with an essay contemplating the lure of the Italian vernacular, established for so many Romantic writers by Dante, but sought in countless other venues after, as the Romantics embraced and assessed what they believed to be their very own Italian heritage.

NOTES

1. For a succinct description of the Grand Tour, see Redford, *Venice and the Grand Tour* 17–23.
2. See William Hazlitt, Essay XVI. Hot and Cold [written 1826], in *The Plain Speaker* (1826) (Hazlitt 12:170, 177).
3. This passage is drawn from Hazlitt's *Notes of a Journey through France and Italy* (1826), (Hazlitt 10:196; see also 10:249, 276).
4. The Carbonari (literally "charcoal burners") were members of an Italian protest movement that originated in Naples during the Napoleonic Wars and grew into a loosely organized freemason-style organization scattered across Italy (and into France). It consisted of patriots who generally desired Italian unification, though their political agenda seems to have been undefined. See Smith, *The Making of Italy: 1796–1870*.
5. See Sultana's *Samuel Taylor Coleridge in Malta and Italy* and Zuccato's *Coleridge in Italy*.
6. See Crisafulli's "The Translator as Textual Critic."
7. See Wu's *Wordsworth's Reading 1770–1799* (1993) and *Wordsworth's Reading, 1800–1815* (2007).

CHAPTER ONE

WORDSWORTH'S ITALIAN
ENCOUNTERS

Marilyn Gaull

Even "the most original poet now living," as Hazlitt called
Wordsworth in *The Spirit of the Age* (1818), had "ancestral voices," to
adapt a phrase from *Kubla Khan*. Receptive, studious, a literary life
full of encounter and exchange, Wordsworth acknowledged, among
others, Chaucer, Spenser, Shakespeare, Milton, Homer, Virgil, and
an array of Italian authors including Metastasio, Petrarch, Ariosto,
Michael Angelo, Chiabrera, Machiavelli, and Dante. He worried
about them: "We are all, in spite of ourselves, a parcel of thieves,"
he observed in a letter to Henry Crabb Robinson, when he offered
to send him the sonnets he wrote on leaving Italy if he promised not
to share them with "verse-writers." To explain, he offered a "droll
example": After Mary accused him of plagiarizing one of the sonnets,
he asked: "From whom?" "From yourself," she replied in December
1838 (see Robinson, *Diary* 3:156). In editions of Wordsworth's poetry
and letters, in critical essays, source studies, and biographies, scholars
such as Alan Hill, Stephen Gill, W. J. B. Owen, Duncan Wu, and
others have identified many of the textual echoes and influences from
Italian literature. His relation to Dante, Italy, Italian culture, and
language, however, is beyond words or phrases, images or concept;
it is as original as his poetry—personal, subtle, complicated, pervasive, unlike any other influence, a combination of learning, taste, and
experience. In this essay, I shall consider the range of Wordsworth's

Italian encounters—the textual, cultural, and biographical—how he assimilated and expressed them, and how his originality is revealed by them.

Wordsworth's Italy

Defeated and fallen, divided into city-states unable to protect or govern themselves, Italy had been successively ruled by Spain, Napoleon, and Austria, its one stable institution the Vatican, of which Rome, once the capital of the Western world, was a synecdoche. In spite of its many cultural achievements and creative genius, during Wordsworth's lifetime (1770–1850) Italy experienced a recurrent social, political, economic, and military collapse, expressed (for the British, at least), on the one hand, in Gibbon's *Decline and Fall of the Roman Empire* (1776) and, sixty years later, in Bulwer Lytton's *The Last Days of Pompeii* (1834). Among the poets, some such as Leigh Hunt, Keats, Byron, and Shelley, celebrated the Renaissance Italy of art and epic, of Michael Angelo, Dante, Da Vinci, and the idealized sculpture and architecture reconstructed in British gardens and civic buildings. But a dark side of Italy pervaded the popular culture. Ann Radcliffe, who had never been to Italy, made it the setting for such gothic romances as *Mysteries of Udolpho* with its perilous crossing of the Alps and *The Italian, or the Confessional of the Black Penitents* (in Wordsworth's library), with the fiendish monk Schedoni, depicting the bandits, secret societies, vulnerable women, rapacious aristocracy, and depravities associated with the Catholic church. Shakespeare's image of Italy in such plays as *The Merchant of Venice, Othello,* and *Romeo and Juliet* offered a more subtle but equally intense population of suspicious, treacherous, and tyrannical men; helpless victimized women; passions; conflicts; greed; jealousy; and forbidden love. Nonetheless, and in spite of the imagined and real dangers of continental travel during and after the Napoleonic wars, Italy continued to attract tourists, religious pilgrims, sexual adventurers, some to study art and music or to produce it—such as the Della Cruscans in Florence or later Shelley and Byron. The Italian climate promised recovery from lung and nervous diseases, but, with the recurrent cholera, it was just as likely to be a fatal destination. Even the Italian landscape was made of contradictions: the exquisite light, the mountains and forests celebrated in picturesque paintings grew out of a traumatic earth history, especially after 1783, the volcanic eruptions, earthquakes, and tidal waves that kept the population on the edge of crisis.

In Great Britain, impoverished Italian *émigrés* escaping Napoleon and the political turmoil that followed his invasion led non-heroic and un-Romantic lives in London as language teachers, merchants, domestic servants, street performers, puppeteers (from Pulcinella to Punch and Judy), actors in the spectacles or pantomime—itself naturalized to the British stage from the commedia dell'arte. Among the notables were two generations of Grimaldi and the Great Belzoni, a giant of a man, perhaps the one Wordsworth confessed to seeing at Sadler's Wells "amid the uproar of the rabblement" (*Prelude* 7:273).[1] There were Italian magicians and Italian magic (Giovanni Pinetti, the first magician to hire a legitimate theater) and the electrical discoveries of Luigi Galvani and Alessandro Volta, both popular performing arts. Their skills were adapted for diorama, panorama, and stage settings for melodrama and for Italian opera, the spectacle, music, bel canto voices, lyrics, and tragedies that passed the strict British censorship laws. As Giacomo Casanova scandalized European aristocracy and published his experiences in his memoirs, his contemporary, Cesare Beccaria, in *Of Crimes and Punishments* (1764), began the humane and utilitarian reform of European and British justice.[2] In 1837, while Wordsworth was on his last tour of Italy, Mazzini, a failed revolutionary, was in London to recruit young patriots for a new insurrection that would unify Italy; instead, he encountered countrymen still depicted and sometimes behaving as gothic villains, philanderers, or clowns (Cavaliero 44). In England, especially the North Country, the heroic remains of Italy lay about the countryside, the displaced and anonymous Roman ruins, forts, walls, barrows, and roads, which were Wordsworth's introduction to Rome and Italian history, the closest he came before he attended university. The Roman occupation, which had lasted for four hundred years, from 43 to 410 AD, was a presence in Wordsworth's poetry and haunts his imagination—the ghosts of Roman legions crossing Kirkstone pass, and the "last holds of ambitious Rome" in a relic in Penrith, as he writes in "Roman Antiquities" (1831).

WORDSWORTH'S TRAVELS IN ITALY

Unlike other poets of his generation and later, Wordsworth did not go to Italy for his health, to escape, or to die—although his daughter-in-law, Isabella, John's wife, and two of his grandchildren who had gone to recuperate from a mysterious illness did die in Italy. He attempted three tours, the first at age twenty as a student with Robert Jones, which he records in *The Prelude*. Crossing Simplon Pass, about to enter Italy, he records the threshold moment, the anticipation, the prospective vision, which sets him apart from his retrospective contemporaries who visited Italy:

> Our destiny, our being's heart and home,
> Is with Infinitude, and only there;
> With hope it is, hope that can never die,
> Effort, expectation, and desire,
> And something ever more about to be. (*Prelude* 6:538–541)

The second tour was in 1820, with Dorothy and Mary, Thomas Monkhouse (Mary's cousin) and his new wife on their wedding tour, her sister, their maid, and several others they met along the way. After visiting Annette Vallon and Caroline, her child by William, they travelled by foot, coach, ferry, mule, boat, and encountered many adventures including an eclipse at Lake Lugano, which Wordsworth recorded in one of the thirty-nine poems he wrote, *Memorials of a Tour of the Continent* (1822). The anecdotes that Dorothy, Mary, and Robinson recorded reveal that this journey was more sociable than poetic, sharing his youthful experience with his family and friends, sharing pleasures, some mischievous: "Wordsworth was the greatest poet England has had for generations," a stranger announced at a small inn. Wordsworth replied: "That's a ridiculous remark for you to make. My name is Wordsworth" (Robinson, *Diary* 2:181). On the natives, Robinson says, "The physiognomy of the people does not speak in favour of their ancestors...[they] have a feeble and melancholy character. The children beg...and sing unintelligible songs. But what says the poet: 'Thrice happy burghers, peasants, warriors old,.../ Heroes before your time in frolic fancy bold'" (Robinson, *Diary* 2:176). His sense of the noble peasant, "Through utter weakness pitiable dear" that he had celebrated at their summer festival in Grasmere (*Prelude* 8:1–69) had survived in Italy. The inn where they stayed in Lugano, Robinson reports, had been a refuge for the disgraced Queen Caroline and her Italian lover, Bartolomeo Pergami, he in Robinson's room, and the queen in the adjoining room where Dorothy stayed. They turned back at Milan because of the cholera.

Wordsworth's third Italian journey in 1837, he said, had been delayed for family and economic concerns. At age sixty-four, he hoped it was not too late (he was to live another sixteen years) but, as a poet, he feared it may have been too late to make the best use of the experience. However belated, with Henry Crabb Robinson, he visited Rome, Florence, Bologna, Venice, Savona, the countryside, and far from aged, Wordsworth hiked and climbed for hours, rising at dawn, indefatigable, though early to bed because his failing eyesight kept him from reading at night. He did occasionally socialize with Robinson: he visited Severn and talked about Keats and a sculptor's studio to see the statue of Byron that was rejected by Westminster. Among the three most powerful experiences: at Vaucluse, Petrarch's home, where for two or three hours he climbed " the steep and rugged crags," he recalls (Robinson thought it was "dreary and uncomfortable"); inside St. Peter's where he attended a mass celebrated by the Pope in the Sistine Chapel; and a pine tree atop Monte Morio in Rome that he embraced and commemorated in a poem in honor of his late friend, Sir George Beaumont who had saved it "from the sordid axe."[3]

WORDSWORTH AND ITALIAN

Having completed all the requirements for Greek, Latin, and mathematics while a student at Hawkshead school, Wordsworth was free when he entered Cambridge to concentrate on modern languages, French, Spanish, German, and Italian at which he excelled. His tutor was the accomplished Agostino Isola, exiled from Milan and hired by the Cambridge faculty in 1764 to prepare students for the diplomatic service, or to be tutors to wealthy travelling families.[4] Using a conversational method of dialogue, which he invented and later turned into a text book, he and Wordsworth translated the Renaissance romances, Tasso, Ariosto, Boccaccio, Boiardo, Petrarch's lyrics and Metastasio's, the anti-romance *Don Quixote,* Dante, and Machiavelli whose writings had a profound, positive, and rarely recognized influence on him.[5] Their lives remained entwined: after Isola's death, his granddaughter, Emma, was adopted by Charles and Mary Lamb. She later married Charles Moxon, who became Wordsworth's publisher, financed his third tour of Italy in 1837, and accompanied him as far as Paris, then published the collected poems of 1842, which include the *Memorials of a Tour of Italy.*

Isola's conversational style affirmed Wordsworth's faith in the spoken language while the vernacular epics and romances appealed to his taste for the oral tradition, which was more congenial to his nature than the formal and elaborate literary tradition that he had already mastered. In an eloquent passage in Book Five of *The Prelude,* he attributes his mature strength, his capacity to imagine and endure, "to live / In reconcilement with our stinted powers" to the tales and romances he first encountered as a child, and the romances that sustained him, the "dreamers," "Forgers of daring tales!" "Impostors, drivellers, dotards," "we feel

> With what, and how great might ye are in league,
> Who make our wish, our power, our thought a deed,
> An empire, a possession. (*Prelude* 5:522–529)

Along with Ovid, Basile, and Boccaccio (whom he could quote by heart), with Isola, he read Boiardo's *Orlando Innamorato* (1495), its continuation in Ariosto's *Orlando furioso* (1516–1532), all of them drawing on a common body of familiar tales associated with Roland, the great British hero, and Charlemagne, the French, as they filtered down into the oral communities and circulated in Great Britain, Europe, and the Middle East—where ever the chivalric romance or folk narratives flourished. In episodic verse, they related the tales of aristocrats and folk heroes challenging each other over women, religion, and land, allied with or against competing supernatural forces, pagan or Christian, the enchantments, wizards, magic rings, talking animals, hares, cats, owls, and the hippogriff. If the narratives faded, the figures endured and populated distant tales through many countries and centuries, including Wordsworth's narratives. One example: originating in an Eastern legend, the bleeding tree as a sign of guilt, appears in Dante's *Inferno*, where suicides are turned into trees devoured by harpies, again in *The Juniper Tree*, which the Brothers Grimm collected from various sources, and Wordsworth's *The Thorn*. In this oral recycling, as the tales passed through Italy, the images and narratives acquired conscience and solemnity—in the legend of Cupid and Psyche, for example, after many transformations, in different languages and cultures, Psyche reappears as the lone goddess of harvest and of death in Wordsworth's "The Solitary Reaper." And, like "*Peter Bell*," in which Ariosto is a presence, and *The Excursion*, after passing through Italy, the tales refocus on the tale-tellers' narratives about telling stories.

Raised on such tales, Wordsworth savored romance epics, the courtships, sufferings, contests, the fantastic voyages to the moon (not Hades), and exotic lands, and, in Ariosto's *Orlando furioso*, the madness of unrequited love. He carried *Orlando* with him on his first walking tour of 1791 with Robert Jones through France, Switzerland, and to Lake Como. Such tales fed his rebellious spirit and prepared him for "the long probation," "The time of trial, ere we learn to live / In reconcilement with our stinted powers":

> To endure this state of meagre vassalage,
> Unwilling to forego, confess, submit,
> Uneasy and unsettled, yoke-fellows
> To custom, mettlesome, and not yet tamed
> And humbled down.... (*Prelude* 5:515–522)

Orlando shaped his perceptions. Captain Michel Beaupuy, for example, a French revolutionary officer, "wandered," Wordsworth writes, "As through a book, an old romance, or tale / Of Fairy" (*Prelude* 8:305–307). And walking by the Loire, he imagined Angelica, his ideal love, the heroine of *Orlando furioso*, and Erminia (from Tasso), satyrs, knights, all frolicking in the woods (*Prelude* 9:438; Liu 374 ff.). Orlando's madness and travels, reappear, like the folk characters of oral legend, in Wordsworth's many thwarted romances, his own with Annette Vallon, *The Borderers, The Thorn, The Forsaken Indian Woman,* the Vaudracour and Julia episode in *The Prelude,* and even Coleridge's obsession with Wordsworth's sister-in-law, Sara Hutchinson. Not *The Sorrows of Young Werther,* which inspired a generation of suicidal lovers, but Ariosto was Wordsworth's mentor. And while it appears that he renounced the romance tradition as early as *Peter Bell* (the narrator does at least), where he cites and says farewell to Ariosto's hippogriff, in fact, he continues to publish the romances in all his later editions, even in the collection of 1842, and retains the tribute to the lifelong value of these romances in *The Prelude* passage, Book Five, to be published after his death in 1850. Evolving from his childhood, his Italian readings, and his own experience, the romance voice survives as one of his many voices, an authentic part of his poetic life.

For a time, Wordsworth lived the romance journey: his love affair with Annette, his wandering conversations with Beaupuy, then, returning from France, the revolution failed, his country at war, separated from his love and his first child, he walked through Salisbury Plain, the River Wye, North Wales, obstacles, encounters, a long search for peace and a home recorded in *The Prelude* and in more subtle ways in the *Lyrical Ballads.* The journey itself, like the poem, has Petrarchan, Virgilian, and Miltonic antecedents, but also more significant predecessors in Ariosto and Boiardo, perhaps Dante, personalized, localized, and historicized. Wordsworth's association of the romance legend with Italy reappears after the 1837 journey: Barthold

Niebuhr's *History of Rome* (1828), had rejected the legendary history of Rome, the "old credulities," as Wordsworth called them, in favor of "severe research," to which Wordsworth objects in *Memorials of a Tour of Italy,* Sonnets IV and V.

WORDSWORTH'S TRANSLATIONS

For Wordsworth, a gifted linguist, translation was habitual from his childhood—recreational, social, and therapeutic. Over the years he read in Italian or translated Dante, Petrarch, Tasso, Ariosto, Metastasio, Machiavelli, Michael Angelo, Beccaria, Chiabrera, and many others who are not recorded. Dorothy reports to her friend, Jane Pollard, that after his return to Cambridge from his walking tour, "He reads Italian, Spanish, French, Greek, Latin, and English, but never opens a mathematical book. We promise ourselves much pleasure from reading Italian at some time" (June 26, 1791). And in 1794, following his own dark time, "My Italian studies I am going to resume immediately as it is my intention to instruct my sister in that language." And in April, Dorothy has "begun Italian," reading the annotated copy of Ariosto that he had carried with him on his walking tour (Wu 7). Translating Ariosto was a source of great pleasure, several cantos, up to a hundred lines a day he said at one point, but he never finished and it was not published until 1947.[6]

Although Petrarch was not considered a major poet in the eighteenth century, Wordsworth paid homage by translating his verse, by reviving and retaining the sonnet form, and in *The Convention of Cintra* describing him as "a man of disciplined spirit, who withdrew from the busy world" to "master" his own mind. In the Italian tour of 1837, he took Robinson on a pilgrimage to Vaucluse where he re-imagined the poet, who, in spite of scant citations, served as another subtext in Wordsworth's life and poetry.[7]

In 1802, Wordsworth translated five poems by Metastasio, who, according to Gillen Darcy Wood, in the eighteenth century was the most popular Italian poet in England. Wordsworth published them in the *Morning Post*, in October and November, 1803, but, like his stanzas from *Orlando*, they were not republished until 1947, and the most popular, *La Partenza*, ("Laura, farewell, my Laura") was not recognized as Wordsworth's work until 1962. They did, however, have a profound impact on the *Lyrical Ballads*, as Wood demonstrates.[8] Like Petrarch and Ariosto, Metastasio wrote lyrics that express longing for one's beloved, for lost, unrequited, or forbidden love. Since most of these translations were written after he had married and settled in

Grasmere with Mary and Dorothy, they seem to express the deep and unresolved emotions he experienced parting from Annette and their unborn child (Johnston 566).

In 1804, at the request of Robert Southey's friend, Richard Duppa, who was writing *The Life and Works of Michael Angelo Buonarroti,* (1806), Wordsworth began translating Michael Angelo's sonnets.[9] After about fifteen of the three hundred sonnets, he explained in a letter to Sir George Beaumont, he found the poetry,

> the most difficult to construe I ever met with, but just what you would expect from such a man, shewing abundantly how conversant his soul was with great things. There is a mistake in the world concerning the Italian language; the poetry of Dante and Michael Angelo proves, that if there be little majesty and strength in Italian verse, the fault is in the authors, and not in the tongue...so much meaning has been put by Michael Angelo into so little room, and that meaning sometimes so excellent in itself, that I found the difficulty of translating him insurmountable. (*Letters: Early Years* 1:628)

In 1810, along with Coleridge, Wordsworth began translating Gabriello Chiabrera (1552–1638), whose collected works in many genre appeared in five volumes in 1782. Wordsworth chose to translate ten of the epitaphs, a unique set of portraits or sketches, and published six of them in *The Friend.* Although learned, classical, formal, and in many ways worldly, in the epitaphs Chiabrera's language was colloquial, the verse unrhymed, and the speakers were either local people with an intimate knowledge of the deceased or the dead themselves. The epitaphs depict the obscure and humble, a shepherd, a soldier, a writer, Titus, "invincible" in "the rage of literary wars," Abrosio Salinero, whose life was taken up with "odious litigation," and a "racking malady," Lelio Pavese, "darling of the fascinating Loves," and the rhythmically challenging Francesco Pozzobonnelli, who died at age twenty while his father was in some "foreign" land, and for whom the "eyes of all Savona streamed with tears." In "Musings Near Aquapendente," a meditative verse Wordsworth included in the *Memorials of a Tour of Italy,* he pauses at Savona, the secluded village where "gentle Chiabrera," "pure poetic Spirit," spent much of his life, and with whom Wordsworth finds an affinity so far from Grasmere. Chiabrera's verse, he says, might have come from "a plain English heart": "glory then to words, / Honour to word-preserving Arts, and hail / Ye kindred local influences." Chiabrera was the inspiration for Wordsworth's *Essay on Epitaphs* and, I believe, for the Pastor and his improvisational elegies on obscure local figures in *The Excursion.*[10]

WORDSWORTH AND DANTE

Wordsworth read Dante while still a student with Isola in the 1790s, when there were no complete translations. Although he was a presence in painting, Dante was not popular or familiar in England until Henry Cary's translation of 1814, which Coleridge brought to public attention. Wordsworth had acquired the Parma folio of 1799, "much the grandest book on my shelves," and in 1824, observes in a letter to Walter Savage Landor, "It has become lately the fashion to extol [Dante] above measure. I have not read him for many years; his style, I used to think admirable for its conciseness and vigor, without abruptness; but I own that his fictions often strike me as offensively grotesque and fantastic, and I felt the poem tedious from various causes." The "grotesque and fantastic" accounts for its popularity: it appealed to the same taste as such sordid gothic tales as *The Monk* and *Vathek*, and the grotesque in art, the epitome of everything Wordsworth said in the Preface to *Lyrical Ballads* he objected to in contemporary culture: "For the human mind is capable of being excited without the application of gross and violent stimulants; and he must have a very faint perception of its beauty and dignity who does not know this, and who does not further know, that one being is elevated above another in proportion as he possesses the capability...to endeavour to produce or enlarge this capability is one of the best services in which, at any period, a Writer can be engaged...especially so in the present day. For a multitude of causes, unknown to former times, are now acting with a combined force to blunt the discriminating powers of mind, and, unfitting it for all voluntary exertion, to reduce it to a state of almost savage torpor." To Wordsworth, *The Inferno* was another intense and inescapable example (more dangerous and sinister because Dante was such a powerful writer) of the sickly genres that he believed had destroyed the sensibility of the nation.

The Inferno was offensive to Wordsworth for personal as well as aesthetic reasons; it violated political principles and religious beliefs on which he had built his life. His character, disposition, and even philosophy had been shaped by the Quaker experiences in his childhood in Hawkshead. Although he affiliated as an Anglican, he was raised in a Quaker community in Colthouse, attended Quaker Meeting with Dame Tyson, acquired the language of inner light, the belief in divine leadings and individual conscience, pacifism, egalitarianism, simplicity, forgiveness, charity, a commitment to the present, to community, plain speaking, truthfulness, and a protective mission that extended to all living things—all of which he brought to his poetry, politics, and Anglican faith. His Quaker background prepared him for the penal reforms initiated by Cesare Beccaria's *On Crime and Punishment* (1764), who advocated equality before the law, punishments suited to the crime, presumed innocence, and imprisonment as opposed to torture and corporal punishment—principles adopted in the Napoleonic Codes, by Bentham, and ultimately all of Western civilization (Gibson 82). With its unforgiving, brutal, and retributive justice *The Inferno* was deeply offensive, the arbitrary sufferings, the failure of personal responsibility and of sympathy. For example, in Canto 32, a public favorite (that fades in translation) with Virgil as his guide, Dante visits Antenora, he calls it, where traitors are buried in ice up to their heads, impulsively inflicts more pain on these helpless and suffering figures, and leaves them screaming in anguish, kicking one in the head and pulling out the hair of another who refuses to divulge his name.

Beyond his Quaker instincts, Wordsworth was an ecumenical and religious poet believing that all poetry is a form of worship and that pagans, such as the ancient Greeks, "suckled on a creed outworn," were exemplary—surely nothing could be more unjust than to punish those such as Virgil, who, born before Christ, did not believe in him. Moreover, Wordsworth was a lover, as he often says, of all living things, not a soldier, judge, or priest; his sympathy was with the suffering lovers, those whose forbidden or merely unbridled passion, a torment in life, became, for Dante, demonized, a just cause for eternal damnation based on a religion that equated virtue with celibacy.

Politically, Wordsworth's long life encompassed the most tumultuous period in Western history. His political attitudes, values, and expression were shaped and altered by his experience. Rather than merely abandoning his youthful radicalism, his belief in revolutionary ideals, Wordsworth stopped being a revolutionary because there was no longer a revolution. The alternative: to become, like the Solitary in *The Excursion*, indeed, like Dante himself, alienated and enraged. When the French Revolution became a Reign of Terror and "domestic carnage...filled the whole year / With feast days," as he wrote in *The Prelude*, he was haunted with "ghastly visions...of despair / And tyranny, and implements of death," such as, one might add, in *The Inferno*. When Napoleon became an aggressor, a conqueror, and even threatened to invade England, Wordsworth, a patriot first, shifted his attention from revolution to liberty and order, as he entitled his series of sonnets "Dedicated to Liberty and Order." Among Napoleon's victims was Venice itself, which Wordsworth lamented in 1802 as "the eldest Child of Liberty."

Human violence, Wordsworth wrote, in a sonnet that could have been addressed to Dante, even imagined, even for retribution, is not a divine instrument: "Hath it not long been said the wrath of Man / Works not the righteousness of God?" (see "Sonnets dedicated to Liberty and Order") So, his sonnets addressed to Italy, Venice, Bologna, acknowledge great Italian history as a source of democratic ideals and heroic action, "Fair land!.../ awake / Mother of Heroes, from thy death-like sleep." In keeping with his character and his experiences in France, he advised the fallen and broken city-states of Italy to follow an evolutionary rather than the destructive revolutionary process, "by no mere fit / Of sudden passions roused shall men attain / True Freedom" (see Wordsworth's three sonnets, *At Bologna, in Remembrance of the Late Insurrection, 1837*).

Wordsworth first published the *Memorials of a Tour of Italy,* in 1842, in *Poems Chiefly of Early and Late Years,* a large and diverse collection including several poems he had not yet published at all. Some of them, I believe, respond not only to Dante and *The Inferno,* but also to the theology embodied in the churches, paintings, monasteries, religious retreats, and monuments that he saw in his 1837 Italian tour. He included the early unpublished *Guilt and Sorrow* (1793–1794), originally called "Adventures on Salisbury Plain," and his drama, *The Borderers* (1796). These literally purgatorial poems explore on a secular level the mysteries of evil, crimes committed out of rationality gone wrong or impulse— "Action is transitory a step, a blow, / The motion of a muscle, this way or that / 'Tis done, and in the after-vacancy / We wonder at ourselves like men betrayed" (*The Borderers* 3.i, 405–410; quoted after the Dedication of "The White Doe of Rylstone," in the 1836 edition). By publishing these poems at this moment, after his last tour of Italy, he renews his faith in them, as if a rebuke to Dante and his theology. " The study of human nature," Wordsworth wrote in the introduction, "suggests this awful truth, that, as in the trials to which life subjects us, sin and crime are apt to start from their very opposite qualities, so there are no limits to the hardening of the heart and the perversion of the understanding to which they may carry their slaves" (*Prose Works* 1:69). And to illustrate, he cites a man like "Orlando or Ariosto...a man of great intellectual powers" that are "perverted," his "energies" devoted to "works of devastation," "who lays waste to the groves that should shelter him" (*Prose Works* 1:77)[11]—a mindless, impulsive, and blameless gesture Wordsworth himself recounts in "Nutting."

Wordsworth admired Dante's language. Dante was the "mighty poet," as he called him in the sonnet "To Florence," with a "Patriot's heart," but he was revolted by Dante's system and values, by the exiled and alienated poet who wrote *The Inferno*, self-imprisoned in his resentments and in the past, living out an unrewarding scenario of revenge and retribution. Wordsworth's beliefs, consistent throughout his life, were the very antithesis of Dante's. He was devoted to the community of human life, the inner life, the sacredness of the individual, the terrestrial "the very world that is the world / Of all of us, the place in which, in the end, / We find our happiness or not at all" (*The Prelude*, Book 10: 731–733). Dante was that opposition that Blake considers "true friendship," an opposition that affirmed Wordsworth's characteristic beliefs and practices.

Wordsworth appropriated, internalized and translated not only Dante's sacred spaces but also Milton's and Virgil's into the new subjectivity of his age and into the more personal Quaker idiom of inner light. At times, it sounded as if he were addressing them directly: "Not Chaos, not the darkest pit of lowest Erebus, / Nor aught of blinder vacancy, scooped out / By help of dreams—can breed such fear and awe / As fall upon us often when we look / Into our Minds, into the Mind of man— / My haunt and the main region of my song…"[12] But even as a countervoice, Dante was one of Wordsworth's "ancestral voices." Reading Dante next to Wordsworth reveals what is most original in his poetry: his belief in the present, the terrestrial, the existential self: "while we plough / This seas of life without a visible shore, / Do neither promise ask, more grace implore / In what alone is ours, the living Now."[13]

NOTES

1. All quotations from *The Prelude* are drawn from the 1805 version as printed in Jonathan Wordsworth, M.H. Abrams, and Stephen Gill's 1979 edition, listed in Works Cited.
2. See Draper's "Cesare Beccaria's Influence on English Discussions of Punishment, 1764–1789."
3. For further insights into these experiences of Wordsworth, see Wyatt, *Wordsworth's Poems of Travel, 1819–1842*, and Shackford's still very interesting 1923 article in *PMLA*, "Wordsworth's Italy."
4. See Sturrock, "Wordsworth's Italian Teacher."
5. For more on this topic, see Alan Hill's "Wordsworth and the Two Faces of Machiavelli" (1980), "Wordsworth and Italy" (1991), and "The Triumph of Memory: Petrarch, Augustine, and Wordsworth's Ascent of Snowden" (2006).
6. In "Wordsworth's Ariosto: Translation as Metatext and Misreading," Laura Bandiera attacks Wordsworth's "surprisingly inadequate

translation" "devoid of literary merits," "disgusting licentiousness
that poisons Ariosto," a "parody," that "debases and belittles" the
text. Given Wordsworth's repeated admiration for Ariosto, his taking it as the only text on his first journey over the Alps, using it to
teach his sister Italian, and given that the translation was a personal
exercise, never intended for publication or even for sharing, I don't
understand this criticism.

7. On no evidence, Zuccato, in *Petrarch in Romantic England*, claims
Wordsworth "disliked" Petrarch (ix), accuses him of a "life long cam-
paign of erasure," of being a "conservative opportunist" for dismissing "Petrarch the love poet" as "a rhetorician and a liar" (146).

8. See Wood, "Crying Game: Operatic Strains in Wordsworth's Lyrical
Ballads" (2004) and "The Castrato's Tale" *The Wordsworth Circle*
38 (2008): 74–79, which was later revised as Chapter 3 in Wood's
*Romanticism and Music Culture in Britain, 1770–1840: Virtue and
Virtuosity* (2010).

9. For more on Wordsworth's translations from the Italian, see Kenneth
Curry's 1938 article, "Uncollected Translations of Michael Angelo
by Wordsworth and Southey."

10. See Mortimer, "Wordsworth as Translator from Italian."

11. In a chapter called "Wordsworth, Dante, and British Romantic
Identity," Luzzi proposes that Wordsworth's *Prelude* is shaped by the
Divine Comedy, his "persona" closest to "the spirit and scope of Dante"
and that the revisions after 1837, his tour, reflect his recognition of his
affinity with Dante, which apparently improved his poetry. Illustrating
Wordsworth's defects as a poet and as a human being, Luzzi analyzes
"Tintern Abbey," which begins, he says, in a "ponderous disjunctive
manner" in a "sluggish and opaque" narrative voice which has "con-
founded and even infuriated its audiences for some time now" (no
citations are offered to verify this claim). He attacks "Michael" for its
"communitarian" ideal, which, he claims, accounts for his aversion to
Dante's "radical politics." In passing, he accuses Wordsworth of invok-
ing religion for "sociopolitical" reasons, essentially of being a hypo-
crite. Luzzi's reading of Wordsworth, like Bandiera's and Zuccatto's,
cited above, illustrates the odd judgments contemporary Italian critics
bring to Wordsworth, for which I can find no explanation.

12. This passage was written as the conclusion to *Home at Grasmere*,
1799, and published as the Prospectus to *The Excursion*, 1814.

13. See Wordsworth's Sonnet 10, *Memorials of a Tour of Italy*. He continues to serve the great tradition of Dante in England. In 2007, in
Grasmere, in the English Lake District where he spent his life, in the
museum attached to Dove Cottage, where he wrote his most original
poetry, The Wordsworth Trust mounted an award-winning exhibit
and published a magnificent catalogue called *Dante Rediscovered:
From Blake to Rodin.*

CHAPTER TWO

SITTING IN DANTE'S THRONE:
WORDSWORTH AND ITALIAN
NATIONALISM

Bruce Graver

William Wordsworth visited the city of Florence just once, during a hot week in late May and early June, 1837. It was not the happiest of visits. He quarreled with his travel companion, Henry Crabb Robinson,[1] fell asleep in the Tribuna of the Uffizi, oblivious to the attractions of the Venus de Medici and the snickers of other English visitors,[2] and repeatedly said that his tour of Italy had come "too late."[3] Robinson's visit was not much better: besides the heat and the quarrel, he had to listen to lengthy accounts of domestic violence from Savage Landor's estranged wife, who wanted to enlist him to negotiate a marriage settlement for her daughter—not exactly a holiday pastime (*Robinson on Books* 2:523). But there was one incident that, according to both men, made the stay worthwhile, and generated one of Wordsworth's most curious sonnets. Just outside the cathedral, opposite the south transept, was a large marble stone, called "il Sasso di Dante;" according to local legend, it was the place where Dante, before his exile, loved to sit.[4] And Robinson induced Wordsworth to try it out: "I remember the pleasure he expressed," Robinson recalled, "when I said to him 'You are now seated in Dante's chair'" (Jackson 806). Wordsworth's account, preserved in poem xvi of his *Memorials of a Tour in Italy, 1837,* is somewhat different.

> At Florence
> Under the shadow of a stately Pile,
> The dome of Florence, pensive and alone,
> Nor giving heed to aught that passed the while,
> I stood, and gazed upon a marble stone,
> The laurelled Dante's favourite seat. A throne,
> In just esteem, it rivals, though no style
> Be there of decoration to beguile
> The mind, depressed by thought of greatness flown.
> As a true man, who long had served the lyre,
> I gazed with earnestness, and dared no more.
> But in his breast the mighty Poet bore
> A Patriot's heart, warm with undying fire.
> Bold with the thought, in reverence I sate down,
> And, for a moment, filled that empty Throne.[5]

For Robinson, sitting in the "Sasso" is a kind of tourist stunt, something he seems to have lured Wordsworth into doing, just to check out his reaction. But in the sonnet, Wordsworth—at his most egotistically sublime, or perhaps just having a daffodil moment—represents himself as solitary, "pensive," contemplating his poetic heritage for an undetermined length of time (maybe a full half hour?), and then, "Bold with the thought," he takes his place "for a moment" as Dante's heir and successor. It is as if Wordsworth's face had been Photoshopped onto the Botticelli portrait of Dante, keeping the laurel wreath fully intact.[6]

Wordsworth makes clear what spurred his presumptuousness: Dante's patriotism. In 1837, that can only mean one thing: Wordsworth is claiming Dante's role as poetic advocate for a united Italy.[7] In 1830, when Robinson took up an extended residence in Italy, hopes for the reunification of the country were high, especially when Louis-Philippe of France expressed support for the nationalists, and promised military aid against the Austrians, if they attempted to intervene.[8] "The desire to see Italy united was the fond wish of most Italian politicians," Robinson reported (*Diary* 2:507); he himself spent most of his time reading about and discussing Italian politics, and successful revolts in several northern Italian cities, including Bologna and Urbino, made a united Italy seem more than a poetic dream. But matters changed dramatically in spring of 1831, when Metternich lowered the boom, Louis-Philippe reneged on his promises, and Austrian troops brutally crushed the rebellions, executing or imprisoning their leaders. Not until the revolutions of 1848 would the nationalist movement regain its footing.

In the space, then, between the failed rebellions of 1830 and the Risorgimento that was yet to be, Wordsworth inserts his voice. Sometimes the voice is prophetic, almost Miltonic, as when he apostrophizes Italy in "From the Alban Hills, Looking towards Rome." "Fallen Power,"

> Thy fortunes, twice exalted, might provoke
> Verse to glad notes prophetic of the hour
> When thou, uprisen, shalt break thy double yoke,
> And enter, with prompt aid from the Most High,
> On the third stage of thy great destiny. (ll. 9–14)

A similar apostrophe, this one more reminiscent of the Shelley of "West Wind," closes poem xxiv, "After Leaving Italy." "Italia!" he writes,

> on the surface of thy spirit...
> Shall a few partial breezes only creep?—
> Be its depths quickened; what thou dost inherit
> Of the world's hopes, dare to fulfill; awake
> Mother of Heroes, from thy death-like sleep! (ll. 9, 11–14)

But more often the voice is cautionary, informed by Wordsworth's experience of the French Revolution, and deeply suspicious (in ways that recall Burke) of violent change in the name of liberty. The three sonnets *At Bologna, in Remembrance of the Late Insurrections, 1837* give fullest expression to this point of view. In the first, he asserts that

> by no mere fit
> Of sudden passion roused shall men attain
> True freedom where for ages they have lain
> Bound in a dark abominable pit,
> With life's best sinews more and more unknit. (ll. 1–5)

The image is from Dante's *Inferno*, cantos 21–22, of the Bolgia of the grafters, whose punishment is to be immersed in boiling pitch, while demons "unknit" their "sinews" with grappling hooks. Such an allusion tells us a good deal about how Wordsworth read the *Commedia*. To be in Dante's hell is a moral and historical judgment, more than a theological one. The Italian people cannot be truly free, as long as they wallow in moral and political corruption, and I don't think the reference to graft here is just accidental. Like his American friend George Ticknor—the greatest American Dante scholar of his generation, whom Wordsworth had just run into in Rome—Wordsworth reads the *Commedia* historically, in the context of the politics of fourteenth-century Italy.[9] In addition, the political conclusion he draws is from Burke: a country without a strong native tradition of liberty cannot simply be freed overnight by insurrection. So Wordsworth counsels "gradual progress," a reliance on "Fortitude," "Patience," "Prudence," and the "golden mean,"[10] addressing the passionate Italian reformers as a seasoned counselor and teacher, much in the same way that Michel Beaupuy had taught and counseled Wordsworth in 1792. Thus the third Bologna sonnet ends with a simile that describes the consequences of too hasty reform, a simile that may also allude, more obliquely, to Dante's cantos on the grafters:

> Alas! with most, who weigh futurity
> Against time present, passion holds the scales:
> Hence equal ignorance of both prevails,
> And nations sink; or, struggling to be free,
> Are doomed to flounder on, like wounded whales
> Tossed on the bosom of a stormy sea. (ll. 9–14)

So, as one would expect, the Wordsworth in 1837 Italy is very different from the Wordsworth in 1790 and 1792 France. It is not that he opposes reform; far from it. As a liberal neighbor of his wrote in 1839, "The poet on Italian politics is all we can desire...[he] spoke with strong and deep feeling of the present state of Italy, and the crushing despotism of Austria....I cannot think Milton himself could have talked more loftily...." (Fletcher 244). But Wordsworth had become skeptical of sudden rebellion, carried out in the heat of passion, having seen its effects in France. Too much is lost, and genuine liberty is seldom attained.

It is in this context that we need to understand the poems about monastic life included in the 1837 *Memorials*: "The Cuckoo at Laverna," "At Vallombrosa," three sonnets on the monastery of Camaldoli, and the short lyric "On a Ruined Convent in the Appenines." La Verna, Camaldoli, and Vallombrosa, all in the Tuscan Appenines, were standard stops for the British tourist, recommended in both Forsyth's and Eustaces's Italian tours; Robinson himself had visited them during his Italian residence in 1829–1831.

But Wordsworth gives them an unusual amount of space in his Memorials, especially when we consider that sites like St. Peter's or the Colosseum or the Florentine cathedral are barely mentioned. As we all know, he had been writing about monasteries, ruined and otherwise, all his life, and in *The Tuft of Primroses* went so far as to compare his life in Grasmere to the monastic retreat of St. Basil. But it is another passage written for *The Tuft of Primroses* and later revised for *The Prelude* that is most relevant here: the account of his visit to the Grand Chartreuse. There Wordsworth, startled at the sight of soldiers just outside the monastery walls, "commissioned to expel / the blameless inmates," imagines that the voice of Nature herself speaks in protest: "Let this one temple last, be this one spot / Of earth devoted to eternity." And to her protest, his "heart" responded: "Honour to the patriot's zeal! / Glory and hope to new-born Liberty! / . . . But . . . spare / These courts of mystery. . . . /

> be the house redeemed
> With its unworldly votaries, for the sake
> Of conquest over sense, hourly achieved
> Through faith and meditative reason. . . .
> (*Prelude* [1850] 6: 425–426, 434–435, 441–442, 448, 450–451,
>   456–459)

Now there is no statement this direct in the 1837 *Memorials*, but by giving the Tuscan monasteries so much attention, by investing them with so much cultural value—the legacy of St. Francis at La Verna, of Milton at Vallombrosa, and, although he neglects to mention it in the sonnets, of the Florentine humanists, who held learned symposia at Camaldoli—and by placing them side by side with sonnets on Italian liberty, Wordsworth is expressing the hope that the Italian reformers will show greater wisdom than the French, or for that matter, the English, whose ruined monasteries were one of his favored haunts. It is thus important to note that the "Ruined Convent in the Appenines" was not actually in the Appenines at all: it was in France, as the original manuscript of the poem reveals.[11] Wordsworth translates the ruin to an Italian setting to serve as a warning to his intended audience to protect the life of contemplation and meditative reason—a warning that, in the event, was not heeded.

But who, exactly, does Wordsworth intend this audience to be? Or rather, how does he expect his political counsels to reach the people who, in his own estimation, are in the best position to act upon them? To answer this question, it is necessary to give more attention to the liberal neighbor, referred to above, who so approved of Wordsworth's opinions on Italian politics: Mrs. Eliza Dawson Fletcher. Eliza Fletcher, widow of a prominent Edinburgh lawyer and liberal Whig, first met the Wordsworths in the summer of 1833 when she rented Thorney How, in the Easedale valley just outside of Grasmere and a short walk from Allan Bank, where her friends the Arnolds were spending the summer (Fletcher 212–214). In her Edinburgh days, Fletcher and her husband frequently entertained Italian exiles, whose nationalist sentiments she shared, and through them she met the historian Sismondi, whose works she read and admired (Fletcher 165–166). In 1840, she purchased Lancrigg, the farm adjoining Thorney How, and remained intimate friends of the Wordsworths for the rest of her life (Fletcher 246). In April 1837, while Wordsworth was on his way to Rome, she met

> a young Italian exile who at that time was a friendless stranger in London.... He could not then speak English, and I very imperfect French; but it was impossible not to be favourably impressed at once by his truth and his sadness. He told me he was an exile, and without endeavouring to excite my compassion, or dwelling at all on his wrongs or his circumstances, by relating any particulars of his past life, he said his present object was to obtain admission to some public library, that he might give himself to literary work. He looked so profoundly unhappy, and spoke so despondingly of the condition of his country, and of the genius of Chatterton with such high admiration, that I foolishly took it into my head, after he had left me, that he meditated suicide.... (Fletcher 230)

This young Italian exile was Giuseppe Mazzini, who was not in fact suicidal, but, having been recently released from a Parisian prison, was looking for support for his "giovine Italia" movement. This was a crucial moment in Mazzini's career. As Maurizio Isabella explains, in the 1830s, Mazzini needed the access to journals and reformist political circles that a well-connected person like Fletcher could afford him. He was convinced that earlier nationalist exiles, Foscolo in particular, were too indebted to French political models, and that native models needed to be developed, based on native institutions. In addition, he needed to be able to make his case to the British people at large, who had already been so supportive of the Italian nationalist movement (Isabella 210–212, 214–215). Eliza Fletcher turned out to be instrumental to his efforts: she wrote him letters of introduction and recommendation, both in Whig circles and in the circles of Italian exiles living in Edinburgh (Fletcher 231–233). She remained

Mazzini's friend, correspondent, and, we can assume, financial supporter for the rest of her life.

Two years later, when Lancrigg unexpectedly came up for sale, Mrs. Fletcher's daughter Mary was in the Lake District visiting the Arnolds and the Wordsworths. There she met the poet "with an Italian gentleman of the name of Miers." Wordsworth asked him about Mazzini, and heard a very high character of him in every respect. Mr. Miers said that shortly before leaving Italy he had called on the mother of Mazzini to ask her commands for her son. She was not well, but she said, "Don't tell Giuseppe that you found me ill, but tell him that not a day of my life passes that I do not thank God for having given me such a son." Mr. Miers added that "it was worthy of a Spartan mother; but what made it so valuable was, that it was uttered by a Christian one" (Fletcher 243–244).[12] Now this encounter, and these discussions, are happening at the very time that Wordsworth is writing his *Memorials of a Tour in Italy*, and beginning to conceive of them as a sequence of poems. So although it is perhaps too restrictive to suggest that Mazzini himself is Wordsworth's target audience, the young Wordsworth to the elder Wordsworth's Beaupuy, it seems all but certain that the poet had in mind the growing numbers of Italian political exiles in Britain, men, like his teacher Agostino Isola, who had dreams of a united Italy, and now had the hope and numbers and leadership and financial support to begin to bring it about. It would not surprise me at all to learn that Wordsworth made a small contribution to the great cause.

But let us return to the moment that occasioned Wordsworth's sonnet "At Florence." As Wordsworth was pausing before il Sasso di Dante, and working up the energy to sit down in it, a cholera epidemic was sweeping the city of Naples. Wordsworth knew this: his tour originally included Naples, Pompeii and Herculaneum, and the magnificent ruins at Paestum. But word of cholera forced a change of plans, and he and Robinson decided to head north instead, to Florence and the Tuscan monasteries, and then north to the Italian lakes and Venice.[13] The cholera epidemic claimed many lives, and the most notable among them was Italy's greatest living poet, Giacomo Leopardi.[14] Did Wordsworth know this? Surely not while in Italy, but almost certainly after his return to England, probably soon after landing in Dover. For Robinson knew Leopardi personally, having met and conversed with him during his stay in Florence in 1831 (*Diary* 2:507). Leopardi's death left the throne of Dante, as Wordsworth understood it, empty. When "for a moment" the English poet fills that throne, it may be as a quiet tribute to the passing of the author of "All' Italia" and "Risorgimento."

NOTES

1. Wordsworth gives particulars of his discomfort with Robinson's habits in a letter to Mary Wordsworth, dated July 17, 1837 (*Letters of Williams and Dorothy Wordsworth* 425–427). Robinson, he writes, "takes delight in loitering about towns, gossiping, and attending reading-rooms, and going to coffee-houses; and at *table d'hôtes*, etc., gabbling German, or any other tongue, all which places and practices are my abomination" (426).
2. Of his nap in the Tribuna, Wordsworth wrote: "It was very hot weather during the week we stayed at Florence; and, having never been there before, I went through much hard service, and I am not, therefore, ashamed to confess, I fell asleep before this picture [Raphel's "John the Baptist"], and sitting with my back towards the Venus de Medicis."
3. See Christopher Wordsworth, *Memoirs of William Wordsworth, Poet-Laureate, D. C. L.* 2:232.
4. Wordsworth himself was more than a little skeptical about this legend. In the notes dictated to Isabella Fenwick, he remarked: "Upon what evidence the belief rests, that this stone was a favourite seat of Dante, I do not know; but a man would little consult his own interest as a traveller, if he should busy himself with doubts as to the fact" (Jackson 807). There is now a restaurant of the same name at the site of the stone seat.
5. All quotations from the *Memorials of a Tour in Italy, 1837,* are from Wordsworth's *Sonnet Series and Itinerary Poems, 1820–1845,* ed. Geoffrey Jackson.
6. In fact, Dr. John Davy (Sir Humphry's brother and the attendant physician during Wordsworth's last illness) thought Wordsworth closely resembled the known portraits of Dante. Davy's wife, Margaret Fletcher Davy, concurred: "I thought if the laurel wreath had been there, it would have been nearly the same face as that which we see in the portraits considered authentic of that poet [Dante] of an older time" (quoted in Rice 38).
7. This view of Dante as advocating Italian unification was promoted in England in the writings of two prominent Italian exiles: Ugo Foscolo and Gabriele Rossetti. For a discussion of their role in reviving British interest in Dante, and their political readings of the *Commedia*, see Maurizio Isabella's *Risorgimento in Exile* (204–206).
8. Robinson's account of the political events of 1830–1831 can be found in his *Diary* (2:478 ff).
9. Ticknor's unpublished three-volume commentary on the *Commedia* survives in the Ticknor Collection at Dartmouth College. At the time of Wordsworth's Italian tour, the Ticknors were also in Italy; Wordsworth met them briefly just before leaving Rome, met up with them again in the northern Italian lakes, and traveled with them to Venice and Germany.

10. "Fortitude" is mentioned in the first sonnet of the three, l. 13; "Patience" and "Prudence" are mentioned in the second, ll. 2, 13; "the golden mean" is also from the second sonnet, l. 8.

11. See Jackson's notes to *Sonnet Series and Itinerary Poems*, 781, 807. Unfortunately, Jackson does not give a photograph or transcription of the manuscript version; it must be reconstructed from his *apparatus*. In the Fenwick Note to this poem, quoted by Jackson, Wordsworth comments: "The Political Revolutions of our time have multiplied on the Continent objects that unavoidably call forth reflections such as are expressed in these verses...." (802).

12. Isabella notes that much of Mazzini's success with British radicals was due to "the intense religious dimension of [his] message" (211).

13. Wordsworth first voice fears about the cholera epidemic in a letter to his family, dated April 27 or 28, 1837 (*Letters of Williams and Dorothy Wordsworth* 394). By May 6, he had given up hope of visiting Naples, "on account of the Quarantine" (*ibid.* 398).

14. The standard account in English of Leopardi's death can be found in Origo (251–255).

CHAPTER THREE

BYRON BETWEEN
ARIOSTO AND TASSO

Nicholas Halmi

"I think I can explain myself," wrote Byron in *Don Juan*, "without / That sad inexplicable beast of prey— / That Sphinx, whose words would ever be a doubt" (9.50).[1] I too hope not to need the Sphinx, but I shall not be able to explain myself without elaborating on the implied promise to situate Byron between Ariosto and Tasso—and not merely alphabetically. The question to be addressed here is this: in what relation does *Don Juan*, as a poetic project, stand to Ariosto's *Orlando furioso*, "A new creation with [its] magic line," and to Tasso's *Gerusalemme liberata*, "unsurpass'd in modern song" (*Childe Harold's Pilgrimage* 4.40, 39)? The question is worth asking less for the specific reasons that Byron repeatedly links the two poets and in *Don Juan* adopts their stanzaic form, ottava rima, than for the general reason that none of the three poems conforms fully or uncontestedly to the traditional conventions of the genre with which each asks primarily to be identified, heroic poetry, or epic. But for reasons to be considered, the answer cannot be formulated adequately in the expected terms of personal affinity or literary influence.

Byron's devotion to the Ferrarese poets is clear enough. The catalogue of books he sold at auction in 1816, before leaving England permanently, lists no fewer than two editions of the *Furioso* and four of the *Liberata*, as well as John Hoole's translation of the latter

and John Black's *Life of Tasso*.[2] The epigraph to the fourth canto
of *Childe Harold's Pilgrimage* (1818) applies to Byron himself a
quotation from one of Ariosto's minor poems: "Visto ho Toscana,
Lombardia, Romagna, / Quel Monte che divide, e quel che serra
/ Italia, e un mare e l' altro, che la bagna" ("I've seen Tuscany,
Lombardy, Romagna, / That mountain which divides, and that
which splits / Italy, and the one sea and the other which bathe it")
(Ariosto, *Satira* 3.57–60). Not without justice might Byron claim in
Childe Harold, "I've taught me other tongues, and in strange eyes /
Have made me not a stranger" (4.8). Yet there was nothing strange
about his admiration of "the bard of Chivalry": the latter half of
the eighteenth century saw a revival of interest in Ariosto and other
Italian poets, stimulated by Giuseppe Baretti's *Dissertation upon the
Italian Poetry* (1753), and the publication of new translations of the
Furioso by William Huggins (1755) and John Hoole (1783). Among
Byron's contemporaries, Robert Southey read Hoole's translation
with delight while still a child (Brand, *Italy* 74–75); Wordsworth,
who studied Italian at Cambridge, was sufficiently interested in the
Furioso to take a pocket edition of it on his Alpine walking tour of
1790 and to translate two cantos from it in 1802 (Wu 7 [note 13];
Wordsworth, *Poems* 594–597); and Coleridge, who began reading
Ariosto in Malta in 1805, praised him for the flexibility of his language in treating all manner of subjects gracefully (*Lectures* 1:291,
2:482). Where Byron differed specifically from Wordsworth and
Coleridge was not in his appreciation of Ariosto's poetic skill, but in
his conviction of the suitability of ottava rima to English verse. (In
1846 Wordsworth advised a translator of the *Liberata* against trying to preserve Ariosto's rhyme scheme because "the unfavourable
nature of the English language for finding rhymes would render this
difficult, if not impossible" (Robertson x).) This is a point to which
I shall return after considering Byron's more complex engagement
with the author of the *Liberata*.

Traveling from Venice to Rome in the spring of 1817, Byron made
a detour to Ferrara to see Ariosto's tomb and Tasso's asylum cell
(*Byron's Letters and Journals* 5:217). This visit gave him occasion to
rebuke the city for having treated its two most distinguished poets
illiberally and to vindicate their poetic achievement in the face of the
adversity that both had endured. Black's *Life* entertained the possibility that Tasso had been confined for having offended his patron,
Alfonso II d'Este—though not, as legend had it, for having fallen in
love with the duke's sister Leonora (2:78–92)—but Byron chose to
present the poet unequivocally as the victim of a tyrant's persecution.

The fulfillment of the prophecy that Byron assigns to the imprisoned
poet in "The Lament of Tasso" (1817),

> I shall make
> A future temple of my present cell,
> Which nations yet shall visit for my sake.
> While thou, Ferrara! when no longer dwell
> The ducal chiefs within thee, shall fall down,
> And crumbling piecemeal view thy heartless halls,
> A poet's wreath shall be thy only crown,
> A poet's dungeon thy most far renown,
> While strangers wonder o'er thy unpeopled walls! (ll. 219–227)

is confirmed in the apostrophe to Ferrara in *Childe Harold*, which
incorporates from the prefatory note to "The Lament" Byron's observation of the city's decayed and depopulated state:

> Ferrara! in thy wide and grass-grown streets,
> Whose symmetry was not for solitude,
> There seems as 'twere a curse upon the seats
> Of former sovereigns, and the antique brood
> Of Este, which for many an age made good
> Its strength within thy walls, and was of yore
> Patron or tyrant....
>
> And Tasso is their glory and their shame.
> Hark to his strain! and then survey his cell!
> And see how dearly earn'd Torquato's fame,
> And where Alfonso bade his poet dwell:
> The miserable despot could not quell
> The insulted mind he sought to quench, and blend
> With the surrounding maniacs, in the hell
> Where he had plung'd it. Glory without end
> Scatter'd the clouds away—and on that name attend
>
> The tears and praises of all time.... (4.35–37)

Projecting into the past a ventriloquized prophecy that he ful-
fills in his present pilgrimage to Ferrara, Byron implicitly not only
identifies himself with Tasso but, in a sense, becomes the poet's
liberator, affirming his place in a cosmopolitan literary culture. Yet
he was hardly alone in such identification, for the popular legend
of Tasso's suffering—imprisoned for love, slandered by his enemies,
censored by the Inquisition—was powerfully attractive in the eighteenth and early nineteenth centuries, conforming as it did to the

conception of the artist as a solitary genius at odds with conventional society. Rousseau, who claimed that Tasso had "predicted" his own *maleurs*, drafted a ballet (now lost) on Tasso's purported love for Leonora (294 and n. 9). Goethe, who recognized parallels between courtly life in sixteenth-century Ferrara and that in eighteenth-century Weimar (*Gedenkausgabe* 24:635 [to J. P. Eckermann, May 6, 1827]), composed a drama on Tasso with the declared aim "of filling [his] mind with the character and fate of this poet" (19:110 [to Duke Karl August, March 28, 1788])—who consequently appears as a more ambivalent figure than Byron's Tasso, the victim as much of his own solipsistic imagination and unrestrained feeling as of others' mistreatment (Burwick, *Poetic Madness* 106–108, 123–124).[3] Commenting in 1834 on Goethe's drama, from which she translated extracts, Felicia Hemans regretted that Tasso had been depicted as a relatively weak character ("Scenes and Passages from Goethe" 612): the subject of her own poem "Tasso's Coronation" (1828), an awkward combination of triumphalism and pathos, had been the belated public recognition of his poetic powers. Had Shelley completed his planned tragedy on Tasso, the protagonist would likely have been, to judge from the two existing fragments (Cameron and Reiman 6:590–592, 851–865), closer in character to Byron's, still vigorous in mind though oppressed by his imprisonment.

Brief as it is, the foregoing survey indicates that Byron's interest in Tasso's life, or more precisely in a popular, romanticized interpretation of that life, was more characteristic of its time than distinctive to Byron himself. He is not even the only poet for whom the self-identificatory treatment of the figure of Tasso signals an intellectual turning point and confirms a sense of poetic vocation (cf. Cameron and Reiman 7:222–223), for Goethe's *Torquato Tasso*, begun before and finished (in substantially altered form) after his Italian sojourn of 1786–1788, is arguably "in many ways the axis round which his entire literary career revolves" (Boyle 1:607). Yet neither Byron's "Lament" nor Goethe's drama is especially concerned with the *Liberata* itself: it is the conflictual environment in which that poem was composed that provides the thematic medium for artistic self-reflection. The particular interest of "The Lament," for its part, consists not in how it figures Byron's relation to Tasso but in its presentation of a specific place as the focus for historical meditation (Cheeke 94–95), a strategy repeated throughout the fourth canto of *Childe Harold*.

In 1819 Byron returned to the subject of the posthumous vindication of the Ferrarese poets. Like "The Lament of Tasso," *The Prophecy of Dante* takes the form of a proleptic soliloquy. Having

Dante rate Ariosto and Tasso "greater still than" Petrarch (3.107), Byron implicitly privileges the epic tradition, but without thereby clarifying his own relation to it:

> he [Tasso] and his compeer,
> The Bard of Chivalry, will both consume
> In penury and pain too many a year,
> And, dying in despondency, bequeath
> To the kind world, which scarce will yield a tear,
> A heritage enriching all who breathe
> With the wealth of a genuine poet's soul,
> And to their country a redoubled wreath,
> Unmatch'd by time. . . . (3.149–157)

This is a generous but generalized tribute, leaving unspecified the nature of the two poets' respective bequests to posterity, let alone more narrowly to Byron himself—for evidently Dante's prophetic gifts did not extend so far forward in time. If Ariosto and Tasso are the legitimate successors of Dante, in what sense is Byron their successor?

Framing that question in terms of influence will not get us far, regardless of whether we have an affective or an idealist conception of influence. Affective criticism, which assesses writers' originality in the context of their engagement with prior literature, derives from the identification of influence with formal and stylistic imitation, both of which had been recommended since antiquity as essential components of a literary apprenticeship. Bryon himself had little patience for questions of influence or indebtedness in this sense, and he responded dismissively to Lady Blessington, for example, when she broached the topic in conversation: "To be perfectly original," he is reported to have said, "one should think much and read little, and this is impossible, as one must have read much more before one learns to think. . . . But after one has laid in a tolerable stock of materials for thinking, I should think the best plan would be to give the mind time to digest it, and then turn it all well over by thought and reflection by which we make the knowledge acquired our own" (Blessington 364–365). Like the individual ingredients of a stew cooked for hours over low heat, the books one has read should be rendered unidentifiable by the process of reflection on them, the resultant concoction exceeding the sum of its original parts.

To be sure, Byron's insistence on the necessity of assimilating knowledge might seem more compelling, and less defensive, if it were realized more fully his own poetry. In contrast to *Paradise Lost*,

whose overt allusiveness is almost inversely proportional to its pervasive learning, *Don Juan* is constantly advertising its literary contexts
and intertexts:

> My poem's epic, and is meant to be
> Divided in twelve books; each book containing,
> With love, and war, a heavy gale at sea,
> A list of ships, and captains, and kings reigning,
> New characters; the episodes are three:
> A panorama of view of hell's in training,
> After the style of Virgil and of Homer,
> So that my name of Epic's no misnomer. (1.200)
> . . . .
> And if Pedrillo's fate should shocking be,
> Remember Ugolino condescends
> To eat the head of his arch-enemy
> The moment after he politely ends
> His tale. . . . (2.83)

Confronted with such instances, one is tempted to extend to Byron
the criticism that a reviewer in the *New Yorker* once made of the film-
maker Peter Greenway: "He chews with his mouth open—we can identify almost every piece of art that has fed his imagination" (Rafferty).
This is the very opposite of assimilative, digestive reading.

But Byron is not, in fact, like Greenaway, whose allusions betray
an anxious desire to be taken seriously as an artist. The very stagi-
ness of Byron's mock-identification with older poets, no less than
the vehemence of his rejection of the Lake poets, testifies to a fundamental dilemma that confronted him as an epic poet: while he
wanted to dissociate himself from contemporary English practitio-
ners of the genre, particularly Southey and Wordsworth, he could
not do so simply by claiming allegiance to epic tradition, for the
conventions belonging to that tradition were no longer adequate
to the distinctly modern conception of reality that impelled the
open-ended narrative of *Don Juan*.[4] The instances of formal and
stylistic imitation or appropriation, as opposed to parody, that can
plausibly be attributed to him tend, therefore, to be localized and
independent of the overall project of the poem, with the obvious
exception of the stanzaic form. But ottava rima was used in much,
if not most, of the Italian narrative poetry Byron is known to have
read—by Boiardo, Francesco Berni, Luigi Pulci, and Giambattista
Casti, as well as by Ariosto and Tasso—and in the event his most
immediate stimulus to adopt the form came, as he acknowledged to

John Murray (*Byron's Letters and Journals* 5:267), from the mock
Arthurian epic, *Prospectus and Specimen of an Intended National
Work* (1817), by John Hookham Frere, pseudonymously known as
the brothers Whistlecraft. Frere's poem convinced Byron that the
easy grace of the Italian stanza could be managed in English, permitting him the "freedom," meaning variety of tone and subject-
matter, that he admired in Ariosto, Pulci, Berni, and others (*Byron's
Letters and Journals* 6:76–77). His appropriation of the form in
Don Juan was so thorough, in fact, that the archivist and historian Francis Cohen, writing to John Murray in 1819, regretted the
extent of his departure from Ariosto's practice: "Lord B. should
have been grave & gay by turns. . . . And not grave & gay in the same
page, or in the same stanza, or in the same line.—If he had followed
~~Pulci more closely~~ Ariosto more closely, he would have produced a
masterpiece & not a sport of fancy."[5]

In Peter Vassallo's comprehensive study of the influence of Italian
literature on Bryon's poetry, Ariosto and Tasso receive far less attention than the eighteenth-century satirist Casti, whose *Novelle galanti*
Byron read in the summer of 1816, and Pulci, the sixteenth-century
"sire of the half-serious rhyme" (*Don Juan* 4.6), the first canto of
whose *Morgante* Byron translated in 1820. In addition, where the
Ferrarese poets are credited by Vassallo as the sources of incidents
in *Don Juan*, the differences from the originals are more striking
than the similarities. Although it is entirely plausible that for his ship-
wreck scene (*Don Juan* 2.23–110) Byron drew on Ariosto's description of Ruggiero's voyage from Marseilles to north Africa in *Orlando
furioso* (41.8–24), he also drew on contemporary accounts of shipwrecks, as was noted by reviewers—indeed a correspondent to *The
Monthly Magazine* accused him of outright plagiarism[6]—and was
acknowledged by Byron himself in correspondence (*Byron's Letters
and Journals* 8:186). If his purpose in including this episode, and
particularly its cannibalism, is to suggest that even the most powerful
taboos, let alone the tenets of conventional morality, prove dispens-
able when one's survival is at stake, then the accepted factuality of
the nonliterary sources that he exploited, such as Sir John Dalyell's
Shipwrecks and Disasters at Sea (1812), is far more pertinent than are
any literary precedents. This point was not lost on Byron's anonymous accuser in *The Monthly Magazine*: "The interest excited by the
well-imagined sufferings of the hapless crew in the vessel in which
Juan embarked, will not, I am sure, be at all diminished, but, on the
contrary, increased by learning that the horrors of such a scene were
actually experienced by some of our fellow-creatures" ("Plagiarisms"

19). As pure fiction, the cannibalism in *Don Juan* would be completely gratuitous, as it is in Greenaway's *The Cook, the Thief.*

Passing to cantos 5 and 9, we may certainly agree that the episodes involving Gulbayez and Catherine the Great recall the seduction of Ruggiero by Alcina in the *Furioso* (7.2–32) and of Rinaldo by Armida in the *Liberata* (14.55–77). But in so far as both episodes in the Italian epics are "allegorical representations of the triumph of the sensuous over the rational" (Vassallo 95), the parallels with Byron collapse. For whereas allegory assumes the existence of a coherent structure of meaning existing outside the narrative and to which the narrative is subordinate, *Don Juan* refers outside itself to historical facts and human experiences rather than to structures of meaning. Moreover, despite his qualified attraction to the supernatural in drama, Byron did not follow his Ferrarese predecessors in allowing it into his epic: the opulent grounds and palace through which the eunuch Baba leads Juan and Johnson, from its "orange bowers, and jasmine, and so forth" (5.40) to its "magnificent large hall" (5.51) and "glittering galleries, and...marble floors" (5.85), are enchant*ing*, perhaps, but not enchant*ed*. In contrast, Alcina and Armida do practice magic in their respective gardens (*Furioso* 6.51–52, *Liberata* 10.66, 70), which is why Ruggiero must be rescued from the one by means of a magic ring (7.64–65) and Rinaldo from the other by means of a magic shield (14.77). Byron's naturalism, thus, distinguishes him fundamentally from the romance epic tradition, as appears in greatest relief exactly where his possible and probable appropriations from representatives of that tradition are quite specific. His version of the "treacherous earthly paradise" (Vassallo 96) is, precisely, earthly.[7]

Thus far I have been addressing the limits of affective criticism in evaluating Byron's relation to the Ferrarese poets, but his possible allusion to both in the opening of the first canto of *Don Juan* opens a broader perspective in which to view all three writers at once. In the commentary to his edition of the poem, Jerome McGann notes that Byron's introduction of Juan as a hero faute de mieux—"I want a hero: an uncommon want, / When every year and month sends forth a new one"—recalls *Orlando furioso* 1.1–4, in which Ariosto introduces Orlando and Ruggiero, and *Gerusalemme liberata* 1.36, in which Tasso invokes the aid of *Mente* (memory) to recall the leaders and companies of the crusading army. Since Ariosto's passage itself alludes to the opening of the *Aeneid* and Tasso's to the invocation preceding the catalogue of ships in *Iliad* 2.484–493, it is obvious that both writers, and Byron in turn in alluding to them, are addressing themselves not only to the intended audiences of their poems but as it were to the conventions of the genre of which their poems are to be members. The *Furioso* is not only a poem about "ladies, knights, arms, and loves" (1.1), nor the *Liberata* only a poem about "pious armies" (1.1), nor *Don Juan* only a poem about "fierce loves and faithless wars" (7.8): each is also a contribution to the idea of something exceeding itself, heroic poetry in general.

This prompts the question of whether we might not make more progress abandoning an affective for an idealist conception of influence, such as that implied in T. S. Eliot's "ideal order" or Northrop Frye's "total form" of literature. Influence in this sense is not the formal imitation of one writer by another, but form itself as the expression of the participation by all literary works in the totality of literature. The surrender of personality enjoined by Eliot on the poet enables "dead poets, his ancestors," to take possession of him and "assert their immortality" through him (14): thus voided of personality, the poet becomes conscious of "not of what is dead, but of what is already living" within him, namely the tradition (22). The metaphor of spectral possession is all too apt, for despite Eliot's concession that new works modify the existing order "ever so slightly" (15), it is evident from his emphasis on the completeness, self-containment, and timelessness of that order that he conceives it not as an aggregate of individual works but as something autonomous and antecedent: "the historical sense compels a man to write . . . with a feeling that the whole of literature of Europe from Homer and within it the whole of the literature of his own country has a simultaneous existence and composes a simultaneous order" (14). Since the creative process, understood in these terms, consists not in the poet's negotiation with the tradition but in the tradition's self-expression through the poet, the idealist critic cannot, in fact, account for the historicity of generic conventions.

This limitation becomes obvious in Frye's *Anatomy*, which articulates an idealist theory of literature without, as in Eliot's "Tradition and the Individual Talent," the burden of a corresponding scheme of aesthetic evaluation. Individual works can be comprehended as parts of the totality of literature, Frye explains, because the totality can be comprehended in individual works. Each work is, thus, a synecdoche of literature itself: "We said that we could get a whole liberal education by picking up one conventional poem, *Lycidas* for example, and following its archetypes through literature. Thus the center of the literary universe is whatever poem we happen to be reading. One step further, and the poem appears as a microcosm of all literature, an individual manifestation of the total order of words" (121). From this

anagogical perspective, the individual work, itself reduced synecdoch-
ically to a symbol—by which term Frye means "any literary structure
that can be isolated for critical attention" (71)—is to be understood
as the finite and temporal manifestation of "a single infinite and eternal verbal symbol" (121). In appropriating the word *monad* as a syn-
onym for *symbol* in this context, Frye implies a certain affinity with
the metaphysical claims of Leibniz's *Monadology*: that the monads of
which the universe is composed are arranged according to a divinely
preestablished harmony and have no interaction with one another. As
in Eliot, the concept of the whole effectively annihilates the possibility of meaningfully comparing the parts.

   We seem to have reached an impasse. But fortunately we are not
compelled to abandon our three epics to the crowded isolation of a
monadic literary universe, for Frye himself, ironically, insinuates a way
of rescuing them. In his sole reference to *Don Juan* in the *Anatomy*, he
remarks the poem's resistance to literary decorum: "*Tristram Shandy*
and *Don Juan* illustrate very clearly the constant tendency to self-par-
ody in satiric rhetoric which prevents the process of writing itself from
becoming an oversimplified convention or ideal" (234). To be sure,
Frye proceeds to assimilate both Sterne and Byron to his "third phase
of satire," but his observation is sufficient to remind us that, whatever
their ontological status, conventions, genres, archetypes, and the like
are objects of consciousness, and as such can become the subjects of literature (in the older sense of *subject* as that about which judgments are
made, I hasten to add, as opposed to the modern philosophical sense as
that which makes judgments). Brian Wilkie's perceptive consideration
of *Don Juan* from the perspective of genre consists to a large extent in
enumerating the variousness of Byron's engagement with epic conventions, from straightforward mockery, as in the abbreviated invocation
"Hail, Muse! *et cetera*" (3.1), to grimly ironic affirmation, as in the
boast with which he interrupts the narrative of the siege of Ismail:

> Reader! I have kept my word,—at least so far
> As the first Canto promised. You have now
> Had sketches of love, tempest, travel, war—
> All very accurate, you must allow,
> And *Epic*, if plain truth should prove no bar;
> For I have drawn much less with a long bow
> Than my forerunners....(8.138)

   As I suggested above and have argued more fully elsewhere, Byron's
simultaneous identification with and rejection of epic tradition was

rooted in his recognition of a disparity between the historical conditions of which that tradition is expressive and those of modern
European life as he experienced and observed it. While the attractions
of existing epics were too powerful, and Byron's literary ambitions—
not least his desire to distinguish himself definitively from Southey
and Wordsworth—too great for him not to attempt make his own
claim to epic status, the anachronisms of the form were also too bla-
tant for him to ignore. Thus, one way his historical consciousness
manifests itself is in a literary self-consciousness. Recognizing what
might be called the situational analogies between Ferrarese poets and
Byron in this respect assists us in schematizing clearly the distinctive-
ness of the English poet's contention with the formal conservatism of
the heroic genre.

In his lectures on aesthetics, Hegel suggestively attributed the
transformation of epic to the advent of modernity. The impingement
of Renaissance humanism on medieval culture, he explained, found
contrasting expressions in the *Furioso* and the *Liberata*: Ariosto
sought to preserve chivalric romance by ironizing it, Tasso to revive
classical epic by Christianizing it (15:411–412). This distinction is
too simple, inasmuch as Ariosto also classicized his episodic romance
by incorporating into it a Virgilian dynastic plot—the marriage of
Ruggiero and Bradamante as the foundation of the house of Este—
while Tasso also romanticized his historical narrative by including
in its centre a romantic excursus—the detainment of Rinaldo by
Armida. Yet Hegel's basic insight is undeniable. Tasso, who disap-
proved of the *Furioso* but was acutely aware of its popularity, himself
allegorized Rinaldo's subjection as the absence of rational government over the irascible part of the soul (Quint 38); but in generic
terms the episode constitutes that which, while not to be wholly
excluded from epic—for romance and epic are not, he maintains,
different in kind (*Discorsi* 576)—must be prevented from dominat-
ing it. If romance is the sugar with which we rim a glass of bitter medicine to make it more palatable ("porgiamo aspersi di soavi
licor gli orli del vaso," *Liberata* 1.3), the medicine itself is a unified
narrative grounded in a Christian interpretation of history: "I concluded," Tasso states in his *Discourses on the Heroic Poem* (1594),
"that the subject of epic [*l'argomento de l'epopeia*] must be based on
some historical event [*qualche istoria*] or some truth" (*Disorsi* 566).
And truth, he elaborates, *is* fundamentally historical: "If poets are
imitators, it is fitting for them to be imitators of the truth [*il vero*],
because the false [*il falso*] does not exist, and what does not exist cannot be imitated" (*Discorsi* 522).

Appealing to a standard of truth external to the poem, Tasso seeks to restrict the role of contingency within the poem to that of a deviation from the norm. Romance, as the narrative of the irrational force of erotic desire, is the formal expression of contingency: Rinaldo must be freed from Armida's powers before the conquest of Jerusalem can succeed, just as Aeneas must abandon Dido before he can fulfill his destiny in Latium. This connection between contingency and romance must have been evident to Ariosto, who in the *Furioso* frequently attributes to the agency of Fortuna, the personification of contingency, events that cannot be assimilated to a teleological narrative of Providence:

> Si vede per gli esempii, di chi piene
> sono l'antiche e le moderne istorie,
> che 'l ben va dietro al male, e 'l male e bene,
> e fin son l'lun de l'altro e biasmi e glorie;
> e che fidarsi a l'uom non si conviene
> in suo tresor, suo regno e sue vittorie,
> né disperarsi per Fortuna avversa,
> che sempre la sua ruota in giro versa. (45.4)

[AUTHOR'S TRANSLATION: One sees from the examples that ancient and modern history afford that good follows ill and ill, good, that glory ends in misfortune and the other way round, that man had better not trust in his wealth, his rule, or his triumphs, nor despair if Fortune opposes, for she always keeps her wheel turning.]

To be sure, the Christian *deus ex machina* intervenes finally to ensure that Orlando's madness is cured and the Saracen army driven from Paris, but such intervention, like that of God's having made Orlando invulnerable to any weapon ("ferro alcun non lo può mai ferire"), is strictly "outside human custom" ("fuor de l'uman uso") (34.63). Orlando is safe from the swords of other men, but not from the force of his own desire, and his madness is a divine punishment for his becoming enamored of a pagan woman. Human custom, in the *Furioso*, is characterized by irrationality and accidence: "Men and women are frequently shown as weak, fragile creatures, incapable of contriving their own happiness, subject to repeated misfortune through their own passions or the perversity of forces beyond their control" (Brand, *Ludovico* 121). When Astolfo travels to the moon to recover Orlando's wits (in an ampoule helpfully labeled thus), he is—to paraphrase Ariosto closely—astonished also to discover the wits of many others he had not realized lacked them, including himself.

Some lost theirs in love, others in seeking honours, still others in seeking wealth or the favor of princes: "Altri in amar lo perde, altri in onori, / altri in cercar...richezze; / altri ne le speranze de' signori" (34.84–5).

It is not surprising, then, that Byron, who understood reality to be contingently self-realizing rather than divinely ordained and providentially guided, found the open-endedness and multiplicity of romance plots congenial, and choose for his hero a figure less heroic than romantic, the master neither of his own feelings nor of the forces that determine the course of his life. At once flouting and professing faithful adherence to every convention of classical heroic poetry, Byron not only cheerfully confessed his lack of a plan to John Murray—"The 5th. is so far from being the last of D. J. that it is hardly the beginning.... To how many cantos this may extend—I know not" (*Byron's Letters and Journals* 8:78)—but acknowledged it in the poem itself: "I meant to make this poem very short, / But now I can't tell where it may not run" (15.22), he tells us, confirming his earlier assurance "that I have nothing plann'd" (4.5). Contingency is thus an inherent structural (I shall not say organizing) principle of the poem, permitting Byron the encyclopedic expansiveness of the epic while freeing him from the imperial ideology implicit in a teleological narrative. Indeed narrative contingency can become the occasion for reflection on the contingency of human life, as in Byron's astonishing interruption of Juan's story to report on the assassination of the military commandant of Ravenna on December 8, 1820:

> The other evening ('t was on Friday last)—
> This is a fact and no poetic fable—
> Just as my great coat was about me cast,
> My hat and gloves still lying on the table,
> I heard a shot—'t was eight o'clock scarce past—
> And, running out as fast as I was able,
> I found the military commandant
> Stretch'd in the street, and able scarce to pant.
> . . . .
> But it was all a mystery. Here we are,
> And there we go:—but *where?* five bits of lead,
> Or three, or two, or one, send very far!
> And this blood, then, form'd but to be shed?
> Can every element our elements mar?
> And air—earth—water—fire live—and we dead?
> *We*, whose minds comprehend all things? No more;
> But let us to our story as before. (5.33, 39)

As this very passage reminds us, however, if *Don Juan* has no teleology, it does have an author, the contingency of whose own death imposed on the poem the conclusion its narrative did not demand. Perhaps mindful that Astolfo had noticed the wits of many poets on the moon ("di poeti ancor ve n'era molto," *Furioso* 34.85), Byron was not prepared to concede the autonomy of the imagination: as his description of Wordsworth as "crazed beyond all hope" by virtue of his "long seclusion" from society implies (*Don Juan* 1.205, Dedication 5), poetry is vitiated by a failure to acknowledge a reality external and prior to itself: the reality of lived experience. Hence his indignant defense of *Don Juan* to Douglas Kinnaird: "It may be profligate—but is it not *life*, is not *the thing*?—Could any man have written it—who has not lived in the world?" (*Byron's Letters and Journals* 6:232). For Byron as for Tasso, epic justifies its existence by its foundation in and reference to history: the difference is that for Byron history is an immanently self-caused succession of events, which is to say that he accepts no agency outside history by which it is itself organized. The contingency of epic narrative is demanded by the contingency of the world.

NOTES

1. All quotations of the poetry are from Byron's *The Complete Poetical Works*. Ed. Jerome McGann and Barry Weller. 7 vols. (Oxford: Clarendon, 1980–1993). References to *Childe Harold's Pilgrimage* are by canto and stanza number (e.g., in this case 9.50), and all other references are by line numbers (e.g., l. 5 or ll. 8–10).
2. See Byron's *Miscellaneous Prose* 232, 236, and 242.
3. For more extended considerations of Tasso's reception in the context of the cult of artistic genius, see Brand, *Torquato* 205–225, and Burwick, *Poetic Madness* 105–143.
4. See Halmi, "The Very Model of a Modern Epic Poem."
5. Qtd. in Stabler, *Byron, Poetics and History* (34). As Stabler notes, Cohen's substitution of Ariosto's name for Pulci's is symptomatic of the preference among English readers of the time for romance over satire, though Ariosto was widely regarded as a licentious writer (Brand, *Italy* 87–89; and see, for an example, Coleridge, *Lectures* 2:95).
6. See "Plagiarisms of Lord Byron Detected." *The Monthly Magazine, or, British Register* 52.357 (August 1821): 19–22, and 52.358 (September 1821): 105–109.
7. Limitations of space and the complexity of the topic preclude me from considering here another area of apparent similarity and underlying difference between the Ferrarese poets: their concern with conflict between the Christian West and the Muslim East. That conflict

furnishes the historical substratum of the *Furioso*, the primary narrative of the *Liberata*, and the occasion of the extended military episode in *Don Juan*. But Byron does not share with his predecessors the need to affirm (however qualifiedly or problematically) the normative assumption of the superiority of the Christians. On contrary, the siege of Ismail reveals the moral bankruptcy of wars conducted in the name of Christianity:

"So now, my lads, for Glory!"—Here he [General Suvorov] turned
And drilled away in the most classic Russian,
Until each high, heroic bosom burned
For cash and conquest, as if from a cushion
A Preacher had held forth (who nobly spurned
All earthly goods save tithes) and bade them push on
To slay the Pagans who resisted battering
The Armies of the Christian Empress Catherine. (7.64)

For a comparison of Tasso's attempt to subordinate romance to epic to "the Western mastery…of a feminized East," see Quint 40.

CHAPTER FOUR

BYRON AND ALFIERI

Peter Cochran

The Deformed Transformed, Byron's last play, would have, had he completed it, shown a return to the commercial style in which *Manfred* is written. For *Manfred*, despite all Byron's avowals to the contrary, is tailored with great precision for Drury Lane. It features apparitions and demons. Its lead is designed for Edmund Kean, who, first, specialized in angst-ridden parts, and second, didn't like having actors opposite him who might draw the audience's attention from his brilliance. No protagonist could be more angst-ridden than Manfred: and neither the Chamoix Hunter, the Witch of the Alps, Arimanes, nor the Abbot, has any lines or moments to upstage him. Astarte does upstage him, but only for fifteen seconds. So when Byron writes to Murray, "I composed it actually with a *horror* of the stage—& with a view to render even the thought of it impracticable, knowing the zeal of my friends, that I should try that for which I have an invincible repugnance—viz—a representation.—"[1] he is being disingenuous. The scenic demands the play makes—Alpine heights, hellish depths, castle towers—are precisely what the vast machinery of Drury Lane was designed to cater for.

The Deformed Transformed is—or would have been—likewise tailored for popular consumption. Like *Manfred*, it ignores the unities of place and time. It has magical transformations, spectral apparitions, warfare on stage, attempted rape, "four coal-black horses," choruses...even, at one point, an ignis fatuus. But Byron was by now writing into a critical void, and no-one—not Mary Shelley his copyist, Murray his publisher, or even Kinnaird his theater-wise agent (he'd see *Marino Faliero* three times)—had the wit to see what he was doing with his dramatic talent. What he was doing was acknowledging that his period of creative allegiance to Vittorio Alfieri was at last over.

A revealing reminiscence by Byron runs as follows:

> Last night [August 11, 1819] I went to the representation of Alfieri's *Mirra*—the two last acts of which threw me into convulsions—I do not mean by that word—a lady's hysterics—but the agony of reluctant tears—and the choking shudder which I do not often undergo for fiction.—This is but the second time for anything under reality, the first was on seeing Kean's Sir Giles Overreach. (*Byron's Letters and Journals* 6:206)

He saw *Mirra* at Bologna in 1819. The actress who played the lead was Maddalena Pelzet (1801–1854), among whose best roles were not only Mirra but Silvio Pellico's Francesca da Rimini. She was eighteen when Byron collapsed while watching her acting.

The last two acts of Alfieri's tragedy *Mirra* show a family in the last stages of disintegration, despite the goodwill of everyone within and without the family group, and despite everything that the family itself tries to do to discover what's happening, and to prevent it. The tragedy is inevitable: there are no malign characters; everyone loves everyone else, and the harder they try to express their love, the closer the catastrophe approaches. The secret lies in the incestuous love of the daughter for the father; but such is Alfieri's control that her love is never expressed, only implied, and she kills herself (with her father's dagger), before the situation forces a full confession from her. It's a triumph of art expressing maximum horror with maximum correctness: a study in what Byron described as "What I seek to show in 'the Foscaris,'" i.e., "the *suppressed* passion, rather than the rant of the present day."[2] His two Alfierian tragedies, *Marino Faliero* and *The Two Foscari*, imitate Alfieri with increasing fidelity. Faliero's great curse upon Venice in the last scene is hardly an expression of suppressed passion, but consider this, from *The Foscari*, after the death of Jacopo:

Officer: Prince! I have done your bidding.
Doge: What command?
Officer: A melancholy one—to call the attendance
         Of –
Doge: True—true—true: I crave your pardon, I
         Begin to fail in apprehension, and

Wax very old—old almost as my years.
Till now I fought them off, but they begin
To overtake me.

Enter the deputation, consisting of six of the Signory and the Chief of the Ten.

Noble men, your pleasure!
Chief of the Ten: In the first place, the Council doth condole
With the Doge on his late and private grief.
Doge: No more—no more of that. (*Two Foscari*, V.i, 4–14)

Francis Foscari is ruined, deposed, and his son has been, in effect, tortured to death by the state of which he is still the head: but all he is prepared to say is "No more—no more of that." By contrast, Faliero "lets it all hang out."

Sardanapalus shows Byron losing faith in the Alfierian idiom. Jokes are occasionally suggested; they are banned from *Faliero* and *The Foscari*. Violent action is permitted. In the last scene, two people burn themselves to death on stage—no messengers here. But the effect is still relatively chaste, as may be seen in the contrast between the scene in Act I between Sardanapalus and Salemenes and that between Ventidius and Antony in the first act of Dryden's *All for Love*.[3] At one point in *All for Love* Antony laughs—at another, Ventidius weeps—finally, the men embrace. For *All for Love* is a professional play, designed to be acted by actors and to awaken the audience's empathy and feelings. I don't think it's inaccurate to say that there is no laughter, no tears, and no physical affection expressed, in any play by Byron—not even in *Manfred* or *The Deformed Transformed*. All is noble, stoic restraint. Byron, trying to be as like Alfieri and as unlike Shakespeare as possible, fails—or refuses—to draw the audience into the action of the play, by employing a much smaller expressive palette, and by allowing his characters a much narrower range of emotions. There's a much better portrayal of male bonding, ("homosociality"), in *All for Love* than there could be in a classical play by Byron. Here, the major (and sick) male bonding in *The Deformed Transformed* is ("would have been") a new development.

The motive for suppressing passion is the same as the motive for "bamming and humming"[4]: self-disguise; but although Byron was adept at "bamming and humming" himself, it is not until the figure of The Stranger in *The Deformed Transformed* that he puts such a seemer as himself on the center stage.

Drama has a necessary social dimension, without which it can't exist and still call itself drama. Closet drama is a contradiction in terms. It's like secret drinking—a sign that someone's failed somewhere. The Greek playwrights, Shakespeare, and Molière, all had the advantage of writing for professional companies to whom they could tailor their work, and for audiences whose tastes they could educate while exploiting—though Molière had difficulty, as we know, educating some of his audiences. Alfieri worked very hard at writing tragedies—but he had no company in mind when he did so (despite Byron's experience at Bologna), and no theater; indeed, he didn't really write for the stage at all, and had little knowledge of writers who had. He didn't read Aeschylus, Euripides, or Sophocles until his writing career was nearly over (Alfieri, *Memoirs* 281; from *Manhood*, Chapter 24); and he tried to ignore Shakespeare, for he was terrified of being influenced, not just by Shakespeare, but by anyone:

> He who reads much before entering on the task of composition often unconsciously borrows from others and thus destroys all originality. This reason, therefore, induced me to give up in the preceding year the perusal of Shakespeare, a circumstance which I regretted the less because I was obliged to read him in French. In proportion as this author, to whose faults I was not blind, pleased me, the more necessary did I consider it to abstain from reading him. (*Memoirs* 170; from *Manhood*, Chapter 20)

It is a Byronic smoke-screen, for of Racine and Corneille, Alfieri makes no mention. The lightly annotated edition of *Mirra* that I am using[5] lists seven borrowings from Racine's *Phèdre*.

Byron studied Alfieri's plays with care, though we can't tell from which edition—none appears in any of the three sale catalogues. One inspiration for *Marino Faliero* was Alfieri's *La congiura de' Pazzi*, an account of the 1478 conspiracy against the Medicis in Florence, which it fictionalizes as thoroughly as Byron does that of Faliero against Venice. As in Schiller's *Fiesco*, the start of the proposed insurrection is signaled by the sound-effect of a bell tolling. Although Alfieri described it as a "liberty-breathing" work, it depicts the attempted coup, correctly in historical terms, as as much of a failure as Faliero's, and the supposed libertarian motives that are supposed to inspire it are as compromised as those of Faliero.

From Alfieri's *Agide* Byron derived the idea of a ruler pitting himself against the state that in theory he rules: Agide, King of Sparta (the story is from Plutarch), wishes to abolish all debts, and divide the

Spartan lands equally! Naturally Sparta will not tolerate these ideas, and Agide is given a partially rigged trial, and condemned. He kills himself in prison. *Agide* is dedicated ironically to Charles I, from whose selfish story, says the dramatist, no tragedy could be written. Byron's Faliero compares himself to Agide ("Agis") at V iii 20–1.

Assuming that *Faliero* is a libertarian tragedy—a debatable point—other tragedies of Alfieri from which a libertarian position can be deduced are *Bruto Primo*, dedicated to George Washington and about Lucius Junius Brutus and his sons; *Bruto Secondo*, which climaxes in Caesar's assassination, and ends with Brutus triumphant, thereby showing how revolution can succeed in the short term; *Filippo*, about the conflict between Philip II of Spain and his son Carlos—the story more familiar these days in the versions by Schiller and Verdi; and *Antigone*, which tells of the classic conflict between Oedipus's daughter and her tyrant uncle.[6]

But in writing such things, not only does Alfieri observe the unities with great strictness, but his dramas are marked, not by orations in Roman Forums, not by midnight assassinations in Scottish castles, not by plays put on by hysterical Danish princes before their guilty uncles, but by "insistent, tense dialogues or…introspective, self-questioning soliloquies" "in the confined and oppressive settings of royal palaces" (Pizzamiglio 198–199). Like Byron's classical plays, they utilize about twenty percent of the theater's resources.

Alfieri's position in relation to performance was in theory uncompromising, though he relaxed it in real life, and sometimes played his own tragic heroes. His early tragedy *Cleopatra* was acted in Turin on June 16, 1775, along with a farce of his called *The Poets*: "These two pieces were played on two successive nights, and with applause. But, repenting that I had so rashly appeared before the public, though it was very indulgent, I used every effort with the managers to prevent further performances" (*Memoirs* 150–151; from "Youth," Chapter 15).

If anyone did put on one of his plays, Alfieri found it an awkward experience:

> During my stay at Turin I happened, without any great desire to do so, to be present at the performance of my *Virginia*. It was brought out at the same theatre where nine years before my *Cleopatra* had been acted, and by nearly as able performers. One of my old school friends had prepared every thing for this performance before my arrival, which was wholly unexpected. He, however, requested me to coach the actors as I formerly had done for *Cleopatra*; but my powers and above all

my pride being now greater, I refused to lend my aid. I knew our
actors and our audiences only too well and I wished not to be in any
way implicated in the actors' incapacity, which was evident to me even
before having heard them. I knew that it was necessary to start with
an impossibility, that of making them speak and pronounce Italian
instead of Venetian; to make it appear as if the parts were uttered by
them and not by the prompter; in short, that it would be necessary to
make them understand (to feel would be requiring too much) the sensations they ought to excite in the minds of their auditors. (*Memoirs*
232; from "Manhood," Chapter 13)

Part of his problem, as we can see, had to do with the absence
of any effective Italian theater, and of any good professional actors;
but another part was linguistic. Where the Greeks, Shakespeare, and
Molière wrote without problems in the language of their day, Alfieri
didn't know what the language of his day was—or rather, he did
know it, and despised it. He was born in Turin, a city neither Italian
nor French, but Piedmontese. When, as a youth, he first picked up a
copy of Ariosto, he had great difficulty understanding it. He had to
teach himself literary Italian.

At Drury Lane, Byron had (or rather, would have had) no such
barriers. His English was the audience's English, and he would have
had many actors (not just Kean) whose talent he admired:

The long complaints of the actual state of the drama arise, however,
from no fault of the performers. I can conceive nothing better than
Kemble, Cooke, and Kean, in their very different manners, or than
Elliston in *gentleman's* comedy, and in some parts of tragedy. Miss
O'Neill I never saw, having made and kept a determination to see
nothing which should divide or disturb my recollection of Siddons.
Siddons and Kemble were the *ideal* of tragic action; I never saw any
thing at all resembling them even in *person:* for this reason, we shall
never see again Coriolanus or Macbeth. When Kean is blamed for
want of dignity, we should remember that it is a grace and not an art,
and not to be attained by study. In all, *not* SUPERnatural parts, he is
perfect; even his very defects belong, or seem to belong, to the parts
themselves, and appear truer to nature. But of Kemble we may say,
with reference to his acting, what the Cardinal de Retz said of the
Marquis of Montrose, "that he was the only man he ever saw who
reminded him of the heroes of Plutarch." (*Marino Faliero*, Preface)

Part of the reason for Byron's Alfierian period was that Alessandro
Guiccioli—with whose wife he was going to bed—told him that he
looked like Alfieri ("the likeness to Alfieri was asserted very seriously

by an Italian who had known him in his younger days," *Byron's Letters and Journals* 9:11). But a greater reason was the horror he experienced at the ideas either of success or of failure: "Were I capable of writing a play which could be deemed stageworthy, success would give me no pleasure and failure great pain" (*Marino Faliero*, Preface). This is the strangest thing, even given his House of Lords hauteur, and even in what he asserts is the present vitiated state of public taste—his horror at "the roar of the greasepaint and the smell of the crowd."[7] If he ever condescended to write a tragedy in a commercial style, and permit its performance, he really would be afraid in case it succeeded.

Not even Alfieri ever said that.

NOTES

1. Byron to Murray, March 9, 1817, in *Byron's Letters and Journals* 5:183–185.
2. Byron to Murray, September 20, 1821: text from National Library of Scotland Acc.12604 / 4160E; *Byron's Letters and Journals* 8:216–218.
3. See Barry Weller's note in Byron's *Complete Poetical Works* 6:614.
4. That means, "bamboozling and humbugging." See William St. Clair, "Bamming and Humming," *Byron Journal* 7 (1979): 38–47.
5. Alfieri, *Opere I*, Int. Mario Fubini and ed. Arnaldo di Benedetto.
6. For Byron and Alfieri, see also Pudbres, *Lord Byron, the Admirer and Imitator of Alfieri*. I am aware of no other studies during the intervening hundred and three years.
7. Byron may be paraphrasing Sir Fretful Plagiary: "...for if there is anything to one's praise, it is a foolish vanity to be gratified at it; and, if it is abuse—why one is always sure to hear of it from one damned good-natured friend or other!" (see Richard Brinsley Sheridan, *The Critic*, Act I).

CHAPTER FIVE

PICTURING BYRON'S ITALY AND ITALIANS: FINDEN'S ILLUSTRATIONS TO BYRON'S LIFE AND WORKS

Paul Douglass

William and Edward Finden successfully marketed Lord Byron's life and literary works in sleek, well-illustrated packages, including *Landscape and Portrait Illustrations of the Life and Works of Lord Byron* (3 vols., 1833–1834), with a text by collaborator William Brockedon. The Findens published around the same time their *Landscape Illustrations of the Bible* (1836) and a periodical called *The Oriental Annual, or Scenes in India* (1834–1840). The latter work promotes British chauvinistic attitudes to the Middle East, to southern Europe in general, and to Italy in particular. Thus, it is unsurprising that *Landscape and Portrait Illustrations of the Life of Byron* employs Byron as a vehicle to promote an idea of Italy in which, as Joseph Luzzi has said, the reader can imagine the country as a repository of a great civilization, one that would be better-off without the inconvenience of contemporary Italians themselves. Many writers, including Goethe, Staël, and Foscolo, but also Shelley and Byron, participated "in constructing their common European heritage" by creating this "Romantic" myth about Italy (Luzzi 54), and my essay grapples with this charge against Byron. In some ways his work was twisted by Finden and Brockedon, who elided Byron's strong engagement with the politics and daily life of Italy while exaggerating the superfeminine aspects of his women protagonists. At the same time, it must be conceded that *Childe Harold's Pilgrimage* and other Byron works often contrast Italy's fabled history with its contemporary cultural malaise. Nonetheless, Finden's and Brockedon's *Landscape and Portrait Illustrations* is an exploitative work that evacuates most of Byron's violence and energy, focusing upon Orientalized females, ruins, and rustic scenes. The contemporary countryside and city environs are depicted as "the culturally impoverished antithesis of [their] own illustrious heritage," as Luzzi says (54). In this, Finden and Brockedon have done an injustice to the poet, who read and spoke Italian well, and engaged the Risorgimento to the degree that he risked his own life at times.

In all their collections, William and Edward Finden each contributed some of the pictures, but commissioned most of them to other artists, including some, like John Frederick Lewis and Miss Corbaux, whose careers were shaped by the public appetite for Orientalist fantasies. They had previously published *Landscape Illustrations of the Waverley Novels* (1830) and would go on to engrave and print a two volume work titled *Tableaux of National Character, Beauty, and Costume* (1843) with specially commissioned tales, such as Leigh Hunt's "Albania— The Love Letter." Landscapes in Finden's and Brockedon's *Landscape and Portrait Illustrations of the Life of Byron* stand beside portraits of real people from Byron's life, like Teresa Guiccioli and Margarita Cogni. More often, however, the pictures offer female characters from Byron's works, many of whom are drawn from Greek and Italian settings. Images from Byron's works published here were afterward augmented by additional portraits printed in *The Gallery of Byron Beauties* (1836), a strand of Orientalist fabric woven through many publications of the 1830s and 1840s in England. The portraits emphasize exotic themes that had helped to make Byron's early work, such as *Childe Harold's Pilgrimage* (1812), popular. Included, for example is an image of the "Maid of Athens" from lines first published in *Childe Harold*. Finden also gives a portrait of Parisina, the young lady who "walks in the shadow of night" in a poem the first verse of which Byron had given to Isaac Nathan as part of their *Hebrew Melodies* project in 1815–1816.[1] Parisina listens breathlessly for the approaching steps of her lover gliding "through the foliage thick, / And her cheek grows pale—and her heart beats quick" (*Complete Poetical Works* 3:359). Brockedon's description of her glosses over the violence of her story, in which her husband Azo (based upon the Marquis d' Este of Ferrara) puts his bastard son to death for having had an incestuous liaison with her, leaving her to go mad with the grief of erotomania. A similar elision of specifics characterizes Finden and Brockedon's entry describing Theresa, from *Mazeppa*, a poem whose eponymous hero (a young page) is brutally punished for engaging Theresa in "[f]rivolous and foolish play," after he has noticed her exotic mixed-race look: "[S] he had the Asiatic eye, / Such as our Turkish neighbourhood / Hath mingled with our Polish blood" (*Complete Poetical Works* 4:181, 180). The theme of madness noted in "Parisina" is continued in the portrayals of Leonora d' Este, from "The Lament of Tasso" and Laura, from *Beppo: A Venetian Story*, which focuses on the *cavalier servente* tradition. In a typical portrait, Finden produces a placid image of Beatrice, drawn from Byron's apostrophe to her in *The Prophecy of Dante*. The feminine inspiration for Dante's *Vita Nuova* sits immaculately coiffed and garbed, with hands crossed over a book—not reading, but preoccupied by tasteful thoughts.

These women's images may seem tame, but their Orientalized dress and postures were erotic to contemporary male readers, inviting the male gaze, and positioning that gaze in a harem of imaginary lovers—for example in the portrait of Dudú, drawn from *Don Juan*: "A kind of sleepy Venus seemed Dudú...etc." (6.42 ff.; *Complete Poetical Works* 5:311). Dudú's lips are bee-stung. Her bodice is carelessly buttoned, and her bosom strains against the fabric as she lies on an embroidered pillow with eyes half-closed, drugged perhaps by sensuous desire (or laudanum?), as she fingers a flower. Another portrait also engages the harem theme, but even more bluntly. The image stems from a passage in the second canto of *Childe Harold's Pilgrimage* about Ali Pasha's harem:

> Here woman's voice is never heard: apart,
> And scarce permitted, guarded, veil'd, to move,
> She yields to one her person and her heart,
> Tam'd to her cage, nor feels a wish to rove:
> For, not unhappy in her master's love,
> And joyful in a mother's gentlest cares...
> ...
> Herself more sweetly rears the babe she bears....
> (*Childe Harold* 2.61; *Complete Poetical Works* 2:63)

This image, published in *The Gallery of Byron Beauties*, is titled "The Light of the Harem," portraying (presumably) one of Ali Pasha's many wives with her baby. An exotic yet domestic image, engraved by William Finden himself, it is accompanied by a quotation from *Edinburgh Review* cofounder Lord Francis Jeffrey, who remarks appreciatively that "Lord Byron has made a fine use of the gentleness and submission of the Eastern females," drawing out the essence of

"female nature in general," which Jeffrey describes as "Oriental softness and acquiescence" (*Byron Beauties* n.p.).[2]

Byron did often eroticize female characters along conventional
lines, and *Childe Harold's Pilgrimage* is replete with such fantasies.
Harold specifically desires "the maid in her youth," whose "caresses
shall lull me, her music shall sooth" (*Childe Harold* 2.72 ff.; *Complete
Poetical Works* 2:67), and yet the women in *Childe Harold* whose
images Finden engraves appear more complicated and powerful than

the soft-focus portraits and carefully abridged texts allow. This is as true of the Maid of Athens and Laura as it is of Astarte, the Maid of Saragoza, and Jephtha's Daughter. I have argued elsewhere that Byron's debt to female writers like Charlotte Dacre and Madame Staël runs deep, and indicates a strong engagement with female identity.[3] His verse portrayals of women do contain misogynistic attitudes sometimes echoed in his letters: "Of all Bitches dead or alive a scribbling woman is the most canine," he wrote just before *Childe Harold's Pilgrimage* was first published (*Byron's LJ* 2:132). Certainly Byron railed against the "gynocrasy" (*Don Juan* 12.66, 16.52; *Complete Poetical Works* 5:514, 635). But that word in itself recognizes a power singularly absent from Finden and Brockedon's works.

A similar but more troubling problem arises with Finden and Brockedon's "landscape" pictures. These generally convey moods of stasis, calm, and reverie—not those of the energy, dynamism, tension, and even terror that actually cohere in the verse Byron wrote about Italy and Italians, like *Mazeppa*, *Beppo*, *Parisina*, *The Two Foscari*, and *Marino Faliero*. Scene after scene is rendered with placid waters. Bellagio, a military and strategic center during the Napoleonic campaigns—and a place not mentioned by name in Byron's works or correspondence—is depicted as a sleepy, distant waterway plied by a few vessels, while in the foreground four female figures and one male engage in conversation and make unhurried progress toward a shore where nothing awaits but a formal gateway. Similarly portrayed is Messolonghi, where the poet had a band of five hundred Suliote soldiers under his command and where he died supporting the Greek rebellion. The engraving focuses attention on a vessel apparently leaving port (no dock or commercial structures appear) while human figures stand in conversation, walk, or tend a fire on the farther barren shore under the windows of a massive structure virtually devoid of life. The waters of Messolonghi ripple, but no drama is implied thereby. The same can be said of Finden's engravings of Interlachen, The Hague, and Yanina, province of Ali Pasha, that "man of war and woes" whose harem fascinated the Findens, but whose portrayal does not convey how "fierce are Albania's children" (*Childe Harold* 2.62, 2.65; *Complete Poetical Works* 2:63–64). Instead the image offers the now-familiar formulas: placid waters, a few vessels meandering thereon; an imposing domed mosque or other structure; and in the foreground human figures quaintly costumed, engaging in desultory conversation or gazing at the scene themselves.

It will not escape the attention of the consumer of these land-scape images that, like the women's portraits, they seem drugged, passive, inert, and are costumed in the raiments of a distant past. The feminization and pacification of the Italian landscape is part of the general association of Italy with "the feminine categories of caprice, reverie, and weakness," as Luzzi argues, categories that epitomize "generalizations about Italy as a feminine, premodern, and sepulchral space whose present cannot escape the burden of its past" (Luzzi 67, 76). Like his contemporaries, de Staël and Foscolo, Byron admittedly imbibed this attitude. The fourth canto of *Childe Harold*, like *Beppo*, feminizes Italy in a Findenesque manner.

> Italia! oh Italia! thou who hast
> The fatal gift of beauty, which became
> A funeral dower of present woes and past,
> On thy sweet brow is sorrow plough'd by shame,
> And annals graved in characters of flame.
> Oh, God! that thou wert in thy nakedness
> Less lovely or more powerful, and couldst claim
> Thy right, and awe the robbers back, who press
> To shed thy blood, and drink the tears of thy distress....
> (*Childe Harold* 4.42; *Complete Poetical Works* 138)

The distress of "Italia" like that of Greece, stems from its permanent state of ruin, a situation richly illustrated by the Findens's engravings. Byron furnishes all they and William Brockedon could have wished on this theme, as he continues his apostrophe to Italy:

For Time hath not rebuilt them, but uprear'd
Barbaric dwellings on their shattered site,
Which only make more mourn'd and more endear'd
The few last rays of their far-scatter'd light,
And the crush'd relics of their vanish'd might.
The Roman saw these tombs in his own age,
These sepulchres of cities, which excite
Sad wonder, and his yet surviving page
The moral lesson bears, drawn from such pilgrimage.

The city as sepulcher is emblemized in the Findens's engraving of Dante's Tomb (the tomb was constructed in 1780 from plans by Camillo Morigia), a scene that evokes the solemnity of "relics of...vanish'd might." The vanishing point in the picture's perspective lies behind the tall doorway, framed itself by the walls of buildings as they pour shadow on a caped figure who strides toward the tomb.

Reading the "sepulchres of cities" as a book, Byron adopts a cyclical view of history:

> That page is now before me, and on mine
> *His* country's ruin added to the mass
> Of perish'd states he mourn'd in their decline,
> And I in desolation: all that *was*
> Of then destruction *is;* and now, alas!
> Rome—Rome imperial, bows her to the storm,
> In the same dust and blackness, and we pass
> The skeleton of her Titanic form,
> Wrecks of another world, whose ashes still are warm.

"The skeleton of her Titanic form," echoes Shelley's sentiments in "Ozymandias," yet Byron does not turn, as Shelley did, to the image of a wasteland, but instead calls on Europeans and Britons to support the Risorgimento:

> Yet, Italy! through every other land
> Thy wrongs should ring, and shall, from side to side;
> Mother of Arts! as once of arms; thy hand
> Was then our guardian, and is still our guide;
> Parent of our Religion! whom the wide
> Nations have knelt to for the keys of heaven!
> Europe, repentant of her parricide,
> Shall yet redeem thee, and, all backward driven,
> Roll the barbarian tide, and sue to be forgiven.
> (*Childe Harold* 4.45–47; *Complete Poetical Works* 139–140)

This last theme—still chauvinistic, to be sure, yet also a confession of European "parricide"—is not included in Finden and Brockedon's comments, summary, and overview of Italy, nor communicated in their texts and illustrations.

Byron's life and works, though they provide plenty for Finden and Brockedon to exploit, required warping to promote the view of southern Europe and the East they embraced. Arrogant, superior, with intimations of condescension and ownership, the attitude conveyed is of a tourist reviewing the remnants of his own cultural past—someone who feels closer to the long-dead ancestors of the lands he visits than to any contemporary population. This was not Byron's journey. Finden and Brockedon chose to include scenes remotely if at all connected to "the life of Lord Byron" (as their title promises), and they also often abandoned pretense of conveying

Byron's sense of the scenes, people, and places he described in his verse and letters.

For example, their third volume includes a rendering of the ruins of the Ponte Rotto in Rome, another place Byron does not mention in his works. The improvisation of Brockedon is peculiar: "This scene upon the Tiber is one of antiquarian interest. The ruins are of the ancient Palatine bridge; but there are vestiges of the piers of another, the Pons Sublicius, a little lower down the river...." Brockedon then describes a song made up on the spot by an "enthusiastic Frenchman...and chanted with great effect to one of the republican airs," which cites Brutus's betrayal of Caesar as an immolation of the entire Italian race. Brockedon then notes that the engraving includes an island, in the distance, which "in the days of Roman splendour...was covered with temples, and the ground built up, or cut away, until the island was made to assume the form of a gigantic Roman galley." But this titanic achievement is, of course, now gone (Finden and Brockedon 3:n.p.). Brockedon strains to include as much as he can of a barbaric, slavery-inflected, larger-than-life Italian past, even when it isn't represented either in Byron's works or in the engraving the text accompanies.

Similarly Brockedon seizes on Byron's representation of Venice as a text of an empire. Venice is rendered in several engravings in Finden's collection, including more than one scene in the Piazza San Marco, the notes for which quote Byron describing Venice as having lost her

"thirteen hundred years of freedom" and sinking "like a sea-weed, into whence it rose!"

> In youth she was all glory,—a new Tyre,—
> Her very by-word sprung from victory....
> Statues of glass—all shiver'd—the long file
> Of her dead Doges are declined to dust;
> But where they dwelt, the vast and sumptuous pile
> Bespeaks the pageant of their splendid trust;
> Their sceptre broken, and their sword in rust,
> Have yielded to the stranger: empty halls,
> Thin streets, and foreign aspects, such as must
> Too oft remind her who and what enthrals,
> Have flung a desolate cloud o'er Venice's lovely walls.
> (*Childe Harold* 4.14; *Complete Poetical Works* 2:129; printed also in
> Finden and Brockedon 1:n.p.)

The commentary of Brockedon and Finden fixes the meaning of this topos: "The Ducal Palace, in all the grandeur of its massiveness, and all the topsy-turvy of its architectural character," furnishes the observer with the impression of "a vast incumbent structure upon an apparently very inadequate support...." Contrast between contemporary weakness and massive antiquity is emblemized for Brockedon in the fact that, upon one of the columns is set "the bronze winged lion—the companion of St. Mark, and the emblem of the new patron saint; a strange figure, which has been oddly compared by Simond to 'a colossal chimney-sweeper crawling out of a chimneytop.'" Trivializing the column at St. Mark's on the one hand, Brockedon indelibly lays down the point for the British reader: Venice's history "is one of the most interesting, except that of our own country, to which the political inquirer can turn his attention," for it comprises a "majestic combination of former splendour and actual decay," that allows the viewer consciously to engage in "reading a history" (Finden and Brockedon 1:n.p.).

Another depiction of Venice elaborates the theme of the inadequacy of the present to antiquity. Brockedon's description of the Ponte Rialto begins solemnly, and then returns to that theme. His definition of the lowly "modern" Italians includes a period extending back almost to the era of the Medicis!

[The] Rialto was commenced in the year 1588, and completed in three years. Pasquali Cicogna was then Doge of Venice, and his arms appear in the centre of the arch. Vasari says the arch was built from a design

made long before by Michael Angelo; and it is curious to observe,
upon what in our day would by comparison appear to be a contempt-
ible work, how great names are pressed into the honour of having built
it....[With] only [an] eighty-three feet span, [the bridge] is approached
by steps, for the curve of the arch is very abrupt. Upon it are two rows
of shops...chiefly furnished with jewellery, haberdashery, perfumes,
and articles for the toilette. (Finden and Brockedon 2:n.p.)

Brockedon's description of Venice performs the twist on Byron's
themes that this essay has sought to describe, starting with the familiar nostalgia for an imperial past, as Byron expressed it in verse, and
then spinning that dream of an empire into the British bailiwick in
a way he would never have endorsed. Brockedon instructs the reader
that Finden's engraving of Venice, seen from the entrance to the
Grand Canal, evokes "Venice in its glory, [rather] than in this its day
of degradation: these gondolas and gaieties are of other times; now
Melancholy pervades this city, and marks it for her own." Brockedon
quotes Byron:

> In Venice Tasso's echoes are no more,
> And silent rows the songless gondolier;
> Her palaces are crumbling to the shore,
> And music meets not always now the ear:
> Those days are gone...(*Childe Harold* 4.3; *Complete Poetical Works*
>   2:125)

And Brockedon comments, "This feeling will prevail in the mind of every traveller, if he reflect, while he looks upon Venice, and contemplates what she was. Some one has written of Venice that it is 'a huge pleasure-house': his feelings must be strangely constituted who thinks that a gleam of sun-light on a tomb is a pleasurable object." Brockedon elaborates on this macabre degradation of the city by quoting from an anonymous writer in one of the literary annuals of 1829, who asserted that "Venice was always an unintelligible place.... It was always a dream, and will continue a dream for ever...." (Finden and Brockedon 2:n.p.).

Perhaps the preceding analysis is not entirely fair to the efforts of Finden. *Some* of his images respond to one of Byron's recurrent themes in *Childe Harold* and *Don Juan*, namely "The eternal surge / Of time and tide," under whose agency "the graves / Of empires heave but like some passing waves" (*Don Juan* 15.99; *Complete Poetical Works* 5:617–618). Finden's engraving of Cadiz's ocean surface looks more alive in this spirit, as does that of Cape Leucadia. In addition, the plate of Venice's Lido, where Byron rode his horse almost daily, depicts a roiling ocean. Similarly, the waters around the Castle of Chillon are in motion, and some few of these scenes are rife with aqueous turmoil, like the waters at Rhodes or along the coast of Lisbon. The depiction of Gibraltar is an especially good example, with its depiction of tens, if not dozens of squall-tossed vessels under a lowering sky.

But such images capturing water in motion are the exceptions. Violence and energy are absent from the vast majority of these engravings, which instead focus on the dead ruins of a once-great civilization, formerly populated by great peoples, who, Britons are invited to feel, would look down upon their descendants as undeserving of the custody of so great a past—and so, those descendants have been elided. The inhabitants of Italy appear in Finden's and Brockedon's pages as a population in the dress of a rustic past. *Landscape and Portrait Illustrations of the Life and Works of Lord Byron* validated a mixed response of nostalgia and superiority by employing Byron as its register. The poet would protest that rather than validating this response, his work mocked and challenged the imperial pretensions of the British nation-state. Finden and Brockedon skipped over Byron's satirical humor, his engagement with politics, and his gender-bending convention-challenging portraits and language in *Don Juan*. If Byron became Finden and Brockedon's ventriloquist's dummy, however, it was not without his cooperation, for they are, after all, his words, born of an attitude toward Italy and Italians he could satirize effectively because he had shared it.

NOTES

1. See Byron's *A Selection of Hebrew Melodies, Ancient and Modern, by Isaac Nathan and Lord Byron* 62 ff.
2. Finden's collections are not paginated, unfortunately.
3. See Douglass, "Lord Byron's Feminist Canon: Notes toward Its Construction."

CHAPTER SIX

REALMS WITHOUT A NAME: SHELLEY AND ITALY'S INTENSER DAY

Michael O'Neill

PART ONE

Romantic quests for "home" are endless, and often involve the epiphanic or even eerie awareness that the imagination's true dwelling-place is homelessness. Such homelessness in its positive guise occurs at the climax of Book Six of Wordsworth's *The Prelude*.[1] The book makes much mention of houses real and metaphorical. Wordsworth speaks of how he only wished at Cambridge "to be a lodger in that house / Of Letters, and no more" (ll. 32–33); he plays with thoughts of Coleridge's life like "a man, who, when his house is built, / A frame locked up in wood and stone, doth still, / In impotence of mind, by his fireside, / Rebuild it to his liking" (ll. 302–305); visiting France in the heyday of revolutionary fraternity, he enjoyed warm hospitality (ll. 401–414). Yet when the imagination rises up "Before the eye and progress of [his] song" (l. 526), Wordsworth, for all his attachment to place in a poem such as *Home at Grasmere*, recognizes that "Our destiny, our nature, and our home, / Is with infinitude, and only there" (ll. 538–539). The moment is at once sublime and full of an affecting trust in "hope that can never die" (l. 540; see Jonathan Wordsworth 187–188).

Shelley, so often seen as all air and fire compared with a more earthbound Wordsworth, shares with the older poet a sense that the imagination may find a local habitation among particular times and cultures, but cannot be confined to them. This essay will explore how his imaginative engagement with Italian and Mediterranean cultures entwines itself with exploration of what, to adapt a phrase from his disenchantment-laden *The Triumph of Life*, might be called "realm[s] without a name" (l. 396).[2] Even his early encounters with Italy name it as a country of the mind as much as a real place. "The beings of the mind are not of clay" (*Childe Harold* 4.5): so Byron affirms in the teeth of Venice's contemporary decline (see *Complete Poetical Works* 2:126). Shelley does not so much idealize Italy as see that ideals must always be related to and thus can never be identified wholly with realities . "Tramontana at Lerici" by Charles Tomlinson delivers an austere rebuke to the projections of human beings onto an "air / Unfit for politicians and romantics." Given the location, the poem seems to slap down supposedly Shelleyan attention-seeking in its conclusion's recognition that "One is ignored / By so much cold suspended in so much night" (Tomlinson 15). But the Shelley of Lerici poems in which he "sate and watched the vessels glide" (36) as though "They sailed for drink to medicine / Such sweet and bitter pain as mine" (43–44) was affectingly aware of the idealist's fate. Such a fate finds representation in this poem ("Lines Written in the Bay of Lerici") in "the fish who came / To worship the delusive flame" (53–54). Shelley is both a worshipper of such delusive flames in the poem and "the fisher with his lamp / And spear" (50–51) who hunts down the delusions of idealistic projection.

That "delusive flame" burned with a finer brightness for Shelley, among Italian scenes, as a poem such as *Epipsychidion* makes clear in the very setting of its "isle under Ionian skies, / Beautiful as a wreck of Paradise" (422–423) to which the imagined voyage of the final section conducts us. "Ionian" suggests Greek influence, even as the "Ionian Sea lies between southern Italy and western Greece" (*Shelley's Poetry and Prose* 403n). The island's description as "a wreck of Paradise" recalls Julian's apostrophic address to Italy in *Julian and Maddalo* as "Thou Paradise of exiles" (57). In *Julian and Maddalo* "Italy" is a "Paradise" that confirms our exilic state; exiles go there and encounter a beauty that confirms humanity's fallen state, of whom the exemplar is the self-torturing maniac. The best life has to offer, it might seem, are conversations that are "forlorn / Yet pleasing, such as once, so poets tell, / The devils held within the gates of Hell" (39–41). Italy is both "Paradise of exiles" and a site that brings Milton's "devils" and "Hell" to mind. Shelley invests it with an instability that derives from the dynamic of unsatisfied desire. This dynamic drives *Epipsychidion*, where the phrase "wreck of Paradise" concedes early on that the idealized isle, which is at once a remodeled Italy and an erotic Utopia, has fallen away from some perfect state. It is the splintered remnant of some diamond absolute, to adapt a phrase from Seamus Heaney's "Exposure." It is in touch with "the age of gold" (428), inhabited by "some pastoral people native there" (426), as in some idyll, but it is also a place suspended " 'twixt Heaven, Air, Earth, and Sea" (457) and "Bright as that wandering Eden Lucifer" (459), where, though the reference is to the star rather than the fallen angel, the juxtaposition of "Eden" and "Lucifer" brings into play postlapsarian associations.

Italy's doubleness as reality and emblem, as place and screen for idealized or troubled projection, takes us close to the heart of the Shelleyan poetic enterprise project as it comes into full, intricate being after he left England in 1818. *Lines Written among the Euganean Hills* deploys and examines a characteristic strategy in which the mind's desires map and do not map onto Italian geography and culture. The poem sets out to substantiate and instantiate its initial proposition: "Many a green isle needs must be / In the deep wide sea of Misery" (ll. 1–2). "To such a one this morn was led / My bark by soft winds piloted" (ll. 68–69) is Shelley's way of saying that his experience is at once local and generalizable, capable of taking on a particular habitation yet always open to redefinition. The Italian scene is "such a one" and evokes his own "paean" (l. 71), a word that rhymes purposefully with "mountains Euganean" (l. 70). If the reversal of the word-order points up the specificity of the place, the specific place delights the poet because of its promise of something unspecific. The skyscape toward which his gaze is drawn, if only in a simile that compares rooks in sunlight with clouds against "the unfathomable sky" (l. 79), brims with immanent and transcendent possibilities.

Again, when Shelley describes Venice in the poem, he brings to his response multiple ways of looking and thinking. The first impulse in his verse is to respond in Turneresque fashion to Venice as a place that has been alchemized by "that chasm of light, / As within a furnace bright" (ll. 104–105). The description is metapoetic; it suggests that one way in which Venice appeals is that it embodies a capacity for idealized disembodiment, of conversion into the symbol of imaginative activity. Yet Shelley resists this merely sensuous appeal, merging his aesthetic response into his historical reading of the city. He simultaneously rebukes and evokes the lure of the merely aesthetic in these lines: "Those who alone thy towers behold / Quivering through aerial gold, / As I now behold them here, / Would imagine not they were / Sepulchres" (ll. 142–146). Such failure to "imagine" bears witness to ignorance, for the poet, of recent Venetian history, its sorry capitulation to forces opposed to the "Freedom" (l. 150) invoked, as so often in Shelley, as a pervasive yet unlocatable alternative to things as they are. Yet if Freedom is to reassert its "omnipotence" (l. 151), the writing suggests, it will have to do with values that are both inherent and conferred, and cannot, therefore, wholly divorce themselves from "the mind which feeds this verse / Peopling the lone universe" (ll. 318–319) in the epiphanic "now" at the poem's center, a mind that shows its sensitivity to beauty that manifests itself "Quivering through aerial gold." Shelley stages a conflict between a rigorous historicism that would lead him to reject Venice if the city shows itself incapable of regeneration (see ll. 160–166) and a responsiveness to possibilities of betterment that seem momentarily actualized through his imaginative work on the Italian scenes before him.

Part Two

Visionary experience in Shelley often involves a kind of verbal tremor, a series of near-kinetic vibrations between inner and outer. In his poetry of the Italian period, the scenes he describes seem often to work as objective correlatives of his imaginative procedure. So when the third section of "Ode to the West Wind" opens, "Thou who didst waken from his summer dreams / The blue Mediterranean, where he lay, / Lulled by the coil of his chrystalline streams" (ll. 29–31), the terza rima, previously driven and headlong in its movement, enacts its own slowed turning away from onward impetus as the word "Mediterranean" idles for half the line. In this passage the sea occupies the provisional, recurring present of "summer dreams," in which it is "lulled by the coil of his crystalline streams." These streams coil upon one another like a sleepy snake, turning away from flight into the future, composing themselves into a fatally attractive image of reposeful indolence. Ultimately the "blue Mediterranean" is an ally of Burkean conservatism, engaged in retrospection. A watery repository of what has already happened, it is its own somnolent spectator. Shelley's syntax is purposefully ambiguous in line thirty-three, "And saw in sleep old palaces and towers," since it could be the sea or the wind that "saw in sleep." The phrase "in sleep," given that the wind has already appeared as the agent of wakening (l. 29), suggests the sleepy seeing applies to the sea. Yet for a moment transforming wind and dreaming sea seem at one, as though, in the figurative workings of the poem, what is laid bare is a collision that is also a collusion between pleasure in the present (the aesthetic) and the lull before the coming storm (revolutionary history in the making). The syntactical slippages do not stop there; it is conceivable that "in sleep" works forwards, attaching itself to the "old palaces and towers," a possibility that intimates that when the Mediterranean is woken, so, too, the sunken ruins of the classical past will, in some way, return.

What wind and Mediterranean see, to make of them a composite subject, is alive, vibrant, ever-altering, "Quivering within the wave's intenser day." The Mediterranean is classical past and sponsor of reenvisioning present for Shelley; the natural world stands in for the transformative imagination in that last line, which distils, if not a Shelleyan essence, then one of his most typical modes of poetic being. The palaces and towers lose their monumentality, reduplicated yet altered in the medium of water, undergoing a metamorphosis within "the wave's intenser day." The reality surrenders to the greater significance of the reflective medium, which turns out to be, in some way, intenser. This greater intensity derives from the wave's function as imaging and transfiguring medium, as objective correlative for the poet who must come to terms with yet reject the past and hold open an avenue to the future.

This section of the "Ode" opposes yet yokes together a symbol of the Roman classical past, "a pumice isle in Baiae's bay" (l. 32), and an emblem of the democratic future, "the Atlantic's level powers" (l. 37) that "Cleave themselves into chasms" (l. 38) before the wind's approach. Geoffrey Matthews succinctly suggests the significance of "Baiae's bay": "A resort of the fashionable and the great under the Roman empire, but also a scene of luxury and cruelty" (Matthews, in *Shelley: Selected Poems and Prose* 200). Matthews presumably has Tiberius's sybaritic excesses in mind. But Baiae is also, for Shelley, the product of volcanic fallout, hence the pumice isle, and, as Matthews pointed out in "A Volcano's Voice in Shelley" (reprinted in *Shelley's Poetry and Prose*), is associated allusively with revolutionary activity; it occupies the space of its own overthrow. When Shelley visited the bay of Baiae, the sight of "many picturesque & interesting ruins" was disappointing by comparison with the "effect of the scenery": "The colours of the water & the air breathe over all things here the radiance of their own beauty" (*Letters of Shelley* 2:61). An atmosphere enveloping "all things" with "the radiance of [its] own beauty" might stand both for Shelley's own Mediterranean imagination and for his awareness of natural realities that are self-sufficing and do not depend on the imagination. Timothy Morton explores the meanings of nature and culture in Shelley's work, arguing that "If nature is to culture as ground is to figure, then it has become impossible to tell the difference between the two" (Morton 201). Shelley does not only use nature as a means of representing the processes of imagining; he also views it as having an otherness that stands in eternal and eternally redemptive opposition to the ruins of culture and the longings of human beings. "The radiance of [nature's] own beauty" may lure us into imagining a Utopian "windless bower...Far from passion, pain, and guilt" (*Lines Written among the Euganean Hills* ll. 344–345); yet even as it spurs on the transforming, revolutionary imagination, it serves as a kind of rebuke to it, too.

The Mediterranean is set against the Atlantic in this section: "the ruins of antique grandeur" against intimations of the new world. The wind, emblem of inspiration, social change, and something close to necessity, is operative in both, wakening the Mediterranean, forcing the Atlantic to acknowledge its power. Rather as Auden does in his early poem "Consider this and in our time," Shelley here dallies with the doomed realm signified by "old palaces and towers," indicating one way in which the Mediterranean (considered as cultural region as well as maritime location) worked on his imagination. There is, in him a striking absorption in the classical realm, which he reads as both flawed and magnificent. Something of this carries over into his response to Rome in *Adonais*: "Go thou to Rome, —at once the Paradise, / The grave, the city and the wilderness" (ll. 433–434). Building on the earlier "Or go to Rome" (l. 424), 'the opening injunction clarifies Shelley's sense of Rome as paradoxical fusion of triumph and failure, "the sepulchre" (l. 424), not of Keats, "but of our joy" (l. 425), both the place that buried joy and where joy was buried. After Athens, Rome is, for Shelley, the very essence of the Mediterranean civilization on which, inspired by Winckelmann and others, he brooded in his superb travel letters. Its beauty makes it a "paradise"; its history a "grave"; ruination converts it into a "wilderness," even as it is the very type of human endeavor, a "city."

Rome is a failed exemplar, in one sense; in another, a pointer toward what can be recovered from the past so as to make for a better future. It embodies the fact "That ages, empires, and religions there / Lie buried in the ravage they have wrought" ("Adonais" ll. 426–427), that attempts to dominate must, Ozymandias-like, inevitably destroy themselves. But it stands, too, for the mingled greatness and abjectness of human attainment. Shelley's writing about Rome reveals both his acknowledgement of this inextricability and his wish to separate out the aesthetic or spiritual wheat from the militaristic chaff. Arguably his cultural vision benefits from its growing sense of the difficulty of doing so, as when he writes in the Preface to *Hellas* of the fact that Rome "spread...illumination with her arms" (*Shelley's Poetry and Prose* 431). Describing "two winged figures of Victory" on the Arch of Constantine, he conveys something of his commingled admiration and ambivalence: "Never were monuments so completely fitted to the purpose for which they were designed of expressing that mixture of energy & error which is called a Triumph" (*Letters of Shelley* 2:86). Every record of Roman civilization, it would seem, was also for Shelley a record of barbarism.

In *The Triumph of Life* that "mixture of energy & error which is called a Triumph" becomes the dominant image in a poem that drives toward the question at which the fragment breaks off: " 'Then, what is Life?' I said" (l. 544). Again, the past haunts the present, best described in an image (that of the triumph) inherited from the Italian past. Yet it is through his negotiation in the form and figuration of the poem with the work of two poets associated with Italy—Petrarch and Dante—that Shelley attempts to find an answer to that question that does not sell life short. Both provide in their work—Petrarch in his *Trionfi*, Dante in the *Commedia*—models of evolution toward betterment that Shelley may ironize but cannot wholly discard. The energy with which the poem questions error indicates Shelley's refusal simply to acquiesce in the kind of fatalism about history that tempts Byron in the fourth canto of *Childe Harold's Pilgrimage* when he asserts that history involves always "the same rehearsal of the past" (*Childe Harold's Pilgrimage* 4.108; see *Complete Poetical Works* 2:160). Shelley is closer in spirit to Madame de Staël's *Corinne* when, in that work, debate about the significance of Rome includes the following in book two, chapter four: "Rome...presents the melancholy aspect of degradation and misery, but all of a sudden a broken column, a bas-relief half destroyed, stones knit together in the indestructible manner of the ancient architects, remind us that there is in man an eternal power, a divine spark, which he must never cease to excite in himself and revive in others."[3] This discernment of "a divine spark" serves as an ally of Shelley's prayer at the close of the "Ode to the West Wind" that he might "Scatter, as from an unextinguished hearth / Ashes and sparks, my words among mankind" (ll. 66–67). The image brings to mind the Dante who, in seeing Beatrice again in *Purgatorio* canto 30, uses a Virgilian metaphor (applied to Dido) to convey his (unspeakable) feelings. Were Virgil still available as an interlocutor, Dante "would have cried....'The old flame / Throws out clear tokens of reviving fire'" (*Purgatorio* 30.45, 46–47).[4] The "old flame" of previous Roman and Italian culture, one might wish to allegorize the passage in applying it to Shelley, is available as a source of "reviving fire." Yet the poet's unaccompanied loneliness is also suggested. The cultural hearth is "unextinguished." The modern poet, inspired by the best of the past and finding images of a better future in the very Mediterranean air he breathes, seeks to initiate a process that "will quicken a new birth" (30.64). Radical though Shelley's visions of better futures are, they are, for all their Utopianism, grounded in his meditations on and negotiations with the past.

Rome is for Shelley a symbol of the wars of conquest that form one part of the Mediterranean's fractured legacy. Visiting Pompeii ("Pompeii you know was a Greek city" (*Letters of Shelley* 2:73) he tells Peacock), he reads history in complexly evolutionary ways: Pompeii offers a model of how life should be led; its inhabitants "lived in harmony with nature, and the interstices of their incomparable columns, were portals as it were to admit the spirit of beauty, which animates this glorious universe to visit those whom it inspired. If such is Pompeii, what was Athens?" (*Letters of Shelley* 2:73). This Hellenizing zeal will find full flower in Shelley's preface to *Hellas* and his assertion, there, that "We are all Greeks" (*Shelley's Poetry and Prose* 431). But the celebration of Greek culture commingles with lament that incriminates the Roman empire as the source of all that is wrong with modern civilization. The Mediterranean is, thus, the source of all that is best and worst about the past and its legacies: "O, but for that series of wretched wars which terminated in the Roman conquest of the world, but for the Christian religion which put a finishing stroke to the antient system; but for those changes which conducted Athens to its ruin, to what an eminence might not humanity have arrived!" (*Letters of Shelley* 2:75).

Italy and the Mediterranean region is very much for Shelley a cradle of civilization (he is also, of course, aware of the claims of other, older civilizations, as is clear from the setting of *Prometheus Unbound* I and II.i, in the Indian Caucasus), but also a place in which perversions of an original potentiality occurred. It is, in part, Shelley's poetic project to reclaim Mediterranean civilization from its falling off; its literal topography becomes symbolic, much as a west wind blowing in Florence in 1819 turned into one of the major Romantic emblems of poetic inspiration. It is Shelley's job as a poet to resuffer history, yet redirect it. For all his objections to the "Christian religion," in section IV of "Ode to the West Wind" he reenacts Christ's suffering as he seeks to define his condition as a poet fallen on harsh times: "I fall upon the thorns of life! I bleed!" (l. 54). Melodramatic, even distasteful, as the line can seem, it is worth noting how deliberately Shelley stages the need to "fall," if he is to rise again as the poet whose "harmonies" (l. 59) assume an affectingly "deep, autumnal tone, / Sweet though in sadness" (ll. 60–61) in the poem's final section.

PART THREE

Culture for Shelley is never fixed; its meanings alter when they are viewed with altered minds. "All high poetry is infinite; it is as the first acorn which contained all oaks potentially" (*Shelley's Poetry and Prose* 528). In a comparable fashion, as Morton argues, "His cry was not so much 'back to nature'...as 'forwards to nature'" (Morton 204). Nature itself is reborn in Shelley's words. In his fascinatingly sophisticated take on Godwinian perfectibility, Shelley deplores yet celebrates the imperfect, much as Ruskin argues in "The Nature of Gothic": "Nothing that lives is, or can be, rigidly perfect; part of it is decaying, part nascent...to banish imperfection is to destroy expression, to check exertion, to paralyze vitality" (Ruskin 92). Shelley's injunction to "Go...to Rome" in *Adonais* precedes and seems to catalyze subsequent gestures that combine world-weariness with the impulse to transform: "What Adonais is, why fear we to become?" (l. 459). "The One remains, the many change and pass" (l. 460), a line with multiple suggestions, includes the idea that there is a historical essence that "remains," a cultural value that endures, one that Shelley locates, with provisos and qualifications, in the Mediterranean. It turns out, as the stanza in question from *Adonais* reaches its hazardously bravura conclusion, that Rome embodies a portal through which the "many" strain toward the "One": "Rome's azure sky, / Flowers, ruins, statues, music, words, are weak / The glory they transfuse with fitting truth to speak" (ll. 466–468). The poetry here recasts the relation between the "One" and the "many" as the interaction between an ultimate glory that is imperfectly "transfused" and the material constituents of Roman nature and culture. True, they are inadequate to speak of such "glory" with "fitting truth," but they give a closer intimation of such "glory," the lines imply, than anywhere else that the poet can locate. The Mediterranean over which the wind sweeps in the ode turns into, one might think, the transformed sea, by way of an allusion to the opening of Dante's *Paradiso* across which the poet sets out in the final stanza of *Adonais*.

At such a moment Italy is caught up and is almost the medium and objective correlative of Shelley's desire for change. Looking at convicts hoeing weeds in St Peter's square, he experiences a "conflict of sensations," seeing the clash between the clanking chains and the "deep azure beauty" of the sky as producing "the emblem of Italy:

moral degradation contrasted with the glory of nature & of the arts"
(*Letters of Shelley* 2:94). Even the arts could possess a glory that was
tainted; but in Italian nature Shelley found a store of images that
mirrored the workings of his imagination and bodied forth his own
love of process and change, and his interest in relativist, partial perspectives; he admired, for example, "the ever changing illumination
of the air" (*Letters of Shelley* 2:87) over the Pantheon. What is "ever
changing" might result in freedom from reification, monumentaliza-
tion, fixity, the tyranny of the unchangeable. It might also, and here
Shelley moves in a different direction, suggest something or somewhere more unconditioned, that might, like the "One" he hails in
Adonais, "remain."

But what would remain must embody within itself the capacity for
purposive change. Such a capacity, for Shelley, was possessed by those
who could read the past, not as a lifeless scroll, but, in the way that
he read "each word" of Dante, as containing within itself "a burning
atom, a spark of inextinguishable thought" (*Shelley's Poetry and Prose*
528). To this end, his writings in Italy show an astonishing array of
generic experimentation: odes, lyrical dramas, tragedy, elegy, dream
vision, Aristophanic spoof, complexly rhymed sonnets, the epistle,
the epyllion. Always the use of genres and forms bears witness to
a desire to rework, to alter, to stimulate response. The very stanza
form of "To a Sky-lark" imitates in its final alexandrine the trill of
the bird's song, maybe; but it also reflects the leaping acts of imagination as typical of Shelley as they are of Dante who uses this image
of leaping in the *Paradiso* 23 to describe the necessary daring that
his "sacred strain" (23.61) must display in its "figuring of Paradise"
(23.60).[5] It captures the way in which the poet draws inspiration from
the natural to depict his wish to be as one who "singing still dost soar,
and soaring ever singest" ("To a Sky-lark" l. 10). In the Italian light,
Shelley's cultural and historical imaginations gain in resonance and
trenchancy, while his view of poetry alters decisively. "Didactic poetry
is my abhorrence" he declares in the Preface to *Prometheus Unbound*
(*Shelley's Poetry and Prose* 209). It is significant that neither "Ode to
the West Wind" nor "To a Sky-lark" expresses a specific political idea.
In both we go beyond opinion to participate in the very energy of the
imagination. Both are intent on entangling the reader in their own
self-imitations, so that in the former we experience "the incantation
of this verse" (l. 65) and in the latter we imagine what it must be like
to be a "Poet hidden / In the light of thought" (l. 36–37).

This is an Italian poetry of delight in potentiality, the intensify-
ing play of the imagination. Shelley's poetry seeks to give us access

to what Morton, glossing the close of *A Defence of Poetry*, calls "a shading of the not-yet" (Morton 191). But the not-yet derives from the has-been, if only by way of cancellation and annulment. Hence the delight in negative epithets, which Timothy Webb has analyzed in a justly celebrated essay,[6] the hearkening after what *A Defence* calls "the before unapprehended relations of things" (*Shelley's Poetry and Prose* 512), the pleasure taken by the speaker of "The Cloud," at the poem's close, in "unbuild[ing]" (l. 84). When Prometheus names Asia "thou light of life, / Shadow of beauty unbeheld," he sees her in the double way typical of the Italian period, as both "luminous" and yet a "shadow" of "beauty unbeheld" (III.3, ll. 7-8). Over and over, the poetry follows in Dante's tracks as it ascends through modes of sight toward possibilities of vision.

And yet the Italian light could play the imagination false; it could turn into the intolerable, ideal-annihilating radiant blaze that streams through *The Triumph of Life*, in which light is often a demonic parody of paradisal effulgence, in which "a cold glare, intenser than the noon / But icy cold, obscured with light / The sun, as he the stars" (ll. 77–79). It is as though the light that elsewhere Shelley celebrates and associates with Italy has turned on its celebrant. This destructive light threatens the light of the stars. Shelley's figurative pattern keeps open the possibility of some higher, better, former light, even as it records the way such light is "obscured." The sun is the ideal that has turned out to mislead, to ally itself with the erosive effects of a culture that the poem's imagery of a triumph associates with "the heirs / Of Caesar's crime" (ll. 283–284), symbolizing the onward rush of a conquest-bent and corrupting historical drive. The poem allows the course of history since "Imperial Rome" (l. 113) little of value; it traces less "the before unapprehended relations" than a near-archetypal process of yielding "Freedom" (l. 115) to the power of institutions and repressive structures. This aspect of the poem echoes the verdict of that side of Shelley who sees Venetian beauty in *Lines Written among the Euganean Hills* as sepulcher rather than exquisite light-struck architecture. The counterbalance remains as a residue, the sense derivable from the greatest poem in Italian literature, in which "all things are transfigured, except Love" (l. 476), that something still "Glimmers, forever sought, forever lost" (l. 431). That there may, in the future, be possibilities that are still "unapprehended" finds as its unstable guarantee the workings of questions and uncertain imaginings.

Figurations of doubleness are themselves capable of further turnings upon themselves here and elsewhere in Shelley. In *Prometheus*

Unbound, the dazzling paradoxes of a light that obscures and blinds act as tokens of a visionary assault on the visual, which in turn corresponds to an imaginative impulse to redefine. So in Act II, scene 5, the "VOICE (*in the air, singing*)" addresses a figure whose "lips enkindle / With their love the breath between them / And thy smiles before they dwindle / Make the cold air fire" (ll. 48–51). The extravagantly performative rhyme of "kindle" and "dwindle" in Shelley finds an appropriate gloss in the assertion made in *A Defence of Poetry* that "the mind in creation is as a fading coal, which some invisible influence, like an inconstant wind, awakens to transitory brightness" (*Shelley's Poetry and Prose* 531).[7] What the moment captures is the instantaneousness of Shelley's dealings with potentiality; he enacts, now, in the present of composition and reading, tensions involved in the workings of desire. Asia is seen as an unobjectifiable force whose quasi-Dantean "smiles" "make the cold air fire," her beauty the more vivid because it evades the visual: "Fair are others;—none beholds thee" (l. 60). The lyric is a microcosm of Shelley's complexly affirmative Italian poetry, poetry intensely and keenly conscious of its own questing desires.

Act II of the lyrical drama set its first scene in "A lovely Vale in the Indian Caucasus," its second in "A Forest, intermingled with Rocks and Caverns," its third on "A Pinnacle of Rock among Mountains," its fourth in "The Cave of Demogorgon," and its fifth "within a Cloud on the Top of a Snowy Mountain." The topography includes, in the first scene, a transfigured pastoral version of the grim rocky terrain of the first act and, thereafter, scenes that resist yet prompt identification. Matthews in "A Volcano's Voice" makes pertinent connections to "the area round Naples which Shelley explored with such delight in late 1818 and early 1819" (Matthews, in *Shelley's Poetry and Prose* 551). But once again Shelley uses Italy, especially Vesuvius and its environs, in ways that are at once localized and more generalized. He implies in his volcanic imagery a destructive-creative duality: the volcano destroys, but its destruction is of Jupiter's rule, while its fallout results in "extreme fertility" (Matthews, in *Shelley's Poetry and Prose* 552). Moreover, the second act refuses to be identified as solely Italian in locale, and occupies most powerfully its own imaginative and Utopian territory.

Shelley may have found in medieval and Renaissance Italy a model of self-rule, which he hoped to see revived in the future. He may have lamented the fact that Venice had fallen to the Austrians. But his Romantic geopolitics sponsored less a fierce regionalism than a recognition of the threat posed by the tyrannies of empire, political and religious (for relevant discussion see Michael Rossington). Incarnation and realization present poetic and ideological problems to Shelley. The moment of realization is the moment at which the workings of desire are temporarily stilled. The quintessential Shelleyan impulse is to put that arrest under pressure, to convert arrest into further quest.

This self-exiled Englishman, at odds with his national religion, was still able to champion the typical English Protestant virtues of independence and resistance to control. Yet his poetry proposes a restless, un-Procrustean universalism that exists through ceaseless dialogue, such as is set going between the Voice in the Air and Asia in 2.5. of *Prometheus Unbound*. Shelley's Italian politics insist on symbolic voyages, voyages that are made possible through poetry, as in Asia's lines: "My soul is an enchanted Boat / Which, like a sleeping swan, doth float / Upon the silver waves of thy sweet singing" (ll. 72–75). Poets legislate by creating the possibility of inhabiting "Realms where the air we breathe is Love" (l. 95). Throughout this song, Asia unbuilds the past, taking us "Through Death and Birth, to a diviner day" (l. 103). It is such an unbuilding that *Prometheus Unboun* as a whole undertakes. The writing shimmers with recollections of passing over the bay of Baiae, and looking down into a past that hints at "watery paths that wind between / Wildernesses calm and green" (ll. 106–107): paths and wildernesses that, for Shelley, were not solely Italian, but that draw on his acutely rhapsodic response to the Baths of Caracalla as a place in which "The paths still wind on, threading the perplexed windings" (*Letters of Shelley* 2:85).

Those "perplexed windings" through Italian history, culture, and nature include the layering upon layering of histories. There is, in Shelley's poetry, a recognition, that, as Iain Chambers has it, "we are faced with the choice of either remaining prisoners of an implacable past, and hence, of time itself, or of returning to that inheritance to remember and interpret it in a manner that frees the present for further possibilities" (Chambers 104). What prevents Shelley's poetry from being ineffectually angelic is its engagement with the—often Italian—past. Vico is Chambers's hero for his historicizing commitment to the "grounding of thought and truth in time" rather than his fellow Neapolitan Croce, criticized by Chambers for a commitment to the idea that "art proposes an unconditional, disinterested, and self-sufficient image whose character is universal" (Chambers 105, 104). But Shelley develops a vision that sees poetry as grounded in history yet capable of imagining an autonomous state, or at least one in which it is creative as well as imitative. When the Spirit of the Hour describes the redeemed order of things in *Prometheus Unbound*, Act III, scene 4, the speech sways between dismissing history as irrelevant junk and implicitly recognizing the power still possessed by the supposedly discarded: the "Thrones, altars, judgement-seats and prisons" (l. 164, which resembled indecipherable hieroglyphs written on Egyptian "obelisks" (l. 170)) "brought to Rome by the conquering armies of the empire" (*Shelley's Poetry and Prose* 268n). Yet these "ghosts of a no more remembered fame" (l. 169) are the stuff from which Shelley weaves poetic dreams of a state in which humanity might be "Equal, unclassed, tribeless and nationless" (l. 195).

Shelley's imaginative investment in the "wave's intenser day" of Italy and the Mediterranean more generally finds expression in the image he uses in "Ode to Liberty" of Athens's enduring significance:

> Within the surface of Time's fleeting river
> Its wrinkled image lies, as then it lay
> Immovably unquiet, and for ever
> It trembles, but it cannot pass away! (ll. 76–79)

Shelley adapts lines from Wordsworth's "Elegiac Stanzas, Suggested by a Picture of Peele Castle" that express the poet's earlier deceived view that nature was wholly benign. "Whene'er I looked," Wordsworth writes of his former self-viewing the castle's reflection in the sea, "It trembled, but it never passed away" (l. 8). Wordsworth has abandoned, as a result of "A deep distress" (l. 36), such a view; Shelley refuses to let go of the belief that what Athens represented still has continuing force. He sees Athens as a "wrinkled image" in the river of Time, distorted by it, but forever stimulating, "Immovably unquiet." The phrase is a suggestive image for the way in which, for Shelley, the past, especially the Mediterranean and Italian past, continue to open up possibilities for the future, through the "intenser day" supplied by the poetic imagination.

NOTES

1. All references to Wordsworth's poetry are by line numbers to *The Major Works,* ed. with introduction and notes by Stephen Gill (Oxford: Oxford UP, 2000).
2. References to Shelley's poetry and prose are to *Shelley's Poetry and Prose.* Ed. Donald H. Reiman and Neil Fraistat. 2nd ed. (New York: W. W. Norton, 2002).
3. Quotation drawn from *Corinne or Italy,* intro. George Saintsbury, 2 vols. (London: Dent, 1894). Project Gutenberg Ebook.

4. References to Dante's works are to *The Vision, or Hell, Purgatory, and Paradise of Dante Alighieri,* trans. Henry Francis Cary (London: Oxford UP, 1916).

5. See Stuart Curran's "Figuration in Shelley and Dante," in *Dante's Modern Afterlife: Reception and Response from Blake to Heaney,* ed. Nick Havely. (New York: St Martin's P, 1998), 49–59.

6. See Webb's "The Unascended Heaven: Negatives in *Prometheus Unbound,*" reprinted in *Shelley's Poetry and Prose* (694–711).

7. See D. J. Hughes, "Kindling and Dwindling: The Poetic Process in Shelley," *Keats-Shelley Journal* 13 (1964): 13–28.

CHAPTER SEVEN

EPIPSYCHIDION, DANTE, AND THE
RENEWABLE LIFE

Stuart Curran

*The poetry of Dante may be considered as the bridge thrown over
the stream of time, which unites the modern and ancient world.*

—*A Defence of Poetry*[1]

One of the great paradoxes of literary history is the veneration of
the self-professed atheist Percy Bysshe Shelley for Dante Alighieri, to
Shelley, uniquely among his contemporary readers, the master poet
who codified for medieval Europe a dramatic, totalized Christian
mythology and a moral universe centered on the transformative power
of love. Since this is a poetic discipleship that, like a lodestone, has
attracted my concerted attention on several occasions and over almost
four decades, a brief rehearsal of, and perspective on, those previous
pursuits will establish a context for the present inquiry.

As the lengthy comparison in *A Defence of Poetry* alerts us, Dante
was, along with Milton, a major influence on Shelley's writings
(525–528). Indeed, I would argue that, when all is said and done,
he was the preeminent influence. We can trace Shelley's profound
veneration for the republican Milton throughout his writings, and
clearly the "Satanic" version of *Paradise Lost* that we find instituted
in *Prometheus Unbound* as well as, before it, in *Frankenstein* (and
which was appropriately initiated by Godwin a generation earlier in
An Enquiry Concerning Political Justice [1:261–262]), testifies to

how resonantly that model affected the Shelley household. Even so, from Shelley's early maturity he interacted with Dante in a singularly intense manner that defies all simple explanation.

In my study *Shelley's Annus Mirabilis: The Maturing of an Epic Vision* (1975) the epic vision in question was that provided by the *Divine Comedy*. From the perspective of time and the accumulation of scholarship, were I to rewrite that study today, I would make the connection far more explicit than the loosely draped structure that governs the discourse in that book. There, beginning from Shelley's own highly dramatic account to Peacock of reading Dante in the dimly lit space behind the sanctuary of the Milan Cathedral (*Letters of Shelley* 2:8), the essential argument stipulated that this experience of Dante, in Italian and on Italian ground, prompted Shelley to reconsider Dante's mythological model from a modern, secular stance, conceiving within that perspective what would constitute hell (the self-consumed, self-destructive personal and social arenas of *The Cenci* and the first act of *Prometheus Unbound*), paradise (the liberating third and liberated fourth acts of the lyrical drama), and purgatory (the conflicted odes of 1819–1820). Today, I would wish to allow greater room for the model of purgatory, since I think that Shelley, in his interrogation of the function of poets—of himself in particular—in that modern, secular world, was responding to how prominently in the *Purgatorio* Dante confronts earlier poets, Latin, French, and Italian, as he slowly spirals toward the summit of earthly experience and beyond. Ralph Pite, I should note, in his estimable *Circle of our Vision* (1994) devotes his chapter on Shelley directly to his response to the *Purgatorio*.

I returned to the Dantean model again for the major conference— *Shelley e L'Italia*—that Lilla Crisafulli and Allan Christensen organized for the 1992 bicentennial celebration of Shelley in Rome. There, my starting point was the remarkable phrase of Dante's from *Paradiso* 23.61, "figurando il paradiso," which in modern critical parlance we might translate as "configuring paradise," a phrase that reveals how conscious Dante is of the metaphorical limitations of a language that always falls short of a truth that transcends its own instrumentation. Shelley's version of that concept is Demogorgon's vatic "The deep truth is imageless" (*Prometheus Unbound* 2.4; l. 116), and what I wanted to bring to focus in that comparison was how it could be that one poet immersed in a Christian poetics and another committed to a skeptical, if not explicitly atheistical, aesthetic could reconcile themselves so wholly over the problematics of metaphor: both poets, to quote briefly from that essay, "us[e] figuration, against its normative expectation, to disconcert, to dissimulate at first glance, and thus to enforce an act of questioning as prior to any agreement that may be struck between signifier and signified" ("Figurando il Paradiso: Shelley e Dante" 55). So, if I can briefly sum up where these considerations had led me, I would say that over those two decades I had moved from seeing Shelley simply adapting the tripartite model of the *Divine Comedy* to circumscribe the modern world and his place as poet within it, thereby essentially construing Dante from a thematically charged moral and social perspective, to later embracing him as a master of poesies, a maker and breaker of images, revealing there a deeply based intellectual affinity that represented itself poetically in a sophisticated hermeneutical deconstruction.

The third consideration was aired only sketchily in the keynote lecture I gave for the major March 2008 conference, *(Trans)national Identities / Reimagining Communities*, organized by the Centro per Studi Romantici of the University of Bologna along with the British Association for Romantics Studies (BARS) and the North American Society for the Study of Romanticism (NASSR), which was later published along with other papers from that extraordinary gathering in the *European Romantic Review*. A much expanded exposition of that argument lies within the annotations for Shelley's first translation of Dante in the spring of 1814 (a sonnet included in the *Alastor* volume of 1816) to be published in the third volume of the Johns Hopkins University Press edition of *The Complete Poems of Percy Bysshe Shelley*. Although more limited in scope than the other two interventions, this one has a direct bearing on the subject of this present essay. The translation in question is of Dante's sonnet addressed to Guido Calvalcanti, "Guido, i' vorrei che tu e Lappo ed io"—Guido, I would like for you and Lappo [that is, the poet Lapo Gianni] and I—a poem that envisions the poets embarking with their ladies in a poetic boat where they would drift on endlessly conversing about love. Shelley, it is true, had something of an obsession with boats—in the end a fatal one—but this particular model became deeply internalized, resulting in various boat-island configurations we can trace across his poetic oeuvre, from "Alastor" to *Lines Written among the Euganean Hills*, to the end of *Epipsychidion*. Appropriately, he quotes directly from the Cavalcanti sonnet in a letter he addressed to Emilia Viviani in 1821 (*Bodleian Shelley Manuscripts* 170–171). In addition, that fact leads me to the large point behind Shelley's selection of this sonnet as the first concrete sign of his investment in Dante's writings, that what Dante envisions there is the world around which the *Vita Nuova* is structured, one involving a coterie of poets who inspire one another with, and reify their community through, their devotion to chivalric love. "Dante," Shelley testifies in the *Defence*, "knew the secret things of love even more than Petrarch" (525); his *Paradiso* "the most glorious imagination of modern poetry...is a perpetual hymn of ever-lasting love" (526). The model of a community of like-minded poets who believe, to adapt the last line of Shelley's preface to *The Revolt of Islam*, that "Love [should be] celebrated everywhere as the sole law which should govern the moral world" (*Poetical Works* 37), is an absorbing ideal to which Shelley aspires from his days at Bracknell in 1813 reading Dante's sonnets under the tutelage of Cornelia Turner to his encouraging Leigh Hunt's emigration to Pisa in 1821 in order to establish *The Liberal* there with Byron and the Shelleys.

This ideal most directly finds its voice in *Epipsychidion*. That was, it could be argued, the essential view of the poem among Victorian Shelley critics (Brooke), but it has long receded before the necessary deflation of their vague Platonic abstractions. The chief instrument to that end, more than being merely influential, has been the wholly dominant reading by one of the twentieth-century's magisterial Shelley scholars, Kenneth Neill Cameron. Because of this, more than a half century after the publication of his "Planet-Tempest Passage," *Epipsychidion* now stands today as what must be called the most perversely misread poem in Shelley's canon. From Cameron's emphasis on the biographical bases of the poem, it has become an all but universal habit to conceive of the representation of the Moon in this poem as a thinly disguised and a thoroughly unflattering, even to some a morally reprehensible, portrait of Mary Shelley. Similarly, modern readers of *Epipsychidion*—if, indeed, any of them should care any longer to be so forcibly entangled in what this model would suggest are the confessional ramblings of the poet's unbridled egocentricity—may be divided on whether the Comet alludes to Shelley's youthful infatuation with Harriet Grove or to that later, much more salacious target of retrospective gossip, Claire Clairmont. (So eminent a scholar as Marian Kingston Stocking, in her introduction to the Clairmont correspondence, thus identifies her without raising a question—or an eyebrow.) In all fairness, it must be granted that in the postwar exhaustion of absolutes and ethos of reconstruction dominant in 1948 Cameron's attempt to set Shelley's feet on solid ground had then to have seemed salutary. Yet, so overdetermined has the poem been by critical and editorial interventions following his lead and reducing every element in a clearly allegorical poetic universe to a crude biographical base that it is rare that any reader can listen

to the pleadings of the preface—or, more exactly, of the three different versions of the preface—or the literally dozens of rejected cou-
plets foretelling misreadings both inadvertent and deliberate, or the
poet's various letters stipulating the poem's intent, demanding that
we sharply distance the author from his text. Shelley goes so far in the
published preface as to kill the poet off as stipulated agent, leaving
himself as a mere literary executor for a figure who has died—not just
died, we might emphasize, but who (to quote from the first sentence
of that preface) "died at Florence" (P&P 392). We could, of course,
see this as an artful ruse to keep us from looking downriver toward
the menage at Pisa. Or, in deliberate contrast, we might instead want
to revert to that Dantean harmonious coterie of poets as it fell prey
to civil strife and truly "died at Florence," as another way to interpret
the offhand remark of a poet schooled in the allegorical mode of an
earlier century.

To exemplify just how well schooled Shelley is in this mode of
discourse, how his very terminology reflects that of a culture a half
millennium preceding his, let us juxtapose two passages. The first is
from the *Vita Nuova*, (4.1–3 in Michele Barbi's discredited, but still
universally adopted, numbering), where Dante recounts an unsettling
dream that was his response to encountering the mature Beatrice after
an interval of nine years from their first acquaintance:

[I]o divenni in picciolo tempo poi di sì fraile e debole condizione,
che a molti amici pesava de la mia vista; e molti pieni d'invidia già si
procacciavano di sapere di me quello che io volea del tutto celare ad
altrui. Ed io, accorgendomi del malvagio domandare che mi faceano,
per la volontade d'Amore, lo quale mi comandava secondo lo consiglio
de la ragione, rispondea loro che Amore era quelli che così m'avea
governato. Dicea d'Amore, però che io portava nel viso tante de le sue
insegne, che questo non si potea ricovrire. E quando mi domandavano
"Per cui t'ha così distrutto questo Amore?", ed io sorridendo li guar-
dava, e nulla dicea loro (4.1–3)

I soon became of so frail and weak a condition that many friends worried about my appearance; and many who were filled with envy sought
at once to know what I wanted wholly to conceal from others. And I,
aware of the malicious questioning that they put to me, through the
will of Love, who commanded me according to the counsel of reason, replied that Love it was who had so guided me. I spoke of Love
because I bore on my face so many of his signs that it could not be
concealed. And when they asked, "For whom has this Love so ravaged
you?", I regarded them smiling and said nothing. (Trans. Cervigni
and Vasta 53)

The second is from a letter Shelley wrote to Charles Ollier on February 12, 1821, accompanying the manuscript of *Epipsychidion* and directing him how to publish it:

> It is to be published simply for the esoteric few; and I make its author a secret, to avoid the malignity of those who turn sweet food into poison; transferring all they touch into the corruption of their own natures. My wish with respect to it is, that it should be printed immediately in the simplest form, and merely one hundred copies: those who are capable of judging and feeling rightly with respect to a composition of so abstruse a nature, certainly do not arrive at that number— among those, at least, who would ever be excited to read an obscure and anonymous production; and it would give me no pleasure that the vulgar should read it. (*Letters of Shelley* 2:263)

The point in juxtaposing these passages is to demonstrate the extent to which Shelley, in representing his purposes to Ollier, has accomplished a remarkable internalization of the character of the *Vita Nuova*, where Dante continually presents himself as hiding himself from the multitude who gossip among themselves and misconstrue his motives as merely carnal. We might add to this example the carefully distanced language of the preface:

> The present Poem, like the *Vita Nuova* of Dante is sufficiently intelligible to a certain class of readers without a matter-of-fact history of the circumstances to which it relates; and to a certain other class it must ever remain incomprehensible, from a defect of a common organ of perception for the ideas of which it treats. (*P&P* 392)

In an earlier draft, the determining phraseology is even stronger— "it must *& ought ever* to remain incomprehensible" (*Complete Works* 2:376–377, emphasis added), indicating the pains Shelley took to enforce the allegorical character of *Epipsychidion*. In the *Vita Nuova* the more that Dante refuses a simple explanation, paradoxically, the more ineffable is the notion of Love he conveys. That, of course, is exactly the point Shelley labors to make.

It took many years after Shelley's pointed citation of the *Vita Nuova* in his prefatory note before Timothy Webb was led to undertake a systematic comparison of the two poems. He was followed in knowledgeable accounts by Earl Schulze and Alan Weinberg, so that we now have in the critical literature a solid foundation for understanding the ways in which Shelley strove to accommodate as well as to diverge from Dante's model. But Webb and Weinberg, the latter with something of an apologetic endnote, insist that the biographical transferences of the poem cannot be ignored (Webb, *Violet in the Crucible* 200; Weinberg 282, n.22). I would propose, against that admonition, that we must do exactly that. The original readers of *Epipsychidion* in England, particularly the Συνετοί or elect readers Shelley imagined for this text (*Letters of Shelley* 2:363), as he had likewise for *Prometheus Unbound*, would, with a few obvious exceptions, have had no familiarity with the poet's experiences in Italy and, therefore, no basis for reading the poem within the biographical strait-jacket that scholarly diligence has devised for it. Indeed, as the poem was published anonymously, most readers would have had no familiarity with the poet at all. A contemporary Italian like Francesco Pacchiani, who held the chair in logic and metaphysics at the University of Pisa, who was confessor to the Viviani family and tutor to its children, and who both introduced the Shelleys to Emilia and provided the poet with his figure of Emily as "Poor captive bird!" (*Epipsychidion* l. 5), however surprised he might have been by the sexual tenor of the poem, would surely have read *Epipsychidion*, through his formal training as well as his clerical asceticism, within the perspective provided by Dantean allegory. Thus, to dismiss the biographical template is not to distort our reading but, rather, exactly the opposite, to restore the actual conditions in which this poem was originally invested.

But some will say, that still leaves us with a Sun, a Moon, a Comet, at least one lodestar, in addition to the "many mortal forms" in which the poet "rashly sought / The shadow of that idol of [his] thought" (ll. 267–268), all pursued at some point in his harried emotional existence. These, they would aver, surely cannot be ignored: in what Shelley a year after writing *Epipsychidion* called "an idealized history of my life and feelings" (*Letters of Shelley* 2:434), they must have concrete embodiments.[2] My answer is, "not in this poem." It does not necessarily follow that we need wholly to abstract Shelley's principal figures, as Earl Wasserman does, improbably forcing the poem into a context provided by the Song of Songs and collapsing it into a stark polarity between "the Moon of sublunary mutability and the Sun of transcendent eternity" (439), even though certainly Shelley observes and finally valorizes a dialectical tension between these "Twin Spheres of light who rule this passive Earth, / This world of love, this *me*; and into birth / Awaken all its fruits and flowers" (ll. 345–347). What matters most is not, I would argue, where any such figure stands as an allegorical counter within the patterning of Shelley's solar or sidereal system, but their sheer number. In addition, in this Shelley follows and extends the model of Dantean allegory. We might surmise, as well, that the several conflicting accounts of the nature of Love in Plato's *Symposium*, which he translated in 1818, must have come to his mind as reinforcing such emphatic diversity.

To engage *Epipsychidion* in this mode, especially given the existence of several valuable exegeses within a Dantean context on which we can already rely, does not require close reading as much as it does an understanding of what the poets share as a general tenor and in their textual strategies. Shelley himself in his preface, in a customary manner that this late in our experience of him we ought to have learned to recognize, virtually tells us how to approach his poem. First, he cites the *Vita Nuova* as a model for readers to bear in mind. And then, in a move that otherwise is without logical purpose, Shelley quotes the conclusion—admittedly beautifully written—of a translation he had made (and never fully published elsewhere) of a second Dante poem, the first canzone from *Il Convito*, beginning, "Voi ch'intendendo il terzo ciel movete, / udite il ragionar ch'è nel mio core." Shelley translates this without elaboration as, "You who intelligent the third Heaven move, / Hear the discourse which is within my heart." This is the by-now famous poem in which Dante laments to those who preside over the sphere of Venus, the reserve of idealized love, that, accompanied by much agony, a new love has replaced what he had felt for Beatrice. Webb, who first printed Shelley's translation of this poem, bridles a little at Dante's allegorization of this second figure as Philosophy (*Violet in the Crucible* 296–297), but that is how Dante himself characterized the poem in a later commentary, one to which Shelley had access. Shelley knew that this was not the end of the matter either, since Beatrice herself was to be reconfigured once more as divine theology in the *Paradiso*, where, one presumes, she finally trumps human philosophy. What Shelley's prefatory citation calls attention to, however, is not a particularized allegorical reading, but rather the way in which Dante, both in the *Vita Nuova* and in his later writings multiplies the number of idealized figures whom Dante pursues and to whom he finds himself devoted. In the *Vita Nuova* there is, early on, a woman whom he uses as a screen to disguise his devotion to Beatrice (5.3); after Beatrice's demise another woman, particularized by her compassion for his wretched state, threatens to usurp Beatrice's position in his heart (35.2). Dante juxtaposes Beatrice with such other figures so as to underscore how constant is the impulse to love even where we would remark what we call inconstancy in its objects. Shelley surely had this example in mind when, contemplating in retrospect the circumstances that brought him to write *Epipsychidion,* he remarked

> I think one is always in love with something or other; the error, and
> I confess it is not easy for spirits cased in flesh and blood to avoid it,
> consists in seeking in a mortal image the likeness of what is perhaps
> eternal. (*Letters of Shelley* 2:434)

The multiplicity of potential objects for one's love is an essential core to the argument of *Epipsychidion.*

> True Love in this differs from gold and clay,
> That to divide is not to take away.
> Love is like understanding, that grows bright,
> Gazing on many truths; 'tis like thy light,
> Imagination! which from earth and sky,
> And from the depths of human phantasy,
> As from a thousand prisms and mirrors, fills
> The Universe with glorious beams, and kills
> Error, the worm, with many a sun-like arrow
> Of its reverberated lightning. Narrow
> The heart that loves, the brain that contemplates,
> The life that wears, the spirit that creates
> One object, and one form, and builds thereby
> A sepulchre for its eternity. (ll. 160–173)

The citation of imagination within this litany should remind us that composition of the *Defence of Poetry* is only a few weeks away. There poetry replicates these "thousand prisms and mirrors": "It awakens and enlarges the mind itself by rendering it the receptacle of a thousand unapprehended combinations of thought" (517). Immediately thereafter Shelley makes the connection with the Love that he celebrates in *Epipsychidion:* "The great secret of morals is Love; or a going out of our own nature, and an identification of ourselves with the beautiful which exists in thought, action, or person not our own. A man to be greatly good must imagine intensely and comprehensively...The great instrument of moral good is the imagination" (517). Going out of our own nature, essential as it is to the operations of both imagination and love, has a moral end because it involves the free giving of the self to what it contemplates. That voiding of the self is fundamentally recreative, since it requires a continual reconstruction of the self and an attendant recalibration of all its surroundings.

The lengthy allegorical account of shifting lodestars, Shelley's "idealized history," then, should be read not so much as a disguised account of what might be vulgarly termed his love life but as the continuing evolution of a prototypical human being undergoing the incessant transformations by which love manifests itself within one's psychic life. As others, Schulze especially, have emphasized, Shelley distinguishes himself from Dante by emphasizing the physical dimensions of love, but as the extraordinary sexual imagery of his imagined island paradise makes clear, the physical is not meant to be equated with mere carnality. Rather, it is seen as a means to a higher unity, of the sort that Shelley had painstakingly rendered in his translation of Plato's *Symposium* in his first year in Italy.

> We shall become the same, we shall be one
> Spirit within two frames, oh! wherefore two?
> One passion in twin-hearts, which grows and grew,
> Till like two meteors of expanding flame,
> Those spheres instinct with it become the same,
> Touch, mingle, are transfigured; ever still
> Burning, yet ever inconsumable (573–579).

The key concept here is of transfiguration, of being formed anew within what Shelley calls "that calm circumference of bliss" (550). That this is how he conceived of Dante's aim throughout his career is made explicitly evident in Shelley's final tribute to his predecessor, in late lines from the *The Triumph of Life*:

> Behold a wonder worthy of the rhyme
>
> Of him who from the lowest depths of Hell
> Through every Paradise and through all glory
> Love led serene, and who returned to tell
>
> In words of hate and awe the wondrous story
> How all things are transfigured, except Love ... (ll. 471–476)

There are two extensions of this notion of transfiguration that distinguish the arena of *Epipsychidion*. The first is the way in which a transfiguration is by its nature a reconfiguration, both of the self and of what the self contemplates. This might explain the way in which Emily, in this poem, defies any rigidity of conception. Shelley begins *Epipsychidion* apostrophizing her with a dizzying array of figures beginning with "Sweet Spirit" (l. 1); then, adopting Pacchiani's figure of the captive bird, as a "Nightingale" (l. 10); then, resorting to metonymy, as a "spirit-winged Heart" (l. 13), followed by her transcendental assumption as a "Seraph of Heaven" (l. 21)—all this within twenty-one lines. By line 71 he has employed twenty-eight such individual figures. In the end his inability to render any single quality that energizes his devotion and his poetry forces Shelley to fall back on the category that unifies all this figural displacement: Emily is "A Metaphor of Spring and Youth and Morning" (l. 120) but still, and unavoidably, "a Metaphor." If we parse that word carefully, it represents in its Greek roots a carrying across—which is to say once again, a transfiguration, a going out of one's nature.

Yet in Shelley's later poetry there is always a counterthrust to the creative elaborations of figuration, one, as I noted earlier, he shares with Dante, a recognition that all diction, as necessary as it is, is by its nature inadequate to the task it assumes. As the poem reaches for a transcendent climax in its edenic bower, it collapses of its own weight.

> The winged words, on which my soul would pierce
> Into the height of Love's rare Universe
> Are chains of lead around its flight of fire (ll. 588–590)

This sense of inadequacy shares with it the inadequacy of the solitary mind that turns to words to discover itself and relate to its surroundings. Part of how one renews oneself, in this conception, is to write oneself, thus in a second sense to reconfigure the self. No sooner is the self written, however, than, like love, it must be rewritten. Dante's initial sonnet in the *Vita Nuova*, "A ciascun'alma presa e gentil core" (3.10–12), is written specifically to be reinscribed by other poets in his circle. Throughout his developing narrative Dante continually centers attention on the act of inscription through a poetic closure to each episode, emphasizing the importance of his bearing nuanced witness to the alterations in the nature of his love. Even after the death of Beatrice he reveals himself, like Shelley at the end of *Epipsychidion*, as unable to continue in his customary creativity and suddenly breaks off his poetic composition. Although the work concludes enigmatically by announcing its title, "Qui finisce la Vita Nuova di Dante Alighieri" (42.4)—Here ends the new life of Dante Alighieri—the renewing life is what Dante is actually inscribing moment-by-moment throughout the work's progression.

If one locates *Epipsychidion* not just within a particularized series of events in Pisa but rather within the context of the texts that will follow within weeks of its composition, *Adonais* and the *Defence of*

Poetry, Shelley's emphasis on the rudiments of creativity, what draws it forth and what it attempts to realize, is the constant in each of these works. In each the creative process is fundamental to the renewal of the self, and these efforts of recreation are themselves, in the words of the *Defence*, "episodes to that great poem, which all poets, like the cooperating thoughts of one great mind, have built up since the beginning of the world" (522). They are, as this amazing metaphor indicates, not static entities but rather always in motion, always in the process of renewal, through all time.[3] It is here, I believe, and not in the particularized details of Shelley's biography, that we should locate the essential impetus behind *Epipsychidion*.

NOTES

1. *Shelley's Poetry and Prose*. Ed. Donald H. Reiman and Neil Fraistat. 2nd ed. (New York: W. W. Norton, 2002) 526. Unless otherwise indicated, all further references to Shelley's poetry and prose are drawn from this edition and cited by page number, or by line or stanza and canto.

2. It can be no accident that in choosing this language Shelley exactly repeats the formulation by which he had characterized the *Vita Nuova* in *A Defence of Poetry*: "Dante understood the secret things of love even more than Petrarch. His *Vita Nuova* is an inexhaustible fountain of purity of sentiment and language: it is the idealized history of that period, and those intervals of his life which were dedicated to love" (*Shelley's Poetry and Prose* 525).

3. The metaphor of fire that Shelley employs to characterize the islanded union of the lovers in *Epipsychidion* explicitly emphasizes an irreducibly kinetic nature that conflates temporalities: "One passion in twin-hearts, which grows and grew, / ... ever still / Burning, yet ever inconsumable" (ll. 575, 578–579).

CHAPTER EIGHT

THE POETRY OF PHILOLOGY: BURCKHARDT'S *CIVILIZATION OF THE RENAISSANCE IN ITALY* AND MARY SHELLEY'S *VALPERGA*

Tilottama Rajan

In his 1860 book *The Civilization [Kultur] of the Renaissance in Italy*, Jacob Burckhardt argues that because Italy had no overarching system of government, it was free to create different political forms through its multiplicity of competing despotisms and republics. Paradoxically, the very fragmentation of Italy allowed for the birth of individualism, "personality," and political experimentation—an experimentation marked by Burckhardt's use of the term "art" to describe both the Italian states and concomitantly their fascination with war. Yet Italy by the same token could never consolidate itself as a nation and did not build on these experiments (69–71, 79, 98). Its wars constantly disintegrated what its art—in the broad sense—had produced. For war, as Jacqueline Rose argues, marks a "limit" to claims of "absolute knowledge," even as such claims are "offered as one cause—if not *the* cause—of war" (16–18).

For Burckhardt, then, the Italian Renaissance never becomes the "adequate embodiment of the Idea," to evoke Hegel's description of classicism: the position in which, according to Julia Lupton, Burckhardt puts the Renaissance between the Middle Ages and modernity in his tacit version of Hegel's three-part cultural scheme

(8–9).[1] In Hegel's *Aesthetics* classicism moves beyond the indeterminacy of the Idea in the Symbolic phase, and synchronizes inside and outside; yet in Hegel's concave dialectic it is only the midpoint of the historical triad. It is then superseded by the Romantic as a return to the dissonance of spirit and the material forms available to it (77–81), as if Hegel recognizes that the adequate embodiment of the Idea is itself an inadequate idea. But if Hegel disavows his own resistance to perfectibility, Burckhardt embraces it when he criticizes Hegel for seeking "the affirmative in which the negative vanishes" (*Reflections* 19). Yet despite this criticism, and the more materialist and empirical approach that we can also associate both with the increasing dominance of the novel in the middle of the nineteenth century and the shift from philosophy to history in German universities, Burckhardt's work, in Ernst Gombrich's words, can still be described as a "Hegelianism without metaphysics" (26). For Burckhardt also speaks, in residually Hegelian terms, of a history that is inhabited deep down, by a "spirit" that is all the time "building a new house," whose "outward casing" will again and again disintegrate (*Reflections* 37). And in his *Letters*, distinguishing what he calls "contemplation," which is oriented to "the concrete, to visible nature, and to history," from "speculation," which understands things "from the standpoint of first principles," Burckhardt nevertheless uses the vocabulary of German Idealism when he says that "the development of the spirit to freedom, has become my highest conviction." "I respect speculation as in every epoch one of the highest expressions of the spirit," he writes, "only instead of Speculation itself, I am looking for its correlative in history." And this correlative Burckhardt finds in the "facta" of history. "To me history is poetry.... [To] you philosophers...history is a source of knowledge, a science, because you see, or think you see, the *primum agens* where I only see mystery and poetry" (50–51).

Placing it within a broader theoretical spectrum, this paper suggests that Burckhardt's reading of the Renaissance is one lens through which to view Mary Shelley's historiographical project and her fascination with early Renaissance Italy in *Valperga: Or, the Life and Adventures of Castruccio, Prince of Lucca* (1823), published five years after Burckhardt was born. Like Burckhardt, who according to Gombrich, "collected seven hundred excerpts from Vasari's *Lives*" and other sources, "cutting up his notebooks in little slips for use in appropriate places" (18), Shelley read "fifty old books" to write *Valperga* (*Letters of Mary Wollstonecraft Shelley* 2:592). She thus developed a method that, rather than being organized by a master-narrative, was anti-foundationalist in the form that Foucault sometimes characterizes as "genealogy" ("Nietzsche" 139–140) and sometimes as "general" rather than "total history" (*Archeology* 3–10). Like Burckhardt, Shelley was interested in the fragmented political geography of Italy at a time when Walter Scott was using the historical novel in the service of total history to canonize the British nation-state. And like Burckhardt's *Civilization*, Shelley's novel is an encyclopedic bricolage of the political, the historical, and the aesthetic, temporarily focalized through the passions of three distinctive individuals whose emergence as individuals is possible only against the backdrop of Italy's fragmentation.

Philology, which Nietzsche described as "*ephexis* or undecisiveness in interpretation" (169), is one point of convergence between Shelley's and Burckhardt's projects. Burckhardt's presentation of Renaissance life, which he himself describes as a "string of marginal notes, . . . extending over some years" (*Civilization* 271), does not reach conclusions. He provides a cross-section, rather than a "history" in the nineteenth century sense of a coherent narrative. For as Martin Rudwick explains, before the French Revolution history involved an account not necessarily tied to a sense of time (53). Burckhardt's information takes the form of an array; his arrangement is encyclopedic and conjunctive, and does not use a logic of sequence and subordination. Implicit in his method is, therefore, a historiography that sets itself against the more teleological history of spirit's self-organization that was an available and indeed dominant model at the time, even if the seamless functioning of that model in Hegel and German Idealism is often complicated. This historiography is spelled out by Burckhardt in his *Reflections on History*, where he distinguishes his work from Hegel's, noting that he takes "transverse section of history in as many directions as possible," rather than constructing the "longitudinal sections" characteristic of the "philosophy of history current hitherto." His work, he insists, has nothing to do with "system" or "theodicy": "The philosophy of history is a centaur, a contradiction in terms, for history coordinates, and hence is unphilosophical, while philosophy subordinates, and is hence unhistorical" (*Reflections on History* 32–33).

Shelley's choice of Italy as the scene for her reinvention of the historical novel may also have to do with the uniquely Italian focus on what Burckhardt calls the state as a work of art. By this term Burckhardt does not mean that the state is to be conceived as a totality: whether that totality has been achieved or is still coming into being, as in Hegel's *Philosophy of Right*. Indeed contrary to Hegel, Burckhardt does not focus on the state but on that lower grade of organized collective life that Hegel calls civil society: *bürgerliche Gesellschaft*, which for Hegel is "atomistic" (*Philosophy of Mind* 257). Hegel's understanding of civil society versus the state is modeled on his distinction between the plant and the animal or human organism from his early Jena System to the Encyclopedia. The plant "fall[s] apart" into a "number of individuals" and is "impotent to hold its members in its power." By contrast, the animal organism, like the state, is a whole that subsumes its differences, synchronously and teleologically. To do this it must have differences, but conveniently the rights of the part and whole do not come into conflict, as each member is "reciprocally end and means" (*Philosopohy of Nature* 276, 303).

In contrast to Hegel, who criticizes civil society as an aggregate of individual self-interests (*Philosopohy of Mind* 256–257), Burckhardt sees the structural category of individualism as being one of the great achievements of the Renaissance, even if its particular manifestations (in the Borgias for instance) were disastrous. By the state as a work of art, Burckhardt, therefore, does not mean the fusion of aesthetics and governmentality within a traditionally organicist model that Marc Redfield, following de Man, calls aesthetic ideology. Aesthetics in this form participates in "processes of mediation" that are properly called "technical," becoming a technics that produces a certain kind of subject within the collective subject of history (16). Rather Burckhardt means a kind of inventiveness: a conscious focus on constructing, even deconstructing, the state that becomes possible precisely within the atomistic structure of Italy, as well as a formal theorization of policy and statecraft that is also experimental, and of which a "constitutional artist" such as Machiavelli is the prime example (*Civilization* 71). Importantly, despite his fascination with Italy, Burckhardt has little positive to say about it. "Intrigues, armaments, leagues, corruption and treason make up the outward history of Italy at this period," he writes (74), in a comment that resonates with Shelley's presentation of how Castruccio's brief consolidation of fascist power is dissipated by the schemes of Tripalda. Certain forms of statecraft in Italy, Burckhardt writes, "attained a perfection" that is not without its own "beauty and grandeur." But "as a whole" Italy "gives us the impression of a bottomless abyss" (74). For no single form of state emerges untarnished from its history. Indeed the republican state-form, which Burckhardt prefers, does not achieve the same level of development as the tyrannies. Florence, for which he has the highest praise as the "most modern state in the world" (65), is essentially a failed state, riven by the conflict of the Guelphs and Ghibellines that also forms the backdrop to Shelley's novel.

What then does Burckhardt find in Italy? Perhaps precisely that it is the scene of multiple unrealized potentialities. The "work" of art allows the state to be the product of "reflection and careful adaptation" (73), but without any single form of state being permanently implemented. Briefly Burckhardt sees other European countries—like France, England, and Spain—as having transformed the feudal system into a "unified monarchy," or as having given it the outward appearance of cohesiveness in the form of "empire," as in Germany (19). But Italy benefitted from the fact that the papacy was strong enough to hinder "national unity," yet not strong enough "to bring about that unity" (19–20). Just as Coleridge said that lacking England's "deep interest in the affair of the whole" and her sense of "nationality," Germany had many universities and was "forever thinking" (*Lectures* 2.574), so Burckhardt feels that Italy produced a "multitude of political units," republican and despotic, and thus possessed a certain political vitality. To borrow his description of Siena, Italy was a "workshop" (*Civilization* 73) for political forms whose inadequacy deferred any end of history.

From this perspective, Burckhardt is particularly interested in the despots of the fourteenth and fifteenth century, a focus that makes his retrospect on Italy different from Sismondi's emphasis on the republics, and provides a unique perspective on reading Shelley. For Shelley takes as her hero Castruccio "prince" of Lucca, a petty "tyrant" (in the Greek sense), pushing the republic of Florence to the margins of her novel. Moreover, unlike Sismondi she does not celebrate Florence's return to prosperity after the death of Castruccio, nor does she note that Lucca itself returned to being a republic. In a curious way Sismondi's history risked leading to a condescending picture of a once republican Italy overrun and debased in modern times into a touristic relic: a binary we find in Byron's representations of both Greece and Italy. By contrast Shelley's seemingly perverse interest in the potential of the *Signoria* in Lucca—a compromise formation between local autonomy and despotism—results in a less linear and more dialectical view of Italian history, though it is a deeply negative dialectic that refuses both the growing despotism of modernity and the closure of hypostatizing a lost republican moment in the past. Significantly, although Sismondi writes of the "middle ages" and Burckhardt writes of the "Renaissance," and although in terms of our own periodization Shelley's novel occupies an interregnum between the two, for Romantics such as Hegel and the Schlegels, both alike would have been postclassical or "Romantic," which is to say unfinished, inhabited by something still to come.

In line with this Romanticism, Burckhardt is interested in the despotisms, perhaps for the same reasons that Bataille in "The Psychological Structure of Fascism" later valorizes fascism over monarchy, as an expression of heterogeneity. Thus Burckhardt emphasizes Italy's unique tolerance of illegitimate birth. Unlike England, which simulated dynastic lawfulness, Italy often admitted bastards "to the succession," a prime example being Ferrara (*Civilization* 30, 48), where the bastard prophetess Beatrice in *Valperga* is briefly allowed to open a new line of thinking. The most admired form of illegitimacy, Burckhardt notes, was "presented by the *condottiere*" who, whatever "his origin, raised himself to the position of an independent ruler" (31), as Castruccio does in Shelley's novel. Italy is also notoriously the scene of crime. Here the more conservative Burckhardt, a critic of the French Revolution, joins hands with the far more radical Godwin in seeing in this "contempt of law" (*Civilization* 284) an anarchism that contests the force of institution. Alongside this democratizing fascism, where a "servant could become a king," and which fascinates and repels British writers from Middleton and Rowley's *The Changeling* onwards, women also had a higher place in Italy than in Britain. "There was no question of woman's rights or female emancipation," Burckhardt writes, "simply because the thing itself was a matter of course": "the great Italian women...had the mind and courage of men" (*Civilization* 251).

For Burckhardt, then, Italy is the scene of an unbinding that is the beginning of the "modern spirit" (*Civilization* 344): a spirit very different from the Habermasian modernity and modernization promoted by Scott in *Waverley*. For this spirit never consolidates itself within a single paradigm, however diffuse, like commercial society. Rather it consists of loose ends, beginnings to which one can go back, within an economy of the fragment described by Friedrich Schlegel, when he writes that fragments are "tendencies, ruins, and raw materials": promises of a system that they project as "subjective embryo[s]," and also marks of its limitations (1, 20). Or as Julia Lupton explains, commenting on Benjamin rather than Schlegel, the ruin "constitutes a kind of rebirth," wherein rebirth consists precisely in ruin, "namely, the survival of a work beyond its period of cultural currency." This survival blocks the narrative of modernity, since for Benjamin "ruins do not simply represent the devastated foundations of new and more glorious buildings" but "persist beyond their supersedure" (Lupton 28). Lupton, to be sure, sees Burckhardt in very different terms from Benjamin and Warburg. Picking up his own image of Italy as Esau, "the first-born among the sons of Europe" (*Civilization* 98), she sees his humanist *Kulturgeschichte as* having absorbed Italy's falling short into a straightforward narrative of modernity, in which the very "prematurity" of its innovations "makes possible the maturation of Europe" (Lupton 35).[2] But leaving aside the placement of Burckhardt in post-Hegelian art-history, I want to insist here on the usefulness of his presentation of Italy to a historiography also articulated by Percy Shelley, when he writes of time in terms of the shadow, the ghost or *Geist*, "which futurity casts upon the present" (*Shelley's Poetry and Prose* 535). For both Shelleys history is a future haunted by a past that bears the future within it, but containing as much shadow and ruin as it does seed.

As a mise-en-abime of how Italy's art falls short, it is worth pausing over Burckhardt's discussion of the emphasis on festivals as a site where the Italians "developed their artistic powers" (*Civilization* 256), because Shelley too gives a certain prominence to such ceremonial forms of collective life. Chapter Two of *Valperga* describes the representation of Hell on May 1, 1304 in Florence, when the Ponte al Carraia broke down under the weight of the spectators (65–67), an episode also mentioned by Burckhardt. Of significance here is both writers' choice of an event that falls apart. In addition, *Valperga's* first volume ends with an elaborate account of Euthanasia holding court, as a variety of "story-tellers, *improvisatori*, musicians...jugglers and buffoons" perform for her (173).This somewhat tedious account is at odds with Godwin's editing of the novel to reduce the epic and extensive elements that resembled the method of Scott, and his preference for the intensively psychological in the relationship of Euthanasia and Beatrice. It may reflect Shelley's desire to make use of her research into "fifty old books." But beyond that, her empiricism, and her bifocal inclusion of the psychological story alongside a history of Castruccio's career framed within a broader cross-section of Italian history, also reflects a reluctance to succumb to a narrativity that could only produce a story of disaster, given that the lives of all three protagonists end in death. The attention to documentation, whether of events or festivals, is thus part of a historiography of unconcludedness. This being said, the inclusion of the court episode, simply because it ought to be included for thoroughness, is symptomatic of a frustration with this part of Italian cultural life. For Burckhardt, both the "secular drama" and the "higher poetical development of the mystery" were inhibited by the Italian passion for "extravagant" external "display" (*Civilization* 260). Perhaps like Burckhardt, Shelley too feels the limitations of "art" as it exists at the time, whether in such practices of everyday life as festivals and pageants, or in the high art of Dante to which she pays formal respect at the beginning of the novel (*Valperga* 57). Indeed the fact that her only other reference to Dante involves a spectacle that falls apart stands in marked contrast to the Romantic idealization of Dante, for instance by Friedrich Schelling, who sees *The Divine Comedy* as "a genre in and for itself," "the most complete interpenetration of everything" and "the entire genre of modern poesy" (239–240).

In the remaining space I can only sketch what is opened up by reading Shelley's promissory pessimism with Burckhardt rather than, for instance, with Godwin's traumatic revision of the historical novel in *Mandeville* (1817), which is set in the interregnum between the execution of Charles I and the Restoration, and is, thus, also concerned with a period of republican political experimentation. Shelley's novel unfolds on two planes. On the "external" plane that Burckhardt associates with history (*Burckhardt's Letters* 49), it provides a general history of Italy in the early modern period. This history unfolds around the minor figure of Castruccio, Prince of Lucca: a state that Burckhardt sees as insignificant a century later (*Civilization* 73). But the novel is also the inner narrative of two women not noted in "public histories," and from whose "private chronicles" Shelley draws in questioning the very concept of general history as public history (*Valperga* 439). Euthanasia, an "independent chieftainness and sovereign" in the world of men (252), and a Guelph who admires Florence because of its patronage of the arts, combines Wollstonecraft's emphasis on the rights of woman with Percy Shelley's cultural idealism. Her name evokes both Asia in *Prometheus Unbound* and Godwin's hope for a euthanasia of government. Betrothed to Castruccio, but growing steadily disillusioned with him as he becomes enmeshed in the ambitions of *realpolitik*, Euthanasia is Shelley's only example of feminist autonomy, as she is neither contained within marriage nor limited by destructive passion, like her rival and dark interpreter Beatrice.

Yet there is something old-fashioned about Euthanasia's courtly and feudal life, and her sovereignty functions only within the limited realm of a small principality. Once she moves from culture to history and politics, and becomes involved with Tripalda in the conspiracy against Castruccio, her aims grow incoherent and her authority is compromised. Moreover, admirable as she is on the private level, she becomes interesting as a character only when her aestheticized idealism is challenged by her deep bond with Beatrice. Beatrice, whom Shelley links to "the unfortunate Beatrice Cenci" (*Valperga* 200), is the child of two female heretics. She is adopted and brought up in the Catholic faith by the Bishop of Ferrara when her second mother, Magfreda, is burnt. But at the encouragement of the Bishop's sister, the Marchesana, she constitutes herself as a female prophetess: a very different but no less impressive public figure than Euthanasia. At the peak of her power and charisma, she falls in love with Castruccio, the expansionist ruler of Lucca. But when he deserts her, she loses faith in her powers, degenerating into hysteria and madness, becoming a pawn in the hands of the Macchiavellian witch Mandragola, and then dying. Finally there is Castruccio himself: a minor parallel to Caesar, Cromwell, and Napoleon in the way he ascends from consul to prince, thus perverting the early ideal of a commonwealth. Castruccio enters and exits the women's stories as an object of desire, though we "can know nothing" of his inner feelings (*Valperga* 439). Only in his early life do we glimpse what Godwin in "Of History and Romance" calls the "subtle peculiarities" of an "individual history" that thereafter is interpellated by the necessities of general history (*History of the Commonwealth* 360–361), though for Godwin this necessity itself is contingently formed by rank, circumstance, and historical period rather than being anything innate. And though, like power in Foucault, Godwinian necessity is profoundly decenterd, a process without a subject.

The terms "individual" and "general history" are ones Godwin uses in "Of History and Romance," where he distinguishes the general history practiced by Scottish Enlightenment historians such as Hume and Robertson, which can be mapped in terms of "regularities" and "recurrent laws," from individual history as a site of variation and of "contingency"—of possibility, but also increasingly of trauma (*History of the Commonwealth* 360–363). In *Mandeville* the general history of the Cromwellian period is pushed out of focus, its possibilities deformed by the pathological necessity of an individual history that usurps the foreground. Like Shelley a few years later, Godwin also makes his hero someone from the other side: a tormented Royalist in Godwin's case, and a potential despot in Shelley's.[3] Like *Mandeville*, *Valperga* is also organized by an asymmetry between individual and general history, and tellingly it is the individual that Godwin wanted to emphasize in shortening it for publication. He was struck by Euthanasia and Beatrice, but complained that the novel "contain[ed] the quantity of four volumes of 'Waverley'."[4] But significantly Shelley herself never allows the vividness of individual character to take over completely from the pedantry of historical detail—the philology that Buckhardt saw as the "poetry" in history (*Burckhardt's Letters* 49, 51), or the poetry of a world of prose.

To read Shelley with Burckhardt, then, is to resist the tendency, based on following the narratives of the female protagonists, to view the novel in "longitudinal sections" that emphasize the closing down of each character's possibilities by the necessity of death. Rather it is to organize the novel in transverse sections that also allow for a general history of the individual that has yet to find a place in general history, a dialectic between the two histories whose possibilities are fore-closed by *Mandeville*'s claustrophobic focus on a single pathological individual. For Euthanasia is not described as definitively drowning; rather she is "lost" and "never heard of more," and "sleep[s] in the oozy cavern of the ocean" (*Valperga* 437–438), as the text's materials are returned to the cultural unconscious. They are restored, in other words, to a world inhabited by the "shadows of all forms that think and live," to evoke Percy's resonant phrase in *Prometheus Unbound*, where he describes a world "underneath the grave" (Act I, l.197), in which the real reverts into its image and the actual is returned to its potential. Here the ruins of Euthanasia's project remain fragments to which we can go back, as it is unclear whether she lived too early or too late: whether as a female ruler she is an anticipatory figure, or whether her republicanism and idealism make her a nostalgic figure at odds with modernity.

Beatrice, to be sure, is "ruined" by her involvement with Castruccio. But the novel's use of the witch to trivialize her pro-phetic power and the Jacobin legacy it figures in the period of the Regency contrasts strongly with Shelley's romanticization, earlier in the novel, of heresy as the socially produced, anamorphic distortion of a still censored and inexpressible female creativity. Thus Beatrice too survives her author's move to dissolve and dissipate what she has created. Although Beatrice's power rests on a (self)-deception—the subterfuge used by the Bishop to protect her when she is asked by the Inquisition to walk on hot coals—the real reason for her fall is not the falsity of her pretensions, but her sexuality. For Beatrice loses faith in herself only when Castruccio leaves her, after which her author too loses confidence in her own imagination. Significantly, Shelley never has to suspend her disbelief in Beatrice's "parents," Wilhelmina and Magfreda, because they remain outside the sexual circuit. Beatrice's loss of faith in herself is thus just as much a misrecognition as her earlier appropriation of prophetic power, while her author's manda-tory demystification of the character can be seen as a falling short in her art, a contingent necessity of the time at which she was writ-ing. Finally, though Shelley's contemporary Sismondi celebrated the death of Castruccio because of the period of peace and prosperity it opened for the Guelph state of Florence, Shelley leaves us with a sense of disappointment at the abrupt termination of his career in "the maturity of his glory" (*Valperga* 440). Like Cromwell, who died on the same day, and whom Godwin later describes in terms reminiscent of Shelley's novel as having died prematurely before his "experiments" could be consolidated, the figure of Castruccio haunts us with a Byronic potential, even if this potential is only a phantasm of the affect produced by the very different kinds of love that the two women bear him.

Here the minor status of the hero of Shelley's general history is also significant. Minor literature, as theorized by Deleuze and Guattari, is not written in a minor language but arises from a minor position within a major language, thus deterritorializing this language (16). In this case minor history deterritorializes what was a reality by Shelley's time: the discourse of the emergent nation-state alluded to in the young Castruccio's "romantic conception of a future union of the Italian states" (*Valperga* 250). For this history focuses on Italy a century before the period treated by Burckhardt, and thus before the hardening of the distinction we might now make between despotisc states and republics. Castruccio never actually takes the Macchiavellian title of "prince." Everything about his life is premature: while his promise is unfulfilled, the harm he might cause also never quite comes to pass. Everything about him is in some sense virtual and unrealized. To be sure his ascendancy mirrors the recapture of republican by monarchic impulses that we see in the careers of Cromwell and Caesar, also figures who interested the Godwin family. But Shelley deals with the intertwined histories of Lucca and Valperga at a point when nationalism and the nascent commune are still intertwined within a moment of potential prior to the inscription of this possibility within a narrative of modernization. It is in this sense that, echoing Deleuze and Guattari, we can say that as deterritorialization, the story of a minor career, even if reactionary, "designates... the revolutionary conditions for every literature within the heart of... established literature" (18). "Literature" here means something like what Burckhardt designates by "poetry," namely material that lends itself to further writing.

In line with this further writing, the political map of Italy as traversed by Shelley includes a multitude of city states but no nation-state. It thus contains no dominant state-form, but rather a variety of emergent and residual forms, including the nascent commune that never quite comes into being; the republic of culture, Florence, which seems for the moment unable to sustain itself in the face of modernization; and the *Signoria* of Castruccio, which is not quite a despotism, and whose charismatic leader in some ways foreshadows later figures such as Garibaldi, thus raising the complex issue of local autonomy versus government that is part of the relation between nationalism and "freedom." It includes, as well, the despotism of the Viscontis, the forces of German and papal imperialism, and as against the latter, local bishoprics such as Ferrara, which quietly resist papal domination and protect a space for dissent in the form of the heretic Beatrice and her female parents. In this array of possibilities, nothing has quite come to pass nor has any possibility been definitively negated. This is to say, that minor history, in Deleuze and Guattari's words—or we could say "philology"—destructures and opens the field of history itself, making it an archive with "multiple entrances" (3). Shelley "enters" this field differently, through Castruccio, Beatrice, and Euthanasia. Her archival work and the "imagination" that, according to Burckhardt, "fills up the lacunae" of this work (*Burckhardt's Letters* 49), allows us, in Deleuze and Guattari's words, "to discover what other points our entrance connects to, what crossroads and galleries one passes through to link two points, what the map of the rhizome is and how the map is modified if one enters by another point" (3).

NOTES

1. I would obviously want to qualify Lupton's claim that for Burckhardt the Renaissance, as a resumption of classicism, is an "expressive totality" (7), defined by "the harmonization of subject with object and form with theme" (8). Rather, Burckhardt evokes Hegel's notion of classicism only to turn away from it as an analogue for the Renaissance.

2. As Lupton further elaborates, Burckhardt's Italy "at once resurrects the ancient past and forms the superseded grounds of the modern present." It is "the first born among the sons of modern Europe," but in "Burckhardt's narrative of cultural rebirth, Italy, for all its innovations, is ultimately like Esau, who, logically set up to receive his father's blessing (here classical civilization), ... wittingly and unwittingly facilitates the ascendance of the younger son (the modern nations of northern Europe)" (12–13, 35).

3. For further discussion of Mandeville see my essay, "The Dis-Figuration of Enlightenment: War, Trauma, and the Historical Novel in Godwin's *Mandeville*." *Godwinian Moments: From Enlightenment to Romanticism.* Ed. Robert Maniquis and Victoria Myers (U of Toronto P, 2010).

4. Godwin, letter of February 14, 1823, Abinger papers, Bodleian Dep. C524, quoted in Hill-Miller, 225 n.3; letter of November 15, 1822, quoted in Lady Jane Shelley, 904B–904C.

CHAPTER NINE

HEMANS'S RECORD OF DANTE: "THE MAREMMA" AND THE INTERTEXTUAL POETICS OF PLENITUDE

Diego Saglia

In the autumn of 1827, the American artist William E. West visited Felicia Hemans at her home in Rhyllon, North Wales, and painted three portraits of the popular poet at the request of Alaric Watts, the editor of the *Literary Souvenir*. One of them, later to be used as a frontispiece engraving in the 1839 *Memoirs* of the poet by her sister, represents a woman with elegantly curled hair covered by a white veil, a high-waisted dress with puffed upper sleeves and gauze lower sleeves, and a narrow waist restrained by a plain belt. Reclining on a scroll-ended arm rest, Hemans appears to be dressed in some generic contemporary, late-Romantic or early-Victorian, style. The overall effect, however, recalls the Italian Renaissance.[1] If this is undoubtedly appropriate for the author of *The Restoration of the Works of Art to Italy* (1816) and *The Vespers of Palermo* (1823), still, this image of the poet (almost) in masquerade also conjures up a scenario of cross-cultural interference. Hemans's attire follows contemporary fashion, but, in keeping with the eclecticism of Regency style, it also sports an exotic air that partly distances her from a specifically English or British figurative canon. Presenting her as visually and culturally ambiguous, the engraved portrait posits Hemans as an intercultural subject. At the same time, it intimates how her uses of Italy and Italian culture function through an interaction of forms of appropriation and ventriloquism.

Even a cursory glance at Hemans's output amply confirms her protracted recourse to Italian themes. In poem after poem, she reworked Italian topics and created intertextual links with Italian literature and culture more generally.[2] For instance, although in *Restoration* she clearly speaks from the standpoint of a British poet, she voices fervently patriotic Italian principles so that the text also reads as a "quasi-Laureate" intervention in the cultural politics of the Italian peninsula.[3] Her works also assimilate and rewrite Italian literature by way of translation (e.g., her 1818 *Translations from Camoens and Other Poets* features two sonnets by Petrarch) and incorporation (*Restoration*, for instance, contains embedded "sonnets" and references to Petrarch). Her use of Italy amounts to an assimilation of, and an identification with, this country and its culture that largely follows the path traced by Madame de Staël's *Corinne* (1807) and its Anglo-Italian protagonist.[4] Indeed, Maria Jane Jewsbury indirectly defined Hemans as "the Italy of human beings" and remarked that her "Italian extraction" partly accounted for "the passion which, even in childhood, she displayed for sculpture and melody"; while Letitia Landon noted that Hemans's verse seemed molded on an other, Italian(ate), set of aesthetic principles that brought it in line with "the finest order of Italian singing—pure, high, and scientific" (Jewsbury 561, 565).[5]

However, if Hemans defines Southern cultural geographies (and Italy in particular) as congenial spaces for women, she also entertains less accommodating views on Italy, imagining it as a menacing and dangerous place for female subjects. As West's Italianate painting makes plain, Hemans occupies an intercultural position, and thus, however deeply she may identify with Italy as a feminized and female-friendly geocultural dimension, her works also figure it as a problematic, if not utterly hostile, dimension. And these premises provide an essential context for Hemans's appropriation and reinvention of Dante in "The Maremma," a poem first published in the *Edinburgh Magazine and Literary Miscellany* in November 1820. This text reworks the brief and enormously suggestive reference to Pia de' Tolomei in *Purgatorio* 5.133, where the Siennese woman informs the wandering poet that her husband was somehow instrumental in her death in the malaria-infested Maremma. Hemans takes this typical example of Dante's incisively concise art and turns it into a medium-length metrical tale that recalls other Romantic-period expansions of Italian medieval texts, such as Leigh Hunt's *Story of Rimini* (1816), William Herbert's *Pia della Pietra* (1820), and Edward Wilmot's *Ugolino* (1828), from Dante, or John Keats's *Isabella*, William Wilmot's *Tale of Gismunda and Guiscardo* (1819), and John Hamilton Reynolds's *The Garden of Florence* and *The Ladye of Provence* (1821), from Boccaccio.

Yet, "The Maremma" is an unusual reinvention of an Italian literary source, in that Romantic women writers were conspicuously more attuned to Petrarch than Dante. As Edoardo Zuccato has recently observed, they were actively "involved in the revival of Petrarch," whereas "they generally disliked Dante," altogether an excessively "masculine, muscular figure" (*Petrarch* ix, x). In point of fact, more female writers read, translated, and rewrote the gentle and plangent Petrarch than the virile and sinewy Dante, a commonplace distinction that Ugo Foscolo helped to popularize in his *Essays on Petrarch* (1821; 1823). It is equally true, however, that women authors—Anna Seward, Mary Shelley, and Hemans, for instance—read, discussed, and rewrote Dante between the 1780s and the 1830s as part of their interventions on literary heritage, national culture, history, and the figuration of gender. "The Maremma" offers a significant testimony of Romantic women's engagement with Dante's verse and, therefore, of an alternative form of discursive transposition of human experience than the more immediately congenial mode of (post-)Petrarchan poetics. In addition, Hemans's poem provides a figuration of Italy that corrects more familiar notions of this country as an Edenic, feminized cultural geography by making it complicit in the destruction of the beautiful, innocent, and powerless heroine.

In examining Hemans's Dantean expansion, this essay concentrates on a series of interconnected practices ranging from appropriation and adaptation, to expansion, reinvention, and revision. As it attends to the poet's deployment of these textual mechanisms, it throws light on the complexity and suggestiveness of her engagement with a difficult poet and one of the founding fathers of literary modernity. Moreover, by recovering its intersection of several intertexts besides the *Commedia*, the essay charts the development of Hemans's operation of rewriting out of a dialogic tension between several voices that defines the poem as a national and cosmopolitan utterance concerned with the condition of woman in a male-dominated milieu, the issue of authorial self-positioning and its own cultural status as a "record." In this perspective, Hemans's appropriation and modification of Dante opens up some significant insights not only into her figuration of woman, but also her reflection on the memorializing function of poetry itself.

"The Maremma" and
the Poetics of "Plenitude"

As a manifestation of the Romantic tendency to the amplification of medieval sources, "The Maremma" appears not to have pleased the editors of the recent anthology *Dante in English* (2005). Their annotations convey a dislike for this unnecessary inflation of Dante's concise sketch in such remarks as: "Dante says nothing, one way or the other, about La Pia's moral character; he says nothing *about* her at all" (*Dante in English* 165). Similar observations cast Hemans's poem as a redundant effort and express disapproval of its expansive and expressive mechanisms, which also partly reflects the diminished popularity of narrative verse and sentimental poetics. Taking an alternative route, instead, we may envisage her "overflowing" text not as the product of a poetics of pleonasm, but rather as the expression of a poetics that tends to maximize narrative, thematic, and formal effects—that is, a poetics of "plenitude" tasked with developing all the possible implications of narrative and lyrical material. In an introductory note to the first publication of "The Maremma," Hemans interestingly observed that her "little Tale...was intended to have been enlarged by the introduction of other characters and incidents, and afterwards published separately" ("Maremma" 395). In other words, she had originally entertained the idea of making an entire metrical tale out of Dante's lines, had it not been for the appearance of "a poem on the same subject by a writer of considerable celebrity" (ibid.), possibly Byron's *Parisina* (1816). Though it could not be given free rein to the full, this quasi-novelistic drive to amplification through characterization and plot complications is integral to the poem. It pervades and qualifies a text that encapsulates the poet's interest in the recreation of emblematic female figures from history or literature, her creation of a sentimental idiom that may adequately convey the themes of the domestic affections and woman's destiny, and her concern with the socially and culturally prescribed nature of gender. As with much of Hemans's production, "The Maremma" becomes meaningful once we have found ways of assessing its textual abundance not as repetitive redundancy, but rather as the pursuit of expressive plenitude— the representation of the entire thematic and ideological potential of a given poetic material.

Composed of 246 iambic pentameter lines divided into sestets, Hemans's poem is written in the "Venus and Adonis" stanza, similar to the sestet in a Shakespearean sonnet, a form Hemans also used in her *Tales, and Historic Scenes, in Verse* (1819). The text is preceded by a quotation from Ugo Foscolo's essay on Dante in the *Edinburgh Review* for February 1818, which also contains the original lines on Pia de' Tolomei. To these, Hemans adds an excerpt from François de Malherbe's celebrated poem "Consolation à Monsieur Du Périer" (1607) about the death of his daughter. The poem combines narrative and descriptive sections, with a decisive prevalence of the latter mode that emphasizes the emblematic nature of the tale. In terms of narrative structure, instead, the text broadly follows the cycle of the seasons and the transition from summer to autumn and winter.

The opening section of "The Maremma" contrasts the natural beauty of Italy and its hidden threats (the invisible miasmas of malaria), and thus reads as an adaptation of the Virgilian topos of *latet anguis in herba*. In this panoramic view, death lurks in the beautiful and fruitful landscape of Italy. The poem then depicts the wedding of Bianca (Hemans's name for Pia) and Pietra—"A voice of music, from Sienna's walls, / Is floating joyous on the summer air" ("Maremma" 396, ll. 55–56)—as well as providing portraits of the two characters. But soon the joyful tone gives way to a gloomier atmosphere induced by the husband's jealousy and suspicion. As Pietra decides to send his wife and child to his ancestors' house in the Maremma, the text evokes the natural features of this beautiful but unhealthy region as a prelude to the death of the child and, then, Bianca herself. The final stanza seals the poem with a memorial to the unfortunate woman.

Narrative is a distinctive component of this phase in Hemans's production, when she visibly aligns her production to the metrical tales made popular by Byron, Scott, and Thomas Moore. However, "The Maremma" also visibly inclines to emotional evocation and exploration and the use of symbolic imagery, all of which impart a clearly lyrical quality to its stanzas. In particular, this intersection of lyrical and narrative characterizes her later collection *Records of Woman* (1828) and its gallery of poetic portraits of fictional and historic women from different times and places. Hemans's use of the term "record" is of course intriguingly polysemous, as it refers not only to women's forgotten achievements, but also to the female affections through its etymological link with the Latin *recordari*, itself derived from *cor, cordis*, the heart. Since all of these formal and thematic features are relevant to "The Maremma," this poem may be seen as an anticipation of the content, style, and ideological concerns of the later collection.

Also from the thematic point of view, the poem reworks several recurrent topics in Hemans's output from the 1810s to the 1820s, which it deals with in accordance with her distinctive poetics of "plenitude." Her Dantean poem thus inflects the themes of gender and the affections by focusing on a family circle that does not bring fulfillment, but rather sadness and death, to the female protagonist. The conflict between husband and wife is then conveyed by gendered contrasts between inflexibility and pliability, hardness and sweetness, or light and darkness. Indeed, the poem pointedly comments on man's inability to understand a woman's emotional and spiritual life: "Oh! can he meet that eye, of light serene, /... / Yet deem that vice within that heart can reign?" ("Maremma" 397, ll. 121–125). In addition, Hemans touches on the theme of the South as a lethal geography that brings death to the female subject through the "sun-bright waste of beauty" (397, l. 141) of the Maremma. This landscape, and Italy more widely, points to further *leimotifs* such as the contrasts between nature and art, music and silence, fertility and sterility, or the imagery of air and breezes, all of which Hemans weaves into her modulation of narrative and lyrical modes. This orchestration of themes and motifs is deployed within what Michael O'Neill has perceptively called "the mournfully stately movement of Hemans's six-line stanzas" to produce a text whose "tone teeters over without toppling into an abyss of sentimentality" (O'Neill 47).

HEMANS'S INTERTEXTUAL REWRITING OF DANTE

Michael O'Neill has also usefully pointed out the presence of echoes from Samuel Taylor Coleridge's "Eolian Harp" and Thomas Gray's "Elegy" in Hemans's text (ibid.). Such references are an integral part of a poem that offers itself as a web of intertexts—a "hypertext," in Gérard Genette's terminology from *Palimpsestes* (1982)—that glosses and reworks a series of preexisting "hypotexts." In point of fact, the poem advertizes its intertextual nature from the outset, in the epigraphic apparatus that simultaneously discloses some of the mechanisms regulating Hemans's engagement with the episode of La Pia. As anticipated, "The Maremma" begins with three clearly identified intertextual presences—Foscolo, Dante, and Malherbe. Of course, the medieval poet and the *Commedia* play a pivotal role. But the Romantic commentator and the Renaissance poet provide further relevant keys to understand Hemans's assimilation of Dante's lines into her own poetry and poetics.[6]

The first and most substantial epigraph is from Foscolo's review of Giosafatte Baglioli's *Dante: with a New Italian Commentary* (1818) and Henry Francis Cary's *The Vision of Dante* (1818). Foscolo's piece was Hemans's main source of inspiration and information for her poem, and she followed it so faithfully that, as the editors of

Dante in English remark, it misled her into some glaring factual mistakes (165, 170). However, questions of accuracy aside, Foscolo's essay opens up some crucial insights into Hemans's rewriting of Dante's lines. Indeed, he notes that La Pia's "few words draw tears" from readers, her brief account being a "deeply pathetic" blend of "domestic unhappiness" with "death" and "cruelty" (Foscolo 460). Concentrating both on the psychological contents of the story and its effect on readers, Foscolo emphasizes the emotional potential of Dante's character and points to the possibility of rereading it by way of an aesthetics of affect, which is precisely what Hemans's poem does.

Foscolo also provides an important clue to Hemans's "anglicization" of Dante by comparing the Italian bard's characterization with Shakespeare's, "[o]f all tragic poets" the one who "most amply develops character" (Foscolo 459, 458).[7] Moreover, for the benefit of his British readers, Foscolo highlights how "The history of Desdemona has a parallel" in the story of Pia, a remark that Hemans reproduces in the first publication of "The Maremma" but which disappears from the version published in her 1839 *Works* (Foscolo 459).[8] Fixing the terms of the comparison and contrast between Dante's compressed portraits in the *Commedia* and Shakespeare's multifaceted figures, the Italian poet and critic envisages the possibility of reinventing a Dantean figure through the type of detailed and heightened portraiture associated with the national bard. Hemans would have been naturally alert to these observations, as she was a fervent admirer of Shakespeare who fully endorsed the commonplace view of his works as unsurpassed mirrors of the human soul. In an early poem, she had expressed her enthusiasm for the playwright "whose magic lays impart / Each various feeling to the heart," and singled out for praise Ophelia's empathetic power: "We learn to shed the generous tear / O'er poor Ophelia's sacred bier" (*Works* 1:7–8). Much as in Foscolo's remarks, here the character's complex emotional makeup interacts directly with the reader's and elicits a powerful response. This was exactly what Hemans experienced years later when she saw Edmund Kean in *Richard III* and *Othello*, and, in a letter of October 1820, confessed: "I felt as if I had never understood Shakspeare till then" (*Works* 1:42). Whereas the emotional power of Dante's figures is an effect of textual economy, Shakespeare crafts his characters by way of what Foscolo termed "amplitude," a category that is akin to Hemans's poetics of "plenitude." Thus, the critic's suggestively transcultural presentation of Pia relates to Hemans's reinterpretation of this character through a Shakespearean mediation that bears on her psychological exploration, as well as on her adoption of the "Venus and Adonis" stanza.

If Dante's Pia, Shakespeare's Ophelia, and Hemans's Bianca die because their men reject them, Hemans intensifies further the link with the Shakespearean precedent by placing her character's death in an Italy oxymoronically imagined as a cemeterial "garden of the world." Shakespeare's text famously surrounds Ophelia with floral imagery. Laertes calls her "rose of May" soon after she begins to distribute wildflowers to the other dramatis personae, while her corpse ends up floating among wildflowers, herbs, and water-plants. Hemans's adoption of the link between death, woman, and the floral dimension is also announced by the epigraph from Malherbe ("Et rose elle a vécu ce que vivent les roses, / L'espace d'un matin"), which emphasizes the fragility and transience of life, as well as reechoing the classical connection of youthful womanhood and the freshness and beauty of a rose, as in the topos *collige, virgo, rosas* (from the "Idyllium de rosis" variously attributed to Ausonius or Virgil). Hemans weaves these images into her distinctive use of flowers as symbols of the death and dissolution that inevitably awaits female beauty. In the conclusion, Bianca appropriately mutates into the "fairest flower" that the voice of death calls "in every gale" ("Maremma" 398, ll. 175–176) as it "[b]ids the young roses of [her] cheek turn pale" (398, l. 178). In other words, Hemans rewrites Dante through a language of sentiment that compounds Shakespearean intimations with Malherbe's Petrarchanism and her own distinctive figuration of death through the topos of the broken flower (or, sometimes, the mown ear of corn) that harks back to Catullus, Virgil, and Ovid.

As is customary with Hemans, "The Maremma" collects, interweaves, and recycles fragments from named sources or a general literary repertoire of themes and images, and integrates them into her own poetical idiom. In particular, it reworks these materials as part of a subtle process that threads Dante's and Malherbe's lines into the poem's formal texture, as their stanzaic structure and rhyme schemes converge into those of Hemans's Shakespearean stanzas. Indeed, since Dante's terza rima lines are quoted as a quatrain rhyming *abab*, they present the same structure as Malherbe's excerpt and also mirror the first four lines of Hemans's sestets. Eventually, this almost seamless transition from paratext to main text comes up against the final rhyming couplet of the "Venus and Adonis" stanza. By thus weaving her Italian and French epigraphs into an English literary form, the poem effects a productive appropriation of two eminent voices from what J. C. L. Simonde de Sismondi called the *littératures du Midi* in his homonymous 1813 study, which Hemans greatly admired. A carefully orchestrated choir of different voices, her Dantean recreation is an instance of cosmopolitan verse that resonates simultaneously with questions of personal poetics and the national literary heritage.

HEMANS'S RECORD OF DANTE

At the end of the introductory section, before going on to depict the protagonists' wedding, Hemans refers to Bianca as "…one who perished, left a tale of woe, / Meet for as deep a sigh as pity can bestow" ("Maremma" 396, ll. 53–54). Thus indirectly casting her poem as a "record of woman," she tasks it with an elegiac and monumentalizing function. Furthermore, as it develops, the text reveals yet another typical feature of her "records"—the fact that this act of poetic "remembering" (both "recalling" and "piecing together again" the lost memory of women's achievements) results in a narration of conflicts. All the poems from the 1828 collection present this underlying structure—as in "Properzia Rossi," which contrasts artistic aspirations with reciprocated love; or "The Indian City," where a Muslim mother challenges an entire Hindu city whose inhabitants have slaughtered her son; or "The Switzer's Wife," in which domestic ties are briefly in conflict with the call of patriotic duty. If memories of woman can only be appropriately recovered and represented in terms of an agon, "The Maremma" establishes the ground of this confrontation by making nature—which encompasses the woman-as-rose and determines her "fate" (l. 115)—into a field of contending forces.

As the epigraphs make plain, the ambivalent nature of the Maremma encapsulates the poem's web of conflicts. It is both extraordinarily bountiful, as in the classical topos of *laus Italiae* or Italy as "the garden of the world," and treacherously lethal, according to the equally garden-related Virgilian topos of *latet anguis in herba*. Hemans soon discloses the hidden perils of the luscious Italian landscape by observing that "Mysterious danger lurks, a Syren, there" (395, l. 13). In its destructive incarnation, moreover, nature subjugates civilization by gradually and inexorably dismantling man-made artifacts, and architecture in particular. Since malaria decimates the population, buildings stand empty and silent, a recurrent image in Hemans's elegiac compositions, as in the description of the Alhambra in *The Abencerrage* (1819) or the childless home in "The Graves of a Household" (1825). The poet amplifies and ennobles this scene by introducing a historical perspective, when the "illustrious hills of Rome" and their ruined grandeur also become prey to "that subtle spirit of the air" (396, ll. 43, 45).[9] It is within this overwhelming landscape that Hemans places Bianca, who, as the "fairest flower" of all (398, l. 175), is reminiscent of Ophelia and embodies the fragile and powerless side of nature.

As the battleground of life and death and the antagonist of civilization, nature is also the crucial site of the conflict between man and woman. In point of fact, the text qualifies the male character as a counterpart to, or a human manifestation of, the natural world. As his name implies, Pietra is a stony figure. He is a dark and brooding character in contrast to Bianca's brightness, his "sullen gloom" and "dark…glance[s]" (ll. 119, 131) overtly antithetical to her "eye, of light serene" (l. 121). Moreover, just as the landscape hides terrible dangers, he harbours dark feelings: "…calmly can Pietra smile, concealing, / As if forgotten, vengeance, hate, remorse" (ll. 103–104). Finally, by presenting him as a warrior, the text emphatically associates him with violence, grimly depicting him as he stands "fearless in the ranks of death, / 'Mid slaughtered heaps, the warrior's monument" (ll. 93–94). Thus starkly set out, the contrast between male and female characters generates the incomprehension on the part of Pietra, who fatally misinterprets Bianca's actions and contrives her death and that of their child. Intriguingly, Hemans rereads Dante by placing an episode of misreading at the centre of her own fictional recreation.

Through its combination of narrative and lyrical modes, "The Maremma" inserts this net of conflicts into a tightly knit web of images and figures, which, as seen above, are the building blocks of her poetics of "plenitude." This orchestration of themes and leitmotifs eventually converges into the final stanza, an envoi that seals the tale by projecting it onto the planes of memory and time, and offers a final problematic formulation of the act of inscription:

> No sculptured urn, nor verse thy virtues telling,
> O lost and loveliest one! adorns thy grave;
> But o'er that humble cypress-shaded dwelling
> The dew-drops glisten and the wild-flowers wave –
> Emblems more meet, in transient light and bloom,
> For thee, who thus didst pass in brightness to the tomb! (398, ll. 241–246)

In these closing lines, Hemans elaborates a version of the "trace," that recurrent, concluding figure that encloses a text's unresolved tensions and conflicts and relays them to posterity in the shape of an inscription of memory through the media of nature or art.[10] As it captures the idea and possibility of the poem's survival, the trace is a testimony of its continuing cultural significance. It emphasizes the uninterrupted resonance of the poem's melody and message. Therefore, it is also a point of arrival—and yet not one—a figure of incompletion that confirms the unresolved status of the conflicts laid bare by the text.

Both the echoing effect and the notion of incompletion are central to the trace in "The Maremma," a "record" that works through thematic anticipations and subsequent reelaborations. Indeed, several traces emerge in the poem well before the final stanza. The Roman hills explicitly "bear / Traces of mightier beings" (396, l. 44); Bianca's beauty is on a par with that of the Mona Lisa, "that daughter of the south, whose form / Still breathes and charms, in Vinci's colours warm" (396, ll. 65–66), a reference taken from Giorgio Vasari's *Vite*; and, finally, the text anticipates Pietra's "vain remorse," the dead Bianca's haunting presence as that of an "an accusing angel," and the transformation of her tomb into "a martyr's shrine" that shall be "hallow'd in his eyes" (398, ll. 217–220). Through such references, Hemans assembles a narrative that forcibly withstands the demise and effacement of the subject—intended as the character and the poem's topic—and replaces it with memory and inscription, "Faded, yet scarce forgotten" (396, l. 75). As a result, the network of conflicts in "The Maremma" translates into a text of death and survival.

As the climax of these anticipations, the closing stanza emphatically denies Bianca (and Hemans's poetry, too) the most hallowed of literary formulations of the trace, the Horatian topos *exegi monumentum aere perennius*. Here, no monument is raised to the memory of the woman, not even that of poetry "more lasting than bronze." The trace is here fragile and transient—dewdrops and wild blossoms expressive of Bianca's incarnation of nature and the image of woman-as-flower. Nevertheless, though fragile, these traces are recurrent and self-renewing, and thus may never be effaced. This feminized version of nature is ultimately triumphant within the long-term perspective of the "trace."

Yet, precisely because it elides all poetic records from Bianca's grave, the closing stanza says something crucial about Hemans's poem as a "record of Dante." Initially, the poet asserts that her text reechoes a "tale of woe" (396, l. 53) about Bianca's death, a precedent that, in view of the epigraph from Foscolo, we may identify with Dante's text. Then, in the closing lines, she disallows language and writing as suitable ways of commemorating the woman's tale. This contradiction casts a fascinating metapoetic light on the poem's conclusion. On the one hand, Hemans defines her own text as an appendix to dewdrops and wildflowers, the only appropriate repositories of Bianca's memory. On the other, she relegates Dante's lines to the same secondary position. Her poem is thus not an agon with an awe-inspiring forefather and, therefore, the result of competitive *aemulatio*. Instead, in the face of the woman's "tale of woe" (emblematic of the fact that "It is our task to suffer," (398, l. 227)), Dante's seminal lines and Hemans's own amplification are equally faulty and inadequate. In consequence, the last stanza squarely puts "The Maremma" at the same level as the *Commedia*, at least as far as the proper way of producing a "record of woman" is concerned. On the whole, a rather daring thing to do with one of the foundational works of Western literature and one of the tutelary father figures of literary modernity.

The final lines of "The Maremma" visibly redirect what Michael O'Neill terms the "epitaphic economy" of Dante's lines (47). For, if in Dante it is Pia herself who voices her own epitaph, Hemans awards this task to a poetic voice who, simultaneously, disinvests (written, engraved. or sculpted) epitaphic inscriptions to provide an open-ended finale to a "record of woman" that is also a "record of Dante," and one in which Hemans's voice has the last word.

The Fate of Inscription

As is customary with Hemans's shorter compositions, "The Maremma" is not an immediately evident text. It does not present itself as an arduous, intellectual achievement, but rather as an effortlessly melodious and transparent composition. Nevertheless, if we attend to the connections between the epigraphs and main text, the poem becomes visible as a work in which amplification contributes crucially to its manipulation of a composite hypotext. In this perspective, "The Maremma" is not a mere rehearsal of familiar images, an instantly recognizable reproduction of a repetitive poetical formula. Instead, it is a skillful elaboration of themes and forms, complete with suggestively metapoetic intimations, which draws on national and foreign literary modes and precedents, and holds a precise place in the development of Hemans's corpus.

Far from being a transparent and thus easily readable composition, "The Maremma" is a multilateral intertextual conversation that is centered primarily on Dante's lines about Pia as mediated by Foscolo's interpretation, yet it also includes Malherbe, Byron, Shakespeare, Madame de Staël, Vasari, and Simonde de Sismondi. A

typical instance of Hemans's output, the poem portrays the unjus-
tified immolation of a woman to male insensitivity and misinter-
pretation, recording her stoic acceptance of adverse events. In her
claustrophobic imprisonment, Bianca embodies missed opportunities, wasted motherhood, and the sacrifice of female generosity and
fertility. Yet, even as it rehearses some of Hemans's familiar tropes
and images, "The Maremma" reflects on the nature of "records,"
the practice of inscription, and the status of cultural memory and
heritage.

Moreover, through its links with the national poem of Italy and
the father of Italian literature, Hemans's text provides further insights
into her relation to this country and its culture. In the early nineteenth century, "Italy" stood for a geopolitical situation of cohesion
in diversity and fragmentation, and a cultural dimension unrelated
to a unitary state. Designating a national canon that was not the pre-
rogative of a single nation, Italian literature had traditionally constituted a shared heritage and cultural currency, its literary wealth
readily lending itself to operations of appropriation and identification. Furthermore, as a deterritorialized dimension, Italian literature
was particularly germane to Romantic-period women writers' perceptions of their own uncertain and fluctuating cultural status. With
these premises in mind, we may take another look at the significance
of Italy for Hemans's verse and her literary status. As it created the
cultural conditions for the emergence of, in Esther Schor's words,
"far more than a frail lyric voice," Italy and its literary heritage were
important loci of identification and intervention, authorial self-positioning, and poetical elaboration (Schor 245). In this light, "The
Maremma" appears as part of a wider process centered on the accli-
matization of foreign literatures and the internationalization of the
national literary tradition. But, as an expression of Hemans's ventriloquism of Italy, the poem also matters as a peculiar instance of Dante's
reception in Romantic-period literature.

Indeed, "The Maremma" subsumes Dante's lines into a figurative and metapoetic discourse that ultimately formulates a judgment
on his poetic achievement and cultural status. Indeed, Hemans's
text revises Dante's foundational role as the primary source of her
poem and, more broadly, as one of the earliest voices in the canon
of modern classics. The author does not question Dante's central-
ity. As her Shakespearean references make plain, she endorses the
Romantic canon of great predecessors, which, with variations, also
comprised such figures as Milton, Aeschylus, and Calderón. By contrast, her text repositions the lines on Pia, which we could read as a

synecdoche for the entire *Commedia*, by placing them in a dialogic relation with other texts in her multifaceted and hybrid narrative-lyrical composition.

This manipulation of Dante is at its most visible in the concluding "trace." There, Hemans questions the epitaphic finality of Dante's lines by appropriating their function and rewriting them into her own last words on Bianca, which, in contrast to the Italian source, convey fragility, fluidity, mutability, and endless self-renovation. The tombstone quality of Dante's lines ("stony," as in Pietra's name) becomes an open-ended utterance contained in such ephemeral natural features as flowers and dew. By thus making the whole tale into an endlessly self-renewing "trace," the poem places Dante's inscription of Pia on the same level as its reinscription of Pia as Bianca. Both narratives have equal dignity, as they belong to a common repository of tales and images from which "records" can be drawn and fashioned. In Hemans's revisioning of the original status of Dante's lines, his words are not the earliest statement on Pia, but rather fragments of a much wider archive of tales and characters. Moreover, by placing Pia's tale in a field of interacting intertexts, Hemans's engagement with Dante produces a reinscription of his verse that questions the nature and aptness of the act of inscription itself. Thanks to its choir of intersecting voices and double-edged implications, "The Maremma" testifies to the aesthetic and ideological complexity of Romantic-period receptions and recreations of Dante by women authors. It also illuminates the wonderfully resonant results of Hemans's recourse to Italian literature and its founding father in order to promote reflections on cultural and literary issues in simultaneously personal, national, and international perspectives.

NOTES

1. Please see Hemans, *Selected Poems*, 467.
2. As Isobel Armstrong notes, nineteenth-century women's poetry features a sustained "movement to Italy" that expresses identification with "an "impassioned land" or emotional space *outside* the definitions and circumscriptions of the poet's specific culture and nationality." This geocultural shift gives them the possibility of "testing out the account of the feminine experienced in western culture by going outside its prescriptions" (Armstrong 324, 325). On Hemans's figurations of Italy, see also Leighton's *Victorian Women Poets* (17).
3. On Stuart Curran's idea of Hemans as a "Laureate manquée," see Sweet, "History, Imperialism, and the Aesthetics of the Beautiful: Hemans and the Post-Napoleonic Moment" (172).

4. Hemans mentions *Corinne* in a footnote to "The Maremma." See "The Maremma," *The Edinburgh Magazine and Literary Miscellany*, 7 (November 1820) 396. All further references, by page and (where appropriate) line numbers, are from this first edition. Line numbers are taken from the version published in *Dante in English*. Ed. Eric Griffiths and Matthew Reynolds (London: Penguin, 2005) 164–175.

5. See also Letitia Elizabeth Landon, "On the Character of Mrs. Hemans's Writings," in Hemans, *Selected Poems, Prose and Letters* (472, 473).

6. On the functions of epigraphs, see Gérard Genette, *Paratexts: Thresholds of Interpretation*. Trans. Jane E. Lewin (Cambridge: Cambridge UP, 1997). 156–60.

7. On Hemans's hallmark "anglicization" of foreign literary and cultural traditions, see Susan Wolfson's remarks in "'Domestic Affections' and 'the spear of Minerva': Felicia Hemans and the Dilemma of Gender" (132).

8. See "The Maremma," 395, and Hemans (*Works* 3:129).

9. On Rome and malaria in Romantic-period culture, see Richard Wrigley, "Infectious Enthusiasms: Influence, Contagion, and the Experience of Rome," *Transports: Travel, Pleasure and Imaginative Geography*. Ed. Chloe Chard and Helen Langdon (New Haven and London: Yale UP, 1996) 75–116; and "Pathological Topographies and Cultural Itineraries: Mapping "Mal'aria" in Eighteenth- and Nineteenth-Century Rome," *Pathologies of Travel*. Ed. Richard Wrigley and George Revill (Amsterdam and Atlanta: Rodopi, 2000) 203–228.

10. See my own essay "Ending the Romance: Women Poets and the Romantic Verse Tale."

CHAPTER TEN

GERMAINE DE STAËL'S *CORINNE, OR
ITALY* (1807) AND THE PERFORMANCE
OF ROMANTICISM(S)

Diane Long Hoeveler

While in the grip of mourning for her beloved father, Germaine de
Staël (1766–1817), made the first stop on an Italian tour in Florence
during December of 1804. She expected it to be warm, but found
instead that it was bitter cold, and she wrote dejectedly to a friend,
"Winter displeases more there [in Florence] than anywhere else,
because the imagination is not prepared for it" (qtd. in Moers 210).
That mixed sense of disappointed expectation, grief, and fierce commitment to the imagination imbues *Corinne, ou l'Italie*, the novel
she published a scant three years later, whose eponymous protagonist
lives in Florence from the ages of ten to fifteen, and who returns to
spend her final exile before dying there in 1803. Corinne becomes the
embodiment of Staël's vision of prospects for a feminine Romanticism
that is doomed to the chill of death even as it struggles to be born.

For the past twenty years literary critics have been approaching
Corinne from a variety of angles: as a performance of heroinism
(Moers), as a work that is situated within the discourses of neoclas-
sicism and pre-romanticism (Gutwirth, Lokke, Vargo), or as a text
about romanticism itself (Furst, Naginski, Vallois, Luzzi, Schoina).
It is sometimes seen as an allegory of the French Revolution (Kadish,
Tenenbaum), a historical record of the romantic craze for *improv-
visatore* (Esterhammer (2005), Simpson, Gonda, Weintraub), a

fictionalized version of the author's own life (Balayé, Starobinski, Sourian); or an early manifestation of Cixous's *l'ecriture feminine* (DeJean). This essay will look at *Corinne* as a series of very literal performances that enact through the exceptional woman's body and voice the emergence of a new but aborted romantic feminine sensibility. In other words, Staël attempted in her novel to explore not just issues of national character and historical destiny, the "Italy" part of the book's title, but to invent a type of female romanticism that would rival in its performative potential the dominant male discourses of Romanticism that she knew all too well, that is, Ossianism, Prometheanism, Faustianism, Rousseauvianism, Alfierianism, or Wertherism. In presenting Corinne's grandiose and heavily coded feminine performances under the censorious *gaze* of Oswald, Staël suggests to her female readers how they too can and indeed must perform a feminization of culture, history, and social institutions. But Staël seems to have also known from the beginning that her noble intentions were doomed, and the choice of performances that Corinne enacts throughout the text makes this, in fact, very clear to us.

John Isbell has claimed that Corinne has to die at the end of the novel because the Revolution and Liberty were dead by the time of Napoleon's *coup d'etat* in 1799 (xiii), while he also has asserted that the name "Corinne" became shorthand for "suffering heroine" throughout nineteenth-century Europe after the publication of the book in 1807 (xi). Yes, *Corinne* the novel allegorizes the process by which modern nation-states attempted to be born, but the other, more important issue is that Corinne the character does not merely or passively suffer; she *performs* her suffering in what Balayé has called a "specularizing" manner; she displays it as a text writ large for her reading audience. She would not let them look away from the spectacle of what they had done to her. All of which is to say that Napoleon did not like this book (Gutwirth, *Madame de Staël* 235).

When Juliet, the young daughter of Oswald and Lucile asks her father, "What is a Corinne?" (396),[1] she might be anticipating A. O. Lovejoy's famous query, what is romanticism? Sprawling, contradictory, complex, and hyperbolically grandiose, Corinne the character and romanticism the cultural and literary movements are difficult if not impossible to neatly define. By my count, Corinne plays twenty-four different roles throughout the novel, very close to the number of definitions that Lovejoy proffered for "romanticism" with a capitol "R."[2] But the final role played by Corinne is as the harbinger of her own death, the stage-manager of her own demise. An enthusiastic translator of Goethe's "Bride of Corinth," Staël praised the poem's "funereal pleasure...where love makes an ally of the tomb, where beauty itself is a frightening apparition" (qtd. in Gutwirth, *Madame de Staël* 274). Like Sappho flinging herself off Cape Leucade out of frustrated love for Phaon, or Corinna, the Greek lyric poetess who was virtually erased from history by her student/rival Pindar, Corinne seems to have been destined to lose her creativity and die as soon as she spotted Oswald in her audience. His seems to have been the face she was waiting for, the reincarnation of the lost and dimly remembered disapproving British father/son who says no to the attempts of the warm and passionate hybridized Italian/British woman to make a place and seize a name for herself in the emerging and contested culture of romantic creativity.

But before looking at *Corinne* as a series of performances that circle around female mourning, *liebestod*, melancholia, and finally death, I want briefly to acknowledge Angela Esterhammer's pioneering work on the "romantic performative," as well as the studies that a number of anthropologists have done on performance as a species of speech-act theory. As Esterhammer notes, "The identity of an individual or a group can be called performative if that identity is established through the very process of practicing it—so that doing and being, or saying and being, or becoming and being, are indistinguishable" (*Romantic Performative* xii). Corinne becomes who she is by performing as a "Corinne," whether as an *improvisatore*, a dancer, a poet, a musician, an artist, an actress, a sibyl, a Catholic theologian, a tour guide, an Amazonian, or a ghost who haunts her dead father's estate. Corinne says something very similar to this in a conversation with Oswald, "Why ask a nightingale the meaning of his song? He can explain it only by starting to sing again; we can understand it only by letting ourselves go to the impression it makes" (109).

Esterhammer also notes that this aspect of the social performative recalls Aristotle's definition of *energeia*, "an action that contains its end within itself, or acting that does not stop when some external terminus is reached" (*Romantic Performative* xii). But Aristotle's *energeia* can be understood as strikingly similar to what Corinne calls her "supernatural enthusiasm...the definite feeling I have that the voice within me is of greater worth than myself" (46). In *On Germany* (1810), Staël had defined enthusiasm as the God within us (qtd. in Lewis 26), and it is this core of her creative energy that is finally sapped during her disastrous return to England when she is relegated from being a performer to a voyeur.

After studying a variety of tribal groups, the anthropologist Elinor Keenan defines what she calls the practice of "ceremonial speech or oratory," and contrasts it to what Michelle Rosaldo has called "invocatory speech" (Bauman 12–13), both of which are very similar to the improvisational style that Corinne uses in her extemporaneous recitals in Rome and Cape Miseno. But such performances are generally culturally specific acts that serve the needs of a particular community, and that is precisely the question that is raised by the performances of Corinne. What and whose needs are being served by Corinne's improvisations, ethnic dances, or theatrical performances? Is she enacting a relevant cultural past or is she in fact a living, animated ruin, an anachronism that can only remind her society of what it has lost and can never replace? Victor Turner, for instance, claims that performance is a practice or event that reveals a culture's "deepest, truest, and most individual character" (qtd. in Diana Taylor 4). And more recently, Diana Taylor has defined "performance" as a "vital act of transfer, transmitting social knowledge, memory, and a sense of identity through reiterated twice-behaved behavior" (2–3).

The larger debate on performance has in fact occurred over precisely this point: can any performance be understood as universal and transparent in its significance and meaning, or is it in its very nature artificial and constructed, bracketed and framed as standing apart from other social practices that occur within a culture?[3] Corinne's many performances throughout the novel raise precisely this question: how "true" is anything she does apart from that one act that contains within itself an undeniable meaning—her death. And doesn't she in fact know this from the very beginning of the novel? Doesn't she know that staging her own death as a performance-piece can be finally the only act that her culture will accept from her? A desperate romantic performance, inspired perhaps by the examples of both Sappho and Werther, Corinne's death can be read as an act of bitter anger directed toward a culture that had rejected her gifts and love and, by extension, the place of the exceptional and creative woman in the new romantic era.

Examining a variety of Corinne's performances will allow an interrogation of Staël's conception of the emerging feminine romantic aesthetic, poised as it was against neoclassicist and masculinist tropes.[4] Set during the period 1794–1803, *Corinne* positions Italy the country and Corinne the woman as a beautiful ruin/siren that beckons the melancholy British aristocrat and naval officer Oswald, Lord Nevil, to a mysterious terrain. In many ways, the love/hate dialectic between them stages an allegorical conflict between an older masculinized,

Ossianic aesthetic and an even older feminized Sapphic one, both of them in thrall to the power of the father as the lost object of desire. Staël would go on to write a short drama entitled *Sappho* in 1811, in which the exceptional woman kills herself after being rejected by her lover, Phaon. As Gutwirth observes, "Only in the *act* of dying can she be restored to the sense of self she had lost in love" (*Madame de Staël* 265). While Ellen Moers reads Oswald as modeled on Richardson's Sir Charles Grandison (201), I think he can more accurately be read as something like the spirit of an Ossianic warrior brought to life— Northern, melancholic, and father-obsessed—who opposes the spirit of Corinne: Southern, Catholic, exuberant, and also, unfortunately, father-obsessed as well. That is to say, on one level the novel is an allegory about how nations and national ideologies attempt to create and renew themselves through the appropriation, control, and dissemination of artistic and cultural capitol.

Arriving in Rome as the hero of Ancona, Oswald encounters a strange spectacle, certainly not something he would have witnessed in London: the crowning of a woman by the laurel wreath of poetic genius on the steps of the Capitoline in Rome. Dressed in white and blue, like a composite of Correggio's Madonna della Scala, Dante's Beatrice, and the Domenichino sibyl, Corinne makes her first appearance in the novel and it is no coincidence that she appears in a public space as a divinely inspired prophetess, giving the impression of "a priestess of Apollo" (23). But this is a muse who has inspired herself, and as a creator and an object of feminine worship, she arrives to deliver the first of her spontaneous improvisations on "The Glory and Happiness of Italy." This performance, with its references to Dante, Tasso, and Petrarch, suggests initially the poet's necessary role as nationalistic herald and preserver of a country's glorious past; but finally her performance politicizes and genders genius and throws into stark relief the glories of the ancient Roman republic as contrasted to the despotism of Napoleon's brutal expansionist campaigns.

The first and most obvious of Corinne's many and disparate performances are her forays into drama, coding as they do Staël's inquiry into the nature and role of dramatic literature for a society, a subject she had treated at length in her essay "On Literature" (1800). During her stay in Weimar in 1803, Staël saw the opera *Die Saalnixe* (*The Saal River Nymph*) based on a tale by La Motte Fouqué. Shortly thereafter she wrote to her friend Hochet: "I saw the other day a German play which gave me the idea of a novel I think charming" (Balayé, "Corinne en Spectacle" 97–98). That novel became *Corinne*, and the origins of its composition in a German opera about a hero who is an earthly knight and a heroine who is a watery river nymph suggest that from the very beginning Oswald and Corinne are meant to represent how impossible it is for the two sexes to ever live together. We see a bit of this operatic residue when Corinne and Oswald coincidentally meet at the Trevi Fountain after a four day separation: "He bent down over the fountain to see better and his own features were then reflected beside Corinne's" (74–75). This watery merger of the two is a momentary illusion, however, and almost immediately their talk turns to the necessity of suffering.

The romantic performative of this text posits public displays of suffering and an adamant division between the sexes as two of its nonnegotiable terms. We hear some of this when Prince Castel-Forte says to Oswald, "Look at Corinne. Yes, we would follow her in her footsteps, we would be men as she is a woman, if men could, like women, make a world for themselves in their own hearts, and if the fire of our genius, compelled to be dependent on social relationships and external circumstances, could be fully set alight by the torch of poetry alone" (27). Trusting one's own genius, finding one's *Coeur*, as in Corinne or the heart, one's authentic voice within, is the challenge that Corinne flings at her audience of mere mortals. Very few, however, can find that voice, let alone perform it successfully in the public sphere.

Translating Shakespeare's *Romeo and Juliet* herself (121), Corinne is not hesitant to take to the boards in order to play the role of Juliet, a role that Staël had seen Mrs. Siddons perform to great acclaim in England. This *liebestod* is performed so convincingly that Oswald is dragged from the theater, groaning loudly during Juliet's death scene. Back in her dressing room still costumed as the dead Juliet, Corinne greets Oswald who finds himself compelled to play the role of Romeo, crying out "Eyes, look your last! Arms, take your last embrace" (127).

Understanding that this self-dramatizing scene is a prelude to his eventual desertion, Corinne accuses Oswald of even now wanting to leave her. The Romeo and Juliet scene is the first of many such performances that suggest that Corinne's love of Oswald is doomed and that in fact she knows this already, has always known it, and wants only for him to acknowledge that both of them are at the end of history, the end of culture as they know it. We know that Staël herself performed something quite similar while writing *Corinne* during the summer of 1806, Jean Racine's *Phèdre* (1677), a neoclassical work that showcases a father's death-dealing curse on his son and the violent lust and anger of a woman hopelessly in love with her stepson and forced finally to suicide. When Corinne takes Oswald on a tour of her art gallery at her estate in Tivoli, she specifically draws his attention to Guerin's painting of Phèdre, Hippolyte, and Thésée, an oedipal triangle that anticipates the doomed curse that will result from the letter that Oswald's own father sends from beyond the grave.

Later, Corinne is persuaded to perform as the sorceress Semiramis in Gozzi's light opera *Daughter of the Air*, a comic work that depicts the female magician as a "coquette gifted by hell and heaven to conquer the world. Brought up in a cave like a savage, skilful as an enchantress, imperious as a queen" (294). The role seems tailor-made for Corinne, and indeed she agrees to perform it despite her growing anxiety about Oswald's intentions. At the point where she appears costumed as the Assyrian queen of Ninevah, as an "Amazon queen," Oswald begins crying in the audience, overwhelmed not simply with Corinne's show of female, castrating power, but with a very real fear for his reputation because their affair is now the subject of public scandal in the London "news-sheets" (297). Performing this role of female political and military power is quickly punished as Oswald criticizes Corinne, she faints and bloodies her head, allowing Oswald to nurse her back to health and assert his dominance once again (298).

As the dancing partner of the Neopolitan Prince d'Amalfi, Corinne performs the *tarantella*, a folkdance noted for its "ritual steps and the charming tableaux they present to the eye" (91). The highlight of the dance is the ritualized fall to the knees that each participant makes while the other dances in staged triumph around the partner. Turning her bodily performance into a text, Corinne is able to make "the spectators experience her own feelings," "her enthusiasm for life, youth, and beauty" (91). This transfer of emotions from the artist to the audience is very similar to romantic empathy, or what Keats would later call negative capability: "Everything was language for her; . . . an indefinable passionate joy, and imaginative sensitivity, stimulated all the spectators of this magical dance, transporting them into an ideal existence which was out of this world" (91). Again, the reference to the power of performative art to transport its viewers to another world beyond this one suggests a return to a neoclassical, platonic ideal realm above this one, a world that stands in stark contrast to the death-obsessed romantic place that Corinne has just shown Oswald on her tour of Rome.

Another dominant performance undertaken by Corinne is that of tour guide to the sights of Italy for Oswald. The grand tour that was part and parcel of the aristocratic young man's coming of age is manipulated in this novel by Corinne, who appropriates the cultural capitol that is Rome for Oswald's gaze. His visits to the Pantheon, St. Peter's, the Capitol and Forum, St. John Lateran, the tomb of Cestius, the Villa Borghese, and the Vatican Gallery become charged venues by which she seduces his historical imagination (86), aligning herself with the glories that were and forever will be Rome. The set-piece here is the visit to the Coliseum by moonlight (276) that was, of course, inspired by Chateaubriand's 1804 letter from Italy and printed in the *Mercure*: "Rome sleeps amidst its ruins. This star of the night, this globe one imagines as finite and deserted wanders in its pale solitude over the solitude of Rome." After reading this, Staël wrote to a friend: "To stay in Rome, as Chateaubriand says, calms the soul. It is the dead who live in it, and each step one takes here is as eloquent as Bosseut on the vanity of life. I will write a sort of novel that will serve as framework for a trip to Italy and I think many thoughts and feelings will find their proper place in it" (qtd. in Gutwirth, *Madame de Staël* 164). This scene in her "sort of novel" made the Coliseum by moonlight a *locus romanticus* for later poets like Byron in *Manfred* (1817), Percy Shelley in "The Coliseum" (1818), Lamartine in the *Méditations* (1820), Hawthorne in *The Marble Faun* (1860), and James's *Daisy Miller* (1878).

In her last stop before leaving Rome, Corinne visits St. Peter's and imagines "what that building would be like when, in its turn, it would become a ruin" (277). *Corinne* participates in the mania for ruin that was sweeping romantic Europe at this time. Chateaubriand can perhaps be seen as the originator of the romantic ruin, "the ruined ruin," a structure that "suggests that even the record generated by destruction can pass away" (Blix 177). In an event that is somewhat analogous to the British dissolution of the monasteries during the reign of Henry VIII, the royal tombs at Saint-Denis, Paris, had been destroyed by the revolutionaries in 1794, revealing "that the historical thread has been broken, and even the memorial of the bygone monarchy has been wiped away" (Blix 177). This event itself expresses the modern anxiety that history can indeed be lost, for if even the mighty are not immune from the ravages of time, no one is. The Roman ruins that Corinne tours, so evocative of a lost past glory and also ominously predictive of Napoleon's eventual defeat, suggest a sweeping historical pessimism not simply in the novel, but shared by a segment of European elite culture, obsessed as it was with nostalgia, revolutionary regret, and anxiety about political futility.

On Cape Miseno, near the ruins of Pompeii and Herculaneum, and framed by the tomb of Virgil, Corinne gives her last and most brilliant improvisation, on the subject of "the memories aroused by these

places" (233). Speaking more about herself and other female mourn-
ers like Agrippina, Cornelia, and Tasso's sister, Corinne bemoans
"strange destiny" (235), that "fate that pursues exalted souls, poets
whose imagination springs from the force of their love and suffering" (237). When Corinne concludes this improvisation, she states:
"Perhaps our fate will be decided by what we do tomorrow; perhaps
yesterday we said a word that nothing can redeem.... Oh, God, but
what does grief want to tell us?" (238). With a "deathly pale" face,
Corinne has finally performed the question that has haunted this text
from the beginning, exactly what role do fortune or fate play in our
lives versus how much are our decisions and decisive actions, our *performances*, able to counter this force, worshipped by the ancients as
the goddess *Tyche*, luck.

It would appear that Corinne's fate caught up with her on the
grounds of her dead father's estate, as well as in a London theater
and in Hyde Park. When Corinne attends David Garrick's revision of
a play by Thomas Southerne, *Isabella, or the Fatal Marriage* (1694)
in London (1782), she not only witnesses the performance of Mrs.
Siddons as the suicide Isabella onstage, but the mirroring action in
the boxes: Oswald's obsessive gaze on Corinne's own half-sister, the
blond Lucile (328--329). No longer a performer, but now a passive
viewer caught in the triangulated theater of the voyeur, Corinne has
become powerless to alter the fate that Oswald's father had destined
for all of them. Her death as performance-piece in Florence concludes
with the words written by Corinne and read by a young woman in her
stead: "The great mystery of death, whatever it may be, must grant
peace. You assure me of that, silent tombs.... I had made a choice on
earth and my heart no longer has a refuge. You decide for me; my fate
will be the better for it" (402). But to cede one's life to the designs
of fate is to sink back into the origins of human history. Corinne
denounces modernity and instead embraces the sort of fatalism that
art is charged with denying. On an allegorical level, the scene suggests that not only Italy, but also France as a nation will pass from
view and eventually be eclipsed by England, the nation that modernity is destined to reward.

It was not for nothing that Elizabeth Barrett Browning praised
the novel, observing "*Corinne* is an immortal book, and deserves to
be read three score and ten times—that is once every year in the
age of man" (*Brownings' Correspondence* 3:25). Browning, in fact,
chose a depiction of the triumphant Corinne, crowned in the wreath
of a poet, for her own tomb in Florence. The "myth" of Corinne,
of an exceptional, creative woman who is idolized, even worshiped

by her society for her talents and her ability to transform her own and her culture's sufferings into cultural capital, is part and parcel of women's attempts to seize the modern, romantic spirit for themselves. That Staël knew how difficult if not impossible this goal would be is proclaimed throughout the novel in Corinne's many ominous performances. One need only mention the names of Marina Tsvetaeva, Sarah Teasdale, Sylvia Plath, Anne Sexton, and Virginia Woolf to see how fearfully prescient she was.

NOTES

1. All references to *Corinne, or Italy* are to the translation by Sylvia Raphael, in the edition with an introduction by John Claiborne Isbell (Oxford: Oxford UP, 1998).

2. Corinne enacts these twenty-four performances: *improvvisatore*, tour guide, ethnic dancer, actress, painter, musician, "nun," voyeur at theater, debater, Catholic apologist, sibyl, "wife" of Oswald on British ship, water nymph, savior of Oswald after near-drowning episode, epistolary confessor, wreath-bearer to Oswald in Ancona, "Amazon queen" in opera, fallen woman in British scandal sheets, father-haunted, stalker of Oswald in Hyde Park, ghost to Lucile on their father's property, teacher of Juliet and Lucile, Dido to Oswald's Aneas, and stage-manager of her own death.

3. Apropos of Corinne's performances, Peggy Phelan writes: "Performance[s] cannot be saved, recorded, documented, or otherwise participate in the circulation of representations of representation.... Performance's being becomes itself through disappearance" (qtd. in Diana Taylor 5). Joseph Roach makes performance coterminous with memory and history, while J. L. Austin refers to cases in which "the issuing of the utterance is the performing of an action" (qtd.in Diana Taylor 5).

4. In *Madame de Staël, Novelist* (1978), Gutwirth observes that "A rich mass of intuition linking past and present is a ground of Romanticism, and Italy represents Romantic fullness as against the 'masculine' linearity of Enlightenment England" (210). Or, "Italy is Romanticism, England the Enlightenment" (215). Or, "If Romanticism can be characterized as a dissent bathed in despair, *Corinne* is certainly one of its first fruits" (279).

CHAPTER ELEVEN

COLERIDGE, SGRICCI, AND THE
SHOWS OF LONDON: IMPROVISING
IN PRINT AND PERFORMANCE

Angela Esterhammer

Recent research on Romantic literature and performance has shown that the improvisation of oral poetry was one of the features of Italian culture that elicited strong reactions from nineteenth-century British writers.[1] In Italy, improvising poets had long been displaying their talents in venues ranging from courts and salons to theaters and marketplaces; the male *improvvisatore* had a history going back at least to the Renaissance, and by the eighteenth century female improvisers or *improvvisatrici* were not uncommon. During the Romantic period, especially when the end of the Napoleonic Wars brought about an increase in international mobility, the influence of this performance genre became surprisingly widespread across Europe, with eyewitness accounts, commentaries, and literary representations appearing in hundreds of English, French, German, Scandinavian, and Russian texts.

The project of literally and figuratively importing *improvvisatori* to northern Europe proceeded along several routes. Most frequently, foreigners witnessed improvisational performances during visits to Italy; thus, the reception of improvised poetry can be traced in the writings of well-known or lesser-known tourists and expatriates, among them Goethe, Byron, the Shelleys, and Madame de Staël. As descriptions of real-life *improvvisatori* and *improvvisatrici* appeared in travel literature, and as Romantic texts like Byron's *Beppo* or *Don Juan* adopted some of the characteristics of improvisation, fictionalized representations of improvisers also began to feature with increasing frequency in nineteenth-century literature. Parallel to this textually mediated reception, another channel of communication was opened up by *improvvisatori* who travelled northward themselves and performed in other countries. During the 1820s, there was a moment when political events, literary trends, and developments in performance and print media converged to produce a sudden surge of interest in the spontaneous, experiential, interactive genius of poetic improvisers who appeared in France, Germany, and England. This lesser-known encounter whereby British Romantic audiences and authors responded to improvisational performances within the entertainment scene of early–nineteenth-century London merits more attention than it has received. Not only does the experience of real-life *improvvisatori* contrast in interesting ways with the fictional representations of *improvvisatrici* that were being offered to English readers at the same time, but it also gives rise to important reflections on mediation and mediality. In theaters and lecture halls, London audiences had opportunities to encounter poetry as an oral rather than a written medium, to discover how the conditions of immediacy and embodiment affect the composition and reception of literary works. Mediation becomes even more of an issue when print media attempt to reproduce improvisational performances and give them a more permanent form—for instance, when improvised poetry is published or when periodicals review ephemeral performances. The resulting reflections on mediality converge, as I will seek to demonstrate, in Coleridge's intriguing though little-known late text "The Improvisatore."

Studies of the reception of improvised poetry in England have often focused on female writers, and the Italian *improvvisatrice* has been seen as a model for nineteenth-century English poetesses from Letitia Elizabeth Landon to Elizabeth Barrett Browning. The most familiar channel of reception for poetic improvisation, in other words, is one that led from Italy through Switzerland and France to England, having been opened up by the publication of Germaine de Staël's popular novel *Corinne, or Italy* in 1807. Staël's own experience of improvisers and improvisation during her Italian tour of 1804–1805 merges with her ideal of the sociability of the French salon to shape her memorable protagonist, the *improvvisatrice* Corinne. While it has been argued that the *improvvisatrice*-persona provided nineteenth-century women writers with an exotic model of spontaneity and freedom, that it liberated them to express emotion, to write from the heart, and to transgress the boundary between private and public spheres, the importation of Staël's half-Italian *improvvisatrice* to England was in many ways fraught with difficulty.[2] In the novel itself, exposure to the conventions and constraints of English society ruins Corinne's health and happiness. In the process of the novel's reception, the enthusiasm of Landon or Barrett Browning vies with critique and condemnation ranging from *The Corinna of England* (1809), a moralistic satire that appeared soon after the first publication of Staël's novel, to magazine verse of the 1820s and 1830s that warned young women to steer clear of Corinne's literary ambition if they valued their health and reputation. While *Corinne* was undeniably important and sometimes inspiring for the (self-)construction of the nineteenth-century woman poet, the influence of Staël's version of the *improvvisatrice* in Britain is a complex story in which conservative and progressive values, private and public spheres, and natural and performative identities persistently come into conflict.

The story of how poetic improvisation was imported into English culture becomes more multifaceted still when one considers the presence of actual, rather than fictional, performers. Many English readers read about the *improvvisatrice* but few would have seen a female improviser perform; to do so, they would have had to travel to Italy themselves. Other than the great Corilla Olimpica's visit to the Austrian court at Innsbruck in 1765, there is little or no evidence of *improvvisatrici* performing outside of Italy. The few English travelers who ventured to Italy during the Napoleonic Wars might have heard Fortunata Fantastici or Teresa Bandettini improvise poetry in salon settings, and among the much larger number of tourists who took advantage of the reopening of the Continent after 1815, some might have caught a performance by Rosa Taddei in the theaters of Rome. By contrast, male performers enjoyed a much higher profile in English media and culture during the post-Waterloo years, both in reports from English tourists in Italy and in London itself. The public debut of the star *improvvisatore* Tommaso Sgricci in Italy in 1816 was astutely timed to coincide with the resumption of large-scale transalpine travel, and he was accordingly recognized with gushing reviews in London's *Literary Gazette*, the German *Morgenblatt für gebildete Stände*, and other English and European periodicals.

Because male performers who enjoyed success in Italy often went on international tours, English readers intrigued by accounts of the exotic phenomenon of extemporized poetry didn't have to travel to Italy to experience it; it came to them in London. Already during the late eighteenth century *improvvisatori* like Angelo Talassi had visited

England and astounded the circle of Hester Lynch Thrale and Samuel
Johnson with their talent (Piozzi 121–122). During the post-Waterloo era, Italian poets, intellectuals, and numerous *improvvisatori* had
a different kind of motivation to travel abroad: many were compelled
to flee repercussions for their actual or suspected involvement in the
events of the early Risorgimento. Several members of the Italian
diaspora who took refuge in London attempted to continue literary activity and build a reputation among the English as well as the
Italian expatriate community; they became Italian correspondents for
literary magazines, offered public lectures on Italian literature and
culture, and, in some cases, displayed their abilities as *improvvisatori*. One example of the networking involved is recorded in a letter
by the poet Thomas Campbell, who, on March 15, 1824, wrote to
enlist a friend's help in introducing to England "an Italian poet, an
improvisatore" who had just escaped from Naples aboard a British
ship (Beattie 2:428). Circumstantial evidence suggests that this new-
comer, unnamed by Campbell, is very likely Gabriele Rossetti, who
was forced to flee prosecution after his involvement with the recent
Carbonari revolt in Naples, who spent the rest of his life in England
as a professor of Italian, and who became, quite literally, the father
of the pre-Raphaelite movement. Gabriele Rossetti eventually gave
up improvising after his relocation to England, and the account he
includes in his verse autobiography *La vita mia* of why he did so
makes a fascinating story in itself. It was not only a matter of opting
for the high culture of a professorial chair at King's College London
rather than the less distinguished role of a public entertainer, but,
more importantly, the danger that improvisation posed to his health.
Improvising, Rossetti claims, killed his brother Dominick, and he too
suffered spasms and paralysis due to the nervous strain caused by this
stressful mode of composition and performance (Rossetti 34).

Nevertheless, during the 1820s and 1830s Gabriele Rossetti
offered public lectures for London audiences about Italian literature, including the tradition of poetic improvisation, and sometimes
illustrated his point by extemporizing verses himself. Other Italian
exiles as well as touring celebrities gave similar performances: Ugo
Foscolo, Filippo Pistrucci, the Marchese Spinetto, and in one notable
instance that I will return to later, Tommaso Sgricci, the most famous
nineteenth-century *improvvisatore*. Reports of these performances,
along with audience responses that combine fascination, admiration,
bewilderment, and skepticism over the quality or the authenticity of
the improvised poetry can be traced in the diaries of London's fashionable elite[3] and in public print media. But how do printed texts

hold fast and reproduce experiential genres, performances that are by definition unrepeatable and perhaps unreportable? *Improvvisatori* appeared in London just at the time when a rapidly changing media environment brought such questions about experientiality, embodiment, publication, and reading to the fore.

If the two-way exchange of tourists, exiles, and expatriates between England and Italy partly accounts for the surge of interest in poetic improvisation during the post-Waterloo period, the avid reception accorded this art form was also fed by the rapid evolution of print and performance media in England, especially in the metropolis. As Richard Altick demonstrated in *The Shows of London* in 1978, thereby opening up a field of study that is only now being explored in detail, the growth of middle-class audiences with leisure time and money resulted in avid experimentation with new visual and experiential media: panoramas, dioramas, live exhibits, melodrama and other forms of illegitimate theater, public lectures, dramatic readings. The decade of the 1820s was also notable for the plethora of literary magazines that started up, revamped themselves, merged, and often went under again as they tried to interface with the new cultural offerings in such a way as to achieve and maintain a viable readership. Both print and performance media unmistakably reflect the vogue of things Italian, and one of the interesting revelations that comes from studying the international reception of Italian *improvvisatori* as reflected in literary magazines is how sharply the popularity of this performance genre peaked in the year 1824.

This trend takes shape when one notes the density of references to improvised poetry and improvisational performance in textual records of all kinds during the mid-1820s. Literary magazines and newspapers carry advertisements and reviews of performances by *improvvisatori*; they commission feature articles on the topic of improvisation and run translations of such articles that appeared in other languages and other venues; they review scholarly books about extemporized poetry in other cultures and other historical eras. The *New Monthly Magazine*—an especially significant example, since it led the market in terms of circulation and influence (Sullivan 331, 336)—ran the following improvisation-related items in 1824:[4]

- A long documentary essay entitled "Italian Improvisatori" (vol. 11, 193–202).
- An announcement of an upcoming performance in Paris: the improvisation of an entire drama by the French poet Eugène de Pradel (vol. 12, 208).

- Four months later, a favourable review of Pradel's performance (vol. 12, 400).
- A review by Stendhal of a performance by the *improvvisatore* Tommaso Sgricci, also in Paris (vol. 12, 509).
- A long review of a French-language book on "Popular Songs of the Modern Greeks" that enthusiastically highlights the Greeks' "faculty of improvisation, (which they possess even in a more remarkable degree than the Italians)" (vol. 11, 139–148; the quotation is from page 140).
- A favourable review of Letitia Landon's *The Improvisatrice and Other Poems* (vol. 12, 365–366).

The 1825 volumes of the *New Monthly Magazine* followed up with two poems on the improvisation theme by Felicia Hemans (13:369–370 and 14:122–123) and a short story entitled "Giulio: A Tale" and described as an "Improvisation" by, of all people, Napoleon Bonaparte (13:119–128). The popularity of improvisers was also noticeable in visual culture: the annual exhibition at the Louvre in 1824 prominently featured a painting by the Swiss artist Louis-Léopold Robert entitled *L'improvisateur Napolitain*. Byron died in 1824, and the flood of memoirs, reminiscences, and evaluations that immediately began to pour from the press often latched onto the *improvvisatore* persona to describe his genius, sometimes by explicitly calling him an "*English* Improvisatore" (*London Magazine* 10:452) and sometimes by characterizing the style of his poetry and his conversation more generally as spontaneous and responsive to the moment. With surprising suddenness, poetic improvisation became a cultural reference point for periodicals and their readers in London, Paris, and Berlin.

The major improvisational sensation of 1824 was the first international tour of Tommaso Sgricci, the most flamboyant and controversial *improvvisatore* of post-Napoleonic Europe, a law student turned performer who specialized in extemporizing entire multiact dramas. In March and April of that year, Sgricci displayed his talent before large theater audiences in Paris. These performances were highly praised and reported on in detail in French, German, and English magazines, and—as was common practice with *improvvisatori* who achieved celebrity status—his improvised tragedies were immediately printed and offered for sale. A long, laudatory review of Sgricci's extemporized tragedy *Bianca Capello* quickly appeared in the French-language paper *Le Courier de Londres*, which was published twice a week in London for the local émigré community. This review was reprinted in English translation in the April 1824 issue of the

London publication *La Belle Assemblée*, an English-language magazine that addressed a female readership and signaled its pretensions
to cosmopolitan elegance with its French title. The review is notable
for its detailed synopsis of each of the five acts of Sgricci's improvised
tragedy, supplemented by extensive quotations of the speeches that
Sgricci had improvised in Italian verse, which were translated by the
reviewers into French and then into English prose. In this respect,
the review follows the common practice of Romantic-period book
reviews that regularly quote at great length from the book in question. But quoting Sgricci's orally improvised poetry in print involves
a significant change in medium: instead of a public spectacle in a
crowded theater, where the forward movement of time governs the
compositional process of the performer and the listening experience
of the audience, the printed review offers a remediated experience of
potentially solitary reading, where the reader can stop, leave, return,
and reread at any time.

In seeking not only to evaluate Sgricci's Paris performance but
effectively to re-create it for English readers, the review, therefore,
becomes an instance of what Jay David Bolter and Richard Grusin
have recently termed "remediation." Yet the attempt to reproduce
Sgricci's improvisation by means of a full synopsis contrasts ironically with the reviewer's insistence that the performance is by nature
*un*reproducible. "We have been witnesses of this wonderful achievement," the review observes, "and our admiration has been shared by
a numerous and select audience; but we assert, that it is necessary to
witness this miraculous improvisation" (*Belle Assemblée* 29:175). The
review concludes by underlining spontaneity as the defining aspect of
this "literary phenomenon": "We may apply to the improvisation of
such a tragedy, what has been said of the birth of Minerva: '*Elle sort
tout armée de son cerveau.*'—She sprang all armed from his brain!"
(*Belle Assemblée* 29:175). Citing historical as well as contemporary
examples of innovative media, Bolter and Grusin identify a persistent
"contradictory imperative" or "double logic of *remediation*" (5): that
is, the paradoxical need to resort to hypermediacy or multiple layers of mediation in order to simulate *im*mediacy. This double logic
aptly describes the practice of Sgricci's reviewers, as they reproduce
Sgricci's improvised drama through layers of texts translated from one
language and genre into another, all the while seeking to erase mediation by describing improvisation as an art of immediacy and an event
that needs to be witnessed, not read about. As the *Belle Assemblée*'s
reviewer realizes, poetic improvisation appealed to Romantic audiences largely because of the illusion that it provided an immediate

experience of poetic creation, even a direct conduit into the mind of the poet. According to the treatise *Über die Improvisatoren* (On improvisers) by the Romantic-period writer Carl Ludwig Fernow, who was cited throughout the nineteenth century as an authority on this subject, the experience of improvisation is one "where the poet, in the moment of creative enthusiasm, pours his song directly into the listener's soul" (304).

In addition to *La Belle Assemblée*, the *New Monthly Magazine* also recognized Sgricci's Paris performances with a review contributed by the French novelist Stendhal, who was a regular Continental correspondent for London periodicals during the 1820s. Reporting on another of the tragedies that Sgricci improvised in Paris in 1824, *The Death of Charles I*, Stendhal praises Sgricci's talent as a quick thinker and a dramatic actor, although he is more ambivalent about the literary quality of the extemporized tragedy. Indeed, Stendhal puts his finger on the disenchantment that resulted whenever an improviser allowed his or her works to circulate in print (although it rarely dissuaded them from doing so). "The intellectual effort is certainly an extraordinary one to witness," he comments, "but when the result is taken down, printed, and submitted to the calmer judgement of the closet, it must be confessed that there is very little of originality or beauty of composition to be found in it" (*New Monthly Magazine* 12:509). The review is addressed to a London readership who would have the opportunity of experiencing Sgricci in person in the future, since the *improvvisatore* had announced an upcoming tour to England. For any of the *New Monthly*'s readers who propose going to Sgricci's performance Stendhal outlines what kind of experience they could expect and recommends some background reading: "a good preparation for hearing him will be to read, some time in the day before going to his *Academia*, an act or two from the *Aristodemo*, or *Cajo Gracco* of Monti, or from the works of any other Italian dramatic poet" (*New Monthly Magazine* 12:509). Stendhal's review thus sets the media of print and performance into a different relation: in this case, the printed review actually precedes and anticipates the live spectacle, creating specific parameters for the audience's experience of it.

In the end, Sgricci's much-anticipated London performance was much delayed: he did not tour to England until after a second Paris appearance two years later, in the spring of 1826. At that point, his performance was anticlimactic—yet the restrained response to it is worth considering in some detail for what it reveals about the expectations of a London audience in the mid-1820s. The reception of this performance by the most famous of *improvvisatori* also forms a revealing background for Coleridge's "The Improvisatore," a text written in the same place at very nearly the same time. The juxtaposition of these two events, performance and text, shows processes of embodied and written mediation to be distinct yet intertwined.

Sgricci's appearance in London's Argyll Rooms on Monday, June 5, 1826 was reviewed under the heading "Sights of London" by the *Literary Gazette*, a periodical that had enthused about his extraordinary talent ever since his debut in Italy ten years earlier. The London performance was attended, the reviewer begins, by a select audience of about a hundred who were able to afford the high ticket price of one guinea—a pricing scheme in keeping with the Argyll Rooms' pretence to high-class exclusivity, despite their morally dubious reputation. Curiously and crucially, however, on this occasion Sgricci did not improvise at all. Instead, he read aloud from the printed version of *The Fall of Missolonghi*, a tragedy he had improvised two months earlier on a Paris stage. What Sgricci offered his London audience was thus a one-man performance of a once improvised but now scripted drama, in which he played seven different male and female roles and that of the chorus. But the audience clearly missed the excitement of on-the-spot composition, and the *Literary Gazette* reported that Sgricci's performance was at best energetic and passionate, but lacked credibility as drama—or, for that matter, as improvisation. The materiality of the printed book he held in one hand distracted from his performance, as did his habit of stroking his "profusely arranged" coiffure with the other hand. Sgricci further destroyed dramatic illusion by announcing the name of each character before he read that character's lines (*Literary Gazette* 490:365).[5]

In order to explore some nuances of the performance culture of 1820s London, it is worth pushing further on the admittedly speculative question of why Sgricci, the great *improvvisatore*, declined to improvise for his English audience. Indeed, the framework for his performances in London and Paris was completely different. In Paris, especially in the spring of 1824 when Sgricci performed his first improvisations outside of Italy, reviews highlighted the fact that the performance was set up as a rigorous test of his talent. Respected French poets and literary critics served as judges to monitor the circumstances, especially to make sure that Sgricci was not informed of the topics proposed by audience members until moments before he began improvising, in order to eliminate the possibility of premeditation or any other deception. The genuineness of Sgricci's spontaneous genius was the main feature that impressed Paris audiences as well as French, English, and German reviewers who spread word of his triumph across Europe. But at his London performance two years later, the key element of spontaneity was eliminated, leaving Sgricci to impress the audience with his ability to impersonate seven different characters, to move from one into the other instantaneously, and to arouse emotion by an impassioned performance.

But why did Sgricci fail to give the audience exactly that which they had presumably come to see? Unless his motivation was a completely contingent one (such as fatigue or illness), perhaps it could be interpreted as a misguided attempt to adapt to the London performance milieu, and even to the specialized venue of the Argyll Rooms. Instead of leaving the topic for the improvisation up to the whim of the audience, it may have seemed advantageous to retain control over it in this case in order to capitalize on the cachet that adhered to the name "Missolonghi" since the death of Lord Byron. Perhaps Sgricci was also aware that, even at the height of its popularity, poetic improvisation in England tended *not* to take the form of full-scale theatrical spectacle. Rather, extemporized poetry was channeled through the well-established institution of public lecturing. In London, touring celebrities as well as long-term expatriates like Gabriele Rossetti and Ugo Foscolo were more likely to take to the podium than to the stage, to give lectures about Italian literature in general and the tradition of improvised poetry in particular, and sometimes to enliven their presentations with impromptu demonstrations of their own ability to improvise. Reviews and other records indicate that London audiences' exposure to *improvvisatori* was mostly of this kind, rather than full-scale improvisational spectacles or formally judged exhibitions of the sort that were ubiquitous in Italy and that became a fashionable novelty in French and German cities during the mid-1820s. Presumably this was, in part, an issue of language: Italian poets might lecture in English, but they normally improvised poetry only in their native language, often at a speed that made it difficult for English listeners to follow.

When Sgricci came to town in 1826, poetic improvisation was one among several forms of solo oral performance that offered entertainment and instruction. Indeed, the *Literary Gazette* mentions that the expatriate Italian poet and *improvvisatore* Filippo Pistrucci "exhibited" on the same evening as Sgricci's performance and announces their intention to improvise together on a future occasion, although evidence that this team appearance ever came about is lacking (490:365). At the same time, lectures were taking place regularly in London theaters. *La Belle Assemblée* mentions, among others, Mr. Bartley lecturing on astronomy at the English Opera House and Mr. Thelwall lecturing on Shakespeare at the Haymarket (*Belle Assemblée* 29:178–179). Dramatic readings were also enjoying success: *La Belle Assemblée* regularly advertises and recommends Mr. Smart's series of readings from Shakespeare, which he performed each winter for a decade beginning in 1817, and Mr. Putnam had recently presented some well-received evenings of "readings and recitations" at the Argyll Rooms themselves, according to the *European Magazine, and London Review* (*European Magazine* 83:88). Sgricci essentially adopts this format, offering his audience at the Argyll Rooms a dramatic reading of his own pre-improvised tragedy.

Another intriguing English counterpart to the *improvvisatori* were the one-man shows of the comic actor Charles Mathews. Since 1818, Mathews had been appearing each season at the Lyceum Theater in the patented performances he called *At Homes*, in which he impersonated multiple characters in a partially scripted and partially improvised mixture of monologue and patter-song, capping each performance with a finale in which he "became" each of that evening's characters in quick succession. As Jane Moody has shown, the consistent success of Mathews's performances owes much to their wooing of genteel and middle-class audiences by offering them a form of illegitimate theater that, through a domestic stage-setting and the performer's intimate address to the audience, mimicked the conditions of a private drawing room (191–197). While Mathews's comedy contrasts with Sgricci's pretensions to high tragedy, Sgricci's choice of a performance genre lying somewhere between impersonation and dramatic reading might suggest an attempt to accommodate to the formats that were proving successful with London audiences.

The *Literary Gazette* lends credence to this hypothesis by holding up a talent Sgricci shared with Mathews for particular praise: namely, the "diversity of style" and "inflexions of voice" with which he portrayed different characters (490:365). The reviewer further evaluates Sgricci's performance in terms of distinctions between English and Italian tastes, and suggests that his foreign flamboyance was moderated just enough to suit a London audience. "The movements of the body were often foreign,—such as seem extravagant to English eyes," the reviewer notes, "but certainly not excessively so: a medium between the best of the Italian stage and a native preacher, such as Mr. Irving when warmed to the utmost" (490:365). This ambivalent comparison with the popular though controversial Edward Irving, minister of the Caledonian Church at Hatton Garden, is an indication that pulpit preaching had come to be evaluated—and, it follows, experienced—according to many of the same criteria as stage performance. Irving's preaching in particular was noted for theatricality and extemporization. In 1823, the *European Magazine* had even launched a monthly series called "Sketches of Popular Preachers," to which some readers promptly objected because of the disturbing elision of religious services with popular entertainment. Indeed, religion and theater approach one another especially closely in the *European Magazine*'s sketch of Reverend Irving in the July 1823 issue, which likens the preacher to star actors David Garrick and Sarah Siddons and to extemporary speakers (84:47). In this context, it is hardly surprising that the *Literary Gazette* would choose to compare the *improvvisatore* Tommaso Sgricci to Reverend Irving as a way of representing Sgricci to English readers who had not witnessed his performance.

Whether or not it was a calculated attempt to anglicize his art form, Sgricci's nonimprovisation in the Argyll Rooms ultimately has the effect of bringing his performance closer, in terms of mediation, to the experience of reading. In reprising the text that he had improvised for a Paris audience weeks earlier, Sgricci is doing something similar to the reviewers who recreate his performances in print by summarizing the action in detail and quoting extensive speeches. While he is, obviously, still operating in the medium of embodied performance, Sgricci eliminates most of the spontaneity and unpredictability of the improvisational genre, putting correspondingly more emphasis on the qualities of his language and the effectiveness of his dramatic impersonations. Imported into the cultural marketplace of 1820s London, the Italian genre of poetic improvisation undergoes significant remediation.

The middle-aged Samuel Taylor Coleridge must have identified to some degree with the *improvvisatori* who were lecturing and performing in London, given his own long-standing habits of extemporizing public lectures and conceiving ideas in oral conversation. Coleridge's letters and notebooks of 1826 take no note of Sgricci's visit, although Coleridge had other Italian correspondents in London and was closely befriended at this time with John Hookham Frere, the writer and diplomat who had assisted Italian exiles (including some *improvvisatori*) to settle in England. Nevertheless, within weeks of Sgricci's London performance Coleridge wrote "The Improvisatore," a curious text consisting of a supposedly extemporized lyric poem prefaced by five pages of prose dialogue that stage this act of improvisation as an amateur drawing room performance. While any possible relationship between Sgricci's visit and Coleridge's depiction of an

"Improvisatore" is purely speculative, Coleridge's text and Sgricci's performance nevertheless form an intriguing juxtaposition. For, if Sgricci's performance moves away from improvisation and toward the reading of a printed text, Coleridge's "The Improvisatore" goes in the opposite direction. It uses a print medium to re-create the experience of live improvisation, depicting the process by which an impromptu poem arises out of the contingencies of conversation in a distinctly performative social setting.

In Coleridge's text, Catherine and Eliza, two young women attending a Christmas party, encounter a fifty-something gentleman who is identified only as "the Friend" and bears the nickname "Improvisatore." This gentleman converses with the two ladies about love and poetry, then extemporizes a lyric poem on the topic of their choice—that is, on the question of whether true love exists and whether he has personally experienced it. As a hybrid of poetry, prose, and drama, the text presents a generic challenge to readers and editors. The *Collected Coleridge* includes "The Improvisatore" among Coleridge's *Poetical Works* and indeed treats the concluding sixty-seven-line poem as the main text, relegating the much longer dialogue that precedes it to the status of a "prose introduction" (*Poetical Works* 1:1055). Yet the generic hybridity of "The Improvisatore" and its self-conscious contextualization of the lyric poem are precisely the factors that give meaning to Coleridge's title and contribute to the remediation of improvised poetry that seems characteristic for 1820s London.

Coleridge's middle-aged protagonist is a dilettante performer who has acquired his nickname "the Improvisatore" from his habit of "perpetrating charades and extempore verses at Christmas times" (*Poetical Works* 1:1057). The action and diction of the text characterize him as a conjurer who can pull words out of the air, as if doing a party trick. Revealingly, the text begins *in medias res* with Catherine's question "What are the words?" (1056); later in the dialogue, Eliza admits that her formless sentiment "wants the *word* that would make it understand itself" (1058). When the ladies look to the Improvisatore as the one who can conjure up the wanted words, he responds by performing ever more challenging acts of improvisation. After warming up by improvising a four-line paraphrase of one of Thomas Moore's *Irish Melodies*, he goes on to extemporize a brief lecture on the theme "is there any such true love?" As a finale, he simultaneously composes and performs a four-strophe poem "*ex improviso*" (1060), using an irregular mixture of couplet rhymes, alternating rhymes, and tercets, and a variable accentual meter.

While the extemporized poem presents itself as an "ANSWER" (1060) to the assigned question "is there any such true love?" (or might it be answering the initial question "what are the words"?), its most remarkable feature is that it constantly calls attention to its performative status by evading any firm ground or constative meaning. The lyric meditates not on the fact or experience, but rather on the idea or "fancy" of being in love. Encouraged by the young ladies to confess that he has personal experience of true love, the Improvisatore instead avows only that he "fancied that he had" it (1060). Even though his poem ends on a note of "CONTENTMENT," the question of whether the emotion was "real or a magic shew" (1062) remains curiously unresolved. The poem's final lines address a listening lady and anticipate her response to the Improvisatore's utterance: "Lady! deem him not unblest" (1062). But since the lyric and the entire text end here as abruptly as they began, there is no indication as to what either of the young ladies might "deem" or what her response to the poem might be. The dialogue portion of Coleridge's text, on the other hand, explicitly dramatizes the listeners' feedback in response to the Improvisatore's prose discourse. One of the ladies, Eliza, is noticeably more receptive, while her friend Catherine voices mild skepticism and reminds the Improvisatore that she expects a "more sincere" answer (1057). Catherine's and Eliza's responses raise the question of sincerity by returning repeatedly to the question of *whose* feeling the Improvisatore is interpreting: his own? theirs? or is he, in the manner of a stage performer "perpetrating charades" and in the genre of the "magic shew" that his poem self-consciously evokes, feigning an emotion because it's what his audience requests? By embedding an ambiguous lyric poem that dwells on the terms "fancy," "conceit," "uncertainty," "hollowness," "shadows," and "magic shew" within a mini-drama that depicts the poet as a dilettante performer conversing about what it means to be sincere and constant, Coleridge's "The Improvisatore" foregrounds questions of performance and authenticity. It risks juxtaposing the traditional timelessness and transcendence of poetry, especially love poetry, with the time-bound conditions of live performance, including contingency, ephemerality, and the presence or absence of audience response.

When it was first published, Coleridge's brief text featured a still more elaborate frame: in all, the original publication comprised two titles, two subtitles, and three sections. The dialogue and poem discussed thus far bore the main title "The Improvisatore" and a subtitle enclosed in quotation marks—"John Anderson, My Jo, John"—which quotes yet another title, that of a song by Robert Burns to which the speakers allude in their dialogue. Preceding all this was a preamble in prose and an overall title for the series of which Coleridge apparently intended "The Improvisatore" to be only the first installment. While it is futile to try to separate texts from paratexts, the longest and most substantial section of "The Improvisatore" remains the five-page dramatic dialogue. Significantly, the effect of this prominent section is to depict the conditions that give rise to the extemporized poem: the nature of the venue, the characteristics of the interlocutors, the discussion of possible topics and the listeners' request for a specific one. In other words, attention shifts from the lyric poem per se onto the process from which it arises; by depicting the Improvisatore in real-time interaction with his audience, the text reproduces the conditions of live performance.

The outermost layer of the incomplete frame sets the creative process on yet another level. It consists of the series title "New Thoughts on Old Subjects, or Conversational Dialogues on Interests and Events of Common Life. By S. T. Coleridge Esq." and a prose preamble in which Coleridge addresses his reader directly. While this title casts the author in the role of philosopher ("New Thoughts") or talker ("Conversational Dialogues"), the voice that speaks through the preamble is above all that of the poet who takes pleasure in the quotidian yet wonderful "freshness of Sensation" that endows "old and familiar Objects" with "Novelty" (*Poetical Works* 2:1250). As editor J. C. C. Mays notes (*Poetical Works* 1:1055), these formulations closely echo Coleridge's comments in the *Friend* (2:73–74) and *Biographia Literaria* (2:7 and 1:80–81) about Wordsworth's contribution to the *Lyrical Ballads*, which was "to give the charm of novelty to things of every day." In "The Improvisatore," the sudden genial observation that permits a fresh responsiveness to everyday objects takes the form of an *ex improviso* poem. Coleridge's preamble thus sets Wordsworth's poetic practice and the art of the *improvvisatore* on the same level: they become two alternative ways of describing the interaction of the genial spirit with the contingencies of everyday life.

This reading of Coleridge's text seeks to tease out the implications of its elaborate framing while putting the emphasis on its main title, "The Improvisatore." It has been suggested that the title deliberately echoes Letitia Landon's popular *The Improvisatrice*, and Anya Taylor has explored the resonances between the two texts, arguing that Coleridge is here presenting an alternative perspective to Landon's gender politics and her portrayal of unhappy love. While Coleridge's "Improvisatore" is certainly about love, setting it into the context of mediality and performance during the 1820s suggests that it is also about the creative process, the status of poetry, the relationship of poet and audience, and the ephemerality of art, especially in a literary field increasingly dominated by popular, commercial, and consumable forms. This last point gains support from the context in which Coleridge's "Improvisatore" first appeared: it was a hasty, money-making piece published in *The Amulet for 1828*, one of the popular annuals that had rapidly become the main publication venue for original poetry during this decade. In his letters Coleridge describes "The Improvisatore" both as an actual improvisation and as a commodity when he complains that he sold it to the editor of *The Amulet* for less than ten pounds, parting with it too cheaply and impulsively on the day it was written, before he had time to reflect on its value (*Collected Letters* 6:699). Coleridge, like Tommaso Sgricci, finds himself obliged to commodify both poetry and improvisation for the 1820s market—although Sgricci evidently fared better in that regard by performing his improvised text for a live audience at a guinea a head.

Importing poetic improvisation into nineteenth-century England was thus a ramificatory project. Coleridge's "Improvisatore" takes its place among many imaginative and fictional depictions of *improvvisatori* and *improvvisatrici* by Staël, Landon, Mary Shelley, William Godwin, Sydney Owenson, Alexander Pushkin, George Sand, Hans Christian Andersen, and other contemporaries. Concurrently, due to a conjunction of historical, political, cultural, and medial factors, the vogue of the improvising performer spread across Europe and peaked during the year 1824. Fed by the presence of Italian *improvvisatori* and lecturers on Italian literature, nurtured by an experimental—and experiential—performance culture, and promoted by market-conscious periodical publications, improvisation took on distinctive forms in 1820s London that give rise to questions concerning mediation and remediation. How does the experience of reading poetry compare to that of hearing it being improvised—or watching a previously improvised piece being read aloud, or reading an improvised poem in print, or reading a review of an improvisational performance in a magazine? The hypermediality that results when *improvvisatori* are imported onto the London scene and into English print culture highlights the differences among these experiences, yet also blurs the boundaries between media. It is worth recalling that in the early nineteenth century the word "performance" could as easily refer to a book, a poem, an essay, or a painting as to a stage production—just as the word "reading," then and now, can refer to an oral public performance as well as a silent individual experience. Taking place at the intersection of reading and performance, English adaptations of

Italian improvisation become a focal point of medial change in the latter days of Romanticism.

NOTES

1. For an overview of this topic, see Caroline Gonda, "The Rise and Fall of the Improvisatore, 1753–1845" (2000); Erik Simpson, "'The Minstrels of Modern Italy': Improvisation Comes to Britain" (2003); Jeffrey C. Robinson, "Romantic Poetry: The Possibilities for Improvisation" (2007); and Angela Esterhammer, *Romanticism and Improvisation, 1750–1850* (2008).
2. For a fuller discussion of this issue, see Esterhammer, "The Improvisatrice's Fame: Landon, Staël, and Female Performers in Italy" (2007).
3. One example is the diary kept by Frances Williams Wynn from 1797 to 1844, which contains accounts of lectures and performances by Rossetti, Foscolo, Pistrucci, and Spinetto.
4. The issues of the *New Monthly Magazine* are numbered and bound as three volumes per year; thus, the 1824 volumes are 10 (January–June), 11 (July–December), and 12 (Historical Register). Each volume is paginated separately.
5. The review appears in the "Sights of London" section of the *Literary Gazette* No. 490, the weekly issue for Saturday, June 10, 1826. The journal is paginated consecutively throughout each annual volume.

Chapter Twelve

Masaniello on the London Stage

Frederick Burwick

"I want a hero," Lord Byron declared in the opening line of the first canto of *Don Juan*. "An uncommon want," he explained, for the simple reason that there were too many candidates jostling for public attention: "Every year and month sends forth a new one." After reviewing some thirty-two such candidates with political and military credentials in British and French history, Byron observed that none of these heroes or would-be heroes could serve the present need, for inevitably, "the age discovers he is not the true one." The want was not as uncommon as Byron implied. When one turns to Byron's source, the theater, it becomes immediately evident that every new melodrama presented yet another hero to meet the persistent public clamor. After a decade of the Regency, the Prince had now become King. Without agreeing with those who called him inept, it would not be wrong to say that he was less ept than current needs of the 1820s required. The defeat of Napoleon, the Bourbon restoration, and the age of Metternich brought about a repression of liberal reform on the Continent. And in Britain, because theater censorship prohibited satirical or polemical drama directed against the government, there was no opportunity for performances directly advocating changes in the present British rule. Perhaps for that very reason audiences flocked to plays depicting revolution and rebellion in other times and climes. Among the many heroic revolutionaries who gained popularity on the London stage in the 1820s, none was sought by more playwrights nor celebrated in more performances than Masaniello, the rebel of Naples. Here, I shall trace the career of that hero as he and his story evolve and metamorphose, passing through the hands of many playwrights and across the channel to Europe and back, in the process sparking an event unique in theater history, for a performance of *Masaniello* must be credited with a significant role in the Belgian national revolution—a revolution even larger than that of its titular hero.

HEROIC REBELS OF LONDON MELODRAMA

The playbills of the period cautiously celebrate the melodramatic exposition of heroic rebels. In representing heroes of England's historical past who opposed rulers of the time, it was important to make clear that the corruption and cruelty of those rulers justified the rebellion. Robin Hood thus made frequent appearances on the stage, typically with displays of his skills as archer and swordsman. As an outlaw his crimes were fully justified by his practice of robbing from the rich and giving to the poor. An equally crucial element in his assaults and robberies was the understanding that he was agitating against the misrule of King John who held the throne while his absent brother, Richard the Lionheart, was busy leading the Third Crusade. Quite often these plays were performed as comedies ridiculing the Sheriff of Nottingham's persecution of hardworking commoners.[1]

Often billed as the Scottish Robin Hood, Robert Roy MacGregor was another folk hero and outlaw whose exploits were dramatized by playwrights of the period.[2] Just as Rob Roy was billed as the Scottish Robin Hood, Twm John Catty was introduced to the stage as the Welsh Rob Roy.[3] The theater managers apparently thought it would useful to explain that they were not, in fact, celebrating a Welsh hero who fought against the English, but an "Ancient Briton" who contributed to the collective strength of the kingdom:

> The very strong and general interest excited by the various National
> Dramas, which have celebrated the Heroes, and gives a local Habitation
> and a Name to the popular Traditions and Historic Legends of the
> Sister Kingdom, authorize the presumption that a Story characteristic
> of the Country which afforded a shelter to our aboriginal Ancestors
> from foreign Invaders, of a People who are no less justly than emphati-
> cally styled the Ancient Britons, and displaying the Scenery, and
> illustrating the manners of one of the most Picturesque Spots and
> Romantic People in Europe, cannot be less acceptable to the Patrons
> of the Drama.[4]

Another drama of Welsh nationalism, *The Welshman; or, The Prince of Cambria* was staged at the Royal Coburg Theater on May 15 of the following year, and Owen Glendower, too, was celebrated for leading an heroic but unsuccessful rebellion of the Welsh against English rule in Drury Lane's production of *Owen, Prince of Powys; or, Welsh Feuds* (January 28, 1822).

The London audiences were by no means exclusively native Londoners. Indeed, native Londoners would have made up a small minority, for at least 80 percent of the population were recent immigrants or first-generation Londoners.[5] Many had arrived from the provinces, others from Scotland (Lobban 452), Ireland,[6] and Wales (Jones 465–466, 476), and still others from the Continent (Flinn 154–163). Cheering non-British heroes on the stage neither inhibited the applause for rebellion against repressive government abroad nor the zeal for domestic reform. Like Robin Hood, Wilhelm Tell was another folk hero of disputed historical authenticity who held persistent popularity on the London stage for his bold opposition to injustice. His defiance of Hermann Gessler, newly appointed Austrian *Vogt* of Altdorf, was supposed to have sparked a fourteenth-century rebellion that led to the formation of the Swiss Confederation, and it was celebrated in an anonymous adaptation of Schiller's *William Tell, the Hero of Switzerland* at the Royal Coburg Theatre on July 2, 1821. Not just among the rebel heroes of the historical past, playwrights also found their heroes among current conflicts being waged in Europe. Rafael del Riego y Nuñez, a Spanish revolutionary who played a key role in the outbreak of the Spanish civil war of 1820–1823, was applauded as a hero in the London melodrama *Spanish Martyrs; or, The Death of Riego* less than two years later at the Coburg (June 13, 1825). Members of the Spanish- and German-speaking communities would have found their national pride encouraged on repeated occasions.[7]

ITALIANS IN LONDON

The plight of Italian nationalism might well have prompted among the Italian community in London a sense of affinity with the predicament of Tell as a Swiss hero struggling against Austrian control or, more recently, Riego attempting to uphold the Spanish constitution of 1812 abolished by Ferdinand VII. Inspired by the Spaniards, a similar movement was launched in Italy. Guglielmo Pepe, a *Carbonaro*, led his regiment in the army of the Kingdom of Two Sicilies in mutiny. He conquered the peninsular part of Two Sicilies. The king,

Ferdinand I, agreed to enact a new constitution. The revolutionaries, though, failed to court popular support and fell to Austrian troops of the Holy Alliance. Ferdinand abolished the constitution and began systematically persecuting known revolutionaries. Many supporters of Carbonari insurrections were forced into exile, some fleeing to Paris and others to London (Holt 258; Dennis Mack Smith, *The Making of Italy* 137–138).

Many Italians had settled in England during previous centuries, and Italian strolling artists had already wrought changes in British drama. Harliquinades in the theaters and Punch-and-Judy shows in the streets were both legacies of the Italian influence in the late seventeenth and early eighteenth centuries. As documented by Lucio Sponza in *Italian Immigrants in Nineteenth Century Britain* (1988), the pattern shifted following the disintegration of Napoleonic rule and the advent of the insurrections. In the 1820s Italians became a more obvious presence in London street life. In tracing the migration during the earlier nineteenth century, Sponza reveals that many travelled by foot from the north of Italy to Austria, Switzerland, France, Germany, with only a few managing a ship crossing to Britain.[8] Although the great wave of Italian emigration occurred during the latter half of the nineteenth century, Sponza accounts for four thousand Italian immigrants arriving in England from 1820 to 1851 (Sponza 28–34).[9] Half of that number remained in London. "Little Italy," a centre of the Italian community in London throughout the nineteenth century, was situated in Clerkenwell and Hatton Garden (Sponza 46–56).[10] Giuseppe Mazzini, the writer, patriot, and revolutionary, arrived there in exile with his Italian friends in January 1837, lived in Laystall Street, founded an Italian language school in nearby Hatton Garden in 1841, and frequently visited Sadler's Wells Theatre on Rosebury Avenue (Denis Mack Smith, *Mazzini* 211–246). Another large group of Italians in London worked as seamen on British ships, with lodgings on the Southbank, many settling with employment as dock workers, stevedores, chandlers, and watermen. These would have been among the audiences at the Royal Coburg Theatre on Waterloo-road or the Surrey Theatre on Blackfriars Road.

During the 1820s the Carbonari insurrections had been thwarted. At the end of the decade, Ciro Menotti led his revolutionaries against the Duke of Modena, but the Austrian troops intervened and Menotti was captured and executed. The efforts of the Italian unification movement, *il Risorgimento*, were being forcefully crushed. Interestingly, neither Ciro Menotti nor Guglielmo Pepe were the fallen heroes celebrated on the stage. That role was filled by another revolutionary, Tommaso Aniello, the twenty-five-year-old Neapolitan fisherman, who 180 years earlier, in 1647, led the revolt against the rule of the Spanish Habsburgs in Naples. Eight different productions based on "Masaniello" and the revolt appeared in the theaters of London between 1825 and 1829. There had been earlier versions, not without volatile political implications, but those of the late 1820s were also charged with a high degree of melodramatic pathos. The revolutionary spark was by no means dampened by the emotional sentiment.

MASANIELLO IN SEVENTEENTH-
AND EIGHTEENTH-CENTURY DRAMA

The first English play based on the Neapolitan revolt was written just two years after those events. The author of *The Rebellion of Naples, or The Tragedy of Massenello* (1649) identified himself as "a gentleman who was an eyewitness where this was really acted upon that bloody stage, the streets of Naples. Anno Domini MDCXLVII."[11] He signed himself "T. B." and provided a further hint to his identity in his dedication "To the right worshipfull his honoured kinsman, John Caesar of Hyde hall, in the county of Hertford, esquire." As John Genest observed, the author's claim to be an eyewitness would have been more credible if he had adhered more accurately to the known facts of the uprising and the circumstances of Masaniello's death.[12]

Regardless, the Neapolitan's story would prove to have great staying power. As rector of the school in Zittau, Germany, Christian Weise, wrote numerous plays for performance by his students, among them the historical tragedy, *Masaniello* (1682). At almost the same time in England there appeared a Tory satire against Anthony Ashley Cooper, the Earl of Shaftesbury, for his part in the insurrection against the ailing Charles II to block the Catholic succession. Charged with treason, Shaftesbury fled to Holland where he died in January 1683. In the anonymous satirical pamphlet, Shaftesbury is identified as Masaniello, not a hero but a rebel and traitor.[13]

During the course of the eighteenth century, there appeared two further accounts of Masaniello that served as sources for the stage adaptations in London in the 1820s. The first of these was Thomas D'Urfey's two-part tragedy *The Famous History of the Rise and Fall of Masaniello* (1700).[14] The second was the work by Francis Midon,. *The Remarkable History of the Rise and Fall of Masaniello* (1729).[15] Yet another eighteenth-century text set an important precedent because it interrogated the motives of the revolutionary hero. In 1732 David

Fassmann's *Wilhelm Tell und Masaniello* accomplished this by presenting the two heroes in an imaginary dialogue. Because the most popular and widely performed staging of the fate of Masaniello in the 1820s and the decades following was Daniel Auber's opera, *La muette de Portici*, libretto by Eugène Scribe (1828),[16] it is important to acknowledge that the materials had already received operatic interpretation by the German composer, Reinhard Keiser, *Masagniello furioso*, libretto by Barthold Feind (1706).

SOANE'S MASANIELLO

In the 1820s, the insurrections that had commenced in the two Sicilies and in the Piedmont elicited a growing public interest, especially within London's Italian communities. To represent the just claims of the Italian rebels, George Bolwell Davidge, manager at the Royal Coburg, turned to his house playwright, Henry M. Milner, to prepare an historical melodrama with Masaniello as heroic leader of the revolt at Naples. At the very same time Robert Elliston, manager at Drury Lane, who had a penchant for developing rival productions, commissioned George Soane to write a five-act tragedy on Masaniello with music by Henry Bishop.[17] Winning the race against Drury Lane, *Masaniello, the Fisherman of Naples and Deliverer of his Country*, "A Serio-Comic Historical Melo-Drama and Neapolitan Spectacle, in 3 Acts," opened at the Coburg on Monday, February 7, 1825. Ten days later, on Thursday, February 17, 1825, *Masaniello, the Fisherman of Naples* opened at Drury Lane; opened—and closed, for Soane's play was an utter flop. Haste may well have contributed to the failure, but it seems likely that he also misjudged his audience. Cited by one critic as a potential influence on Scribe (Hibberd 152), Soane's *Masaniello* was a disappointment even with Edmund Kean in the title role. Christina Fuhrman has speculated that difficulty with censorship was a contributing factor (Fuhrmann 89–106). As Fuhrman points out, Soane's script caused trouble with the censor, who liberally excised and altered lines before allowing the performance.[18] The problem, however, was not that the political speeches were inflammatory, but rather that Soane's Masaniello sacrifices heroic integrity. When he insists that "noblemen are nothing" and derides statesmen as "state-cankers, who come between us and our monarch's love," he still affirms the "monarch's love" (Soane, *Masaniello* 6, 8). His downfall is in becoming too much like the noblemen he had denounced, moving into a palace, abandoning his wife, and declaring his love for the courtesan Olympia.

Soane's play makes it clear that Masaniello was the man for the moment. In the opening scene, Count Manfred warns the viceroy, Duke D'Arcos, that the new tax "Will drive the people mad," and Caraffa adds that there is one among the masses who could "*organize revolt*," and that one is a Masaniello, "a man for treasons—bold and stubborn;/ A proud contemner of authority" (Soane, *Masaniello*, 2). In Act I, scene iii, a mob has already assembled. Bruno tells them they need a leader. A hero is wanted

> BRUNO: [. . .] you are a body, gentlemen,—a very handsome body,—
> and 'tis fit you should have a head [. . .]
> LUIGI: [. . .] it is a big body, and must needs have a big head to think
> for it, or the whole creature will be preposterous. Therefore,
> unmuzzle neighbour; who shall be the man?
> BRUNO: Who but Masaniello?
> MOB: Right! Right! (Soane, *Masaniello*, 9–10)

In spite of the claim by the reviewer in the *Theatrical Observer* that the tale of Masaniello was "so well known that a description of the plot seems unnecessary,"[19] historical accounts varied in their conclusion to that tale. The challenge to be confronted by each of the playwrights was not in depicting Masaniello's rise to power but in accounting for his fall. A lust for power? For wealth? Or for a woman? Did he suffer madness? Intoxication? Or was he poisoned? Was he betrayed by the Spanish authorities? Or by his own people? In reporting on the sources, Genest asserts that "the most probable and received opinion is, that the Viceroy had given him an intoxicating draught."[20] Soane's resolution, according to the critic in the *Examiner*, was incongruously unfortunate. Although the play pretends to be a tragedy, it is "little more than a Melo-drama, attended with a fault, which from the nature of the story is very extraordinary; that is to say, a surprising want of action." The action has been crowded into the first three acts: Masaniello not only leads the revolt, he prepares for the peace. When the Duke and his retinue take refuge in a church, Masaniello presents the demands of the people, that the charter of Charles V be returned and honored. The Duke promises to grant their request, but offers a parchment that Masaniello recognizes as a forgery. If the true charter is not delivered by daybreak, Masaniello vows to burn down the church. At the close of Act II, Masaniello enters on horseback holding aloft the true charter of Charles V in his right hand. The weakness of Soane's drama is his handling of Masaniello's downfall and the Duke's easy return to power. The turn comes amidst the celebrations in Act III. The critic in the *London Examiner* objects specifically to the "mawkish tissue of feminine interest—why lower the ruling passion of a man in the situation of Masaniello, by a silly and improbable amour with a woman of quality, and the undesigned assassination of a too tender and prying wife?" (qtd. in Genest 9:290–291). In the third act, suspecting her husband's affair, Lorina disguises herself as a man. Failing to recognize her when she tries to reclaim his love, Masaniello kills her with his knife. He immediately succumbs to grief so overwhelming that his sanity fails. Convinced that the hero has vanquished himself, the Duke pretends remorse:

> DUKE: I grieve
>   Too much to see a hero—such a hero—
>   Subdu'd and prostrate.
> MASANIELLO: (Starting up!) No, Duke; he's not subdu'd;
>   Bow'd to the dust, it may be—no subdu'd;
>   He's still Masaniello—still your master.
>   Unfeeling pride!—Were you so visited,
>   I had not trod on your affliction. (Soane, *Masaniello*, 34)

But the Duke is right. Masaniello has already lost his capacity to lead at the end of Act III. Acts IV and V depict Masaniello's slow and agonizing dissolution and death. If Masaniello's purpose had been to reveal the degenerate morality of the court, then Soane might have allowed him to keep his honor by exposing Olympia's fickle turn from Caraffa to Masaniello. Instead, he presents Olympia as an honorable woman, and Masaniello as being swayed by fickle lust. Taking advantage of Masaniello's grief and mental distraction, the Duke seduces the populace to his side. In the fifth act, shot by his own people, Masaniello dies denouncing "the treacherous nobles" and calling on his "brave countrymen" to continue their fight for freedom (Soane, *Masaniello*, 60). The drama, Genest declares, does Soane "no credit—he has not hit off the character of Masaniello happily" (Genest 9:290).

MILNER'S MASANIELLO (1)

The race to be first at Drury Lane resulted in a dramatic failure for Soane, but Henry Milner's first-place version at the Royal Coburg (February 7, 1825), *Masaniello, the Fisherman of Naples*, was a decided success, with repeat performances throughout February and a revival the following year (June 5, 1826).[21] Part of that success was no doubt due to the enthusiastic response from the local southbank Italian community (Sponza 39–45). The two plays are approximately the same length, even though Milner adhered to the three-act division of melodrama (62 pages), while Soane chose the five-act division of tragedy (60 pages). But in dialogue, character development, and plot structure Milner's play is superior to Soane's. Milner adhered closely to Midon's *Remarkable History of the Rise and Fall of Masaniello* as his major source,[22] but may well have consulted as well with one of the Italian expatriates in Southwark or Westminster.

A crucial development in the revolt, not even mentioned by Soane, was the appearance on July 10, 1647 of five hundred banditti in the marketplace of Naples. This occurred after the viceroy restored the charter of Charles V and promised to comply with the demands of the people. Sent by the outlaw Perrone, the arrival of the banditti threatened further bloodshed and destruction. At first Perrone had joined Masaniello, but he was bribed to aid the Duke of Mataloni and his brother Don Pepe. When Masaniello accused Perrone as a traitor, muskets were fired, but Masaniello escaped unwounded. In the ensuing fracas, Perrone and about 150 of the banditti were killed. Don Pepe was taken and put to death. This episode, which might have corrected the "surprising want of action" in Soane's drama, is fully developed in Milner's version in Act I, scenes iii and v, and in Act II, scenes i and ii.

By no means as gifted an actor as Edmund Kean at Drury Lane, nor as gifted as many other members of his famous acting family, Henry Stephen Kemble nevertheless performed the role of Masaniello with considerable power. He had in that role, as Kean unfortunately did not, the advantage of effective dramatic situations and powerful dialogue. Moreover, as suited the character of Masaniello, his lines were tempered and restrained rather than boisterous and ranting.[23] In following his source, Milner took several of Masaniello's speeches verbatim from the transcriptions in Midon's *History* (see Midon 117–126). Following the defeat of the Spanish Guards who had been ordered to fire upon the people of Naples, Masaniello addressed his comrades with a modest pride in being a simple fisherman sharing in their success as loyal patriots (I.v). Masaniello's voice of controlled determination gives way in Act III, scene ii, to the first indications of incipient madness. Because of poor management of situation and action, Soane allowed the hero of his play to be reduced to an embarrassing state of debility for two entire acts. Milner avoids this problem by the simple expediency of a minor plot, drawn not from his historical sources but from popular gothic melodrama.

Like Soane, Milner too has given Masaniello a wife, but he has avoided entirely what the critic in the *The Examiner* called a "mawkish tissue of feminine interest." Leona, wife to Masaniello, was played by Miss Watson, who in 1818 had arrived at the Royal Coburg from the Cheltenham Theatre and soon rose to prominence in such roles as Helen Marr in William Barrymore's *Wallace, The Hero of Scotland*; Lady Calantha in *Glenarvon* (adapted from the novel by Lady Caroline Lamb); Catherine in *Gustavus Vasa* (adapted from the German play by Kotzebue); and Malvina in W. T. Moncrieff's *The Vampire*.[24] Milner presented her with bravery, fortitude, and a revolutionary temperament every bit as bold as her husband's. The gothic villain, Guilio Genovino, a renegade Monk, was played by Rowbotham, a favorite villain on the Coburg stage, cunning and duplicitous—plotting first with the outlaw Perrone to pillage Naples, then plotting with Caraffa, secretary to viceroy, to assassinate Masaniello. Genovino is a lecherous predator as well, determined to bribe or force Masaniello's wife into his bed.

The first indications of Leona's strength occur at the end of Act I. Masaniello has pledged to lead the people in refusing to submit to the tax imposed by the Spaniards. When the magistrates intervene to enforce the law, Leona steps forth to deliver a bold address on behalf of the people. Milner has given her words from one of Masaniello's speeches recorded in Midon's *History* (see 108–112). The attempt to arrest and imprison her is resisted by Masaniello who rallies the people to her side. Before Masaniello meets with Genovino in Act II, scene ii, Leona has already told him of the Monk's lewd advances. Expecting the worst of the low-minded villain, Masaniello is nevertheless shocked at Genovino's demand that Naples be delivered up to the pillage of Perrone's outlaws. Masaniello disavows all connection with the outlaws, who retaliate with an attempt on his life. Again, Milner places Leona at the forefront, displaying her heroic devotion in gathering the citizens of Naples to drive off the attack. Act II ends with the success of the rebels, the reading of the charter of Charles V, and the triumphal procession led by Masaniello.

Act III opens in a chamber in the viceroy's palace, where Caraffa reveals his plot with Genovino to kill Masaniello. In the next scene, Masaniello begins his descent into delirium. Leona and the friends who have gathered attempt to comfort him but are unable to determine either a cause or a cure. In this distraught state, Leona is again approached by the Monk, who renews his lecherous proposal that he now intends to enforce with the threat of having mad rebel imprisoned and executed. Her acquiescence seems to be her only recourse to preserve her husband's life. In the ensuing scene (III.iii) the insanity of Masaniello increases to a fevered pitch. Fearing for his life, he attempts to escape and is assassinated by the contrivance of Genovino. The heroic voice of Masaniello may be silenced, but the voice of Leona still speaks. In an energetic address to the multitude, Leona calls upon the people to secure the success they have gained against the viceroy. And in her striking attack on the villain Genovino, she avenges Masaniello's murder.

SCRIBE'S MASANIELLO

Milner's successful melodrama at the Coburg was performed through February 1825 and revived again the following year in June 1826. The next year, a different version of the story was created by Michele Carafa de Colobrano, whose *Masaniello ou le Pêcheur napolitain* opened on December 27, 1827 in Paris at the Opéra-Comique.[25] Although this opera fared well in France, there were no contemporary performances in England. And the most successful of all the versions discussed here opened not in London but in Paris. It was Daniel-François-Esprit Auber's opera, *Masaniello, ou La muette de Portici*, which had its premiere performance at the Théâtre de l'Académie royale de musique, February 29, 1828. The libretto had originally been drafted by Germain Delavigne and corrected by Eugène Scribe. In France, the circumstances of the Neapolitan insurrection had to be represented with a certain caution because of the ultraroyalist measures of Charles X and the increasing discontent during these years just prior to the July Revolution of 1830 and the overthrow of the Bourbon monarch. Later this same year, 1828, the satiric verses of the French songwriter, Pierre-Jean de Béranger, were the sole provocation for having him arrested, fined 1100 francs, and imprisoned for nine months. Scribe's libretto reflected the current political agitations not only in Italy but in France as well. In Act II, scene ii, Pietro and Masaniello sing a duet (*Amour sacré de la patrie—Sacred Love of the Homeland*) that became popular as a new *Marseillaise*.

As the subtitle reveals, Scribe has introduced a new subplot, a subplot with sufficient melodramatic appeal to counter the exclusive attention to Masaniello. In dramatizing the fate of "La Muette de Portici" (The Mute Girl of Portici), however, Scribe did not shift attention away from the evils of Spanish; he provided, rather, a further instance. Soane had given Masaniello an illicit affair with a courtesan, Olympia, and a jealous wife, Lorina. Milner had provided him with a brave and heroic wife, Leona, pursued by a fiendish predator, Genovino.

Scribe's contribution was not a wife, but a sister, Fenella, a mute girl who has been seduced and kidnapped by Alphonse, son of the Viceroy of Naples. The effect of this change, of course, is to make the offense against his sister, rather than oppressive taxation, the prime cause for Masaniello to lead the revolt against the Spanish authorities. The exposure of Alphonse's transgression occurred on the eve of his marriage to the Princess Elvira. She forgives him, but persuades him to make amends to Fenella. While Alphonse searches for Fenella, Masaniello loses control over the revolutionaries who are bent on the destruction of the viceroy's family. When Alphonse and Elvira seek refuge in the fisherman's hut, Masaniello risks the fury of Pietro, his rebel friend, for wanting to protect them. Convinced that Masaniello is a traitor who is undermining the effort to overthrow the oppressors, Pietro secretly poisons Masaniello. In the last throes of his agonizing death, Masaniello manages to aid Elvira in her escape. Alphonse marches with a Spanish army against the Neapolitans, rescues Elvira, and quashes the insurrection. In the concluding scene, Mount Vesuvius erupts and Fenella throws herself into the lava in despair.

Because the rebellion is crushed and Spanish authority is resumed, it may seem that Scribe's libretto represents a political capitulation to ruling power. Contemporary audiences, however, recognized in the failure of the insurrection and the tragic fate of Fenella, an appeal to revive the revolutionary cause. The very fact that Fenella is confined to silence makes her an articulate representative of a populace denied a political voice. The role of the mute in melodrama frequently served as a symbol of "the defencelessness of innocence," as Peter Brooks has argued in "The Text of Muteness." The silent performance demanded of the audience a heightened attentiveness. Special exertions were required, too, of the performer: "The mute role is in fact a virtuoso role, [...] a role that demands of an actor a deployment of all his dramatic powers to convey meaning" (Brooks 56–58, 61). Although not as violently mutilated as Lavinia in Shakespeare's *Titus Andronicus*, Fenella was still a victimized character intended to arouse sympathy and compassion.

DESHAYES'S MASANIELLO

Following Thomas Holcroft's *Deaf and Dumb* (1801) and *A Tale of Mystery* (1802), the mute may have become a standard character in melodrama, but Fenella is a character in opera (Burwick, *Romantic Drama* 109–113). A nonsinging character in a principle operatic role is a striking innovation, a bold hybridity of opera and ballet.[26]

Dance, of course, was a well-established component of melodrama and opera, but for Fenella in *La muette de Portici* dance was as integral to the exposition of her character as song for any other operatic character. Her silent cry of despair was communicated solely through expressive body language. It should be no surprise, then, that the first adaptation of Auber's *Masaniello* in London was as a ballet. Opening at King's Theatre in March 1829 André-Jean-Jacques Deshayes's *Masaniello*, with music composed by Nicholas Bochsa, retained from Auber's score two vocal numbers, the wedding chorus and the barcarole.[27] The manuscript libretto submitted to the Lord Chamberlain for the obligatory censorship contained Italian text for four choruses and one solo with chorus.[28] One contemporary critic found that "[t]he plot, the action, and the music [...] seemed really to hold out an invitation to mould all these into the shape of an interesting ballet," noting that "the opera itself contains so much dancing" and, even in the originally vocal numbers, "the subjects are so replete with neat and pleasing melody, that they essentially suited the purpose of ballet-music."[29] The ballet-like performance, however, had the effect of flattening the plot. Fenella was no longer estranged, for everyone in this "opera without words" spoke her language.

KENNEY'S MASANIELLO

Less than two months later, on May 4, 1829, Drury Lane and the Royal Coburg theatres were once again competing with rival productions of *Masaniello*. This time the playwrights were not Milner and Soane, but Milner and James Kenney. Both had adapted Scribe's libretto for the English stage. Although still declaring the work to be "a Grand Opera," the production at Drury Lane conformed more to the usual melodrama. Kenney substituted spoken dialogue for the recitative in his *Masaniello: A Grand Opera in Three Acts* (1831) and Barham Levius, the composer, reduced and replaced many of Auber's musical numbers in his version, *Masaniello; or, The Dumb Girl of Portici; a Grand Opera* (1829).

Arguing that Soane's version had been too "pointedly political," Christina Fuhrmann maintained that Kenney sought to avoid similar failure by amending "the more politically provocative aspects of Scribe's libretto" (Fuhrmann 89–106). As I have stated, my own assessment is that Soane's play failed because it was a bad play, with its major action over by Act III, leaving a hero debased and dishonored, driven mad not by his enemies but by himself. Fuhrmann's commentary on Kenney's version, however, impresses me as completely accurate. She effectively counters the contention published in *Harlequin: a Journal of the Drama* on May 16, 1829 that the Drury Lane production was a replication of the original French opera: "So exact is the copy, that we could almost fancy ourselves on the stuffed seats of the *parterre* of the *Academie Royale de Musique*." In listing Kenney's numerous subtle changes, she observes obvious patterns. Whereas Scribe centered the fault in the viceroy's exploitative policies as mirrored in his son's sexual abuse of Fenella, Kenney's version has the blame directed against the injustices imposed at large by the Hapsburg Spaniards. Thus, he adds an exchange in the marketplace scene in which a tax collector aggressively demands money from two peasant women. Kenney also has Masaniello refer directly to the tax as provoking the resistance: "Go to the market-place, and read the new tax-table; that's my weather-glass. Who'll set that to rights?" (Kenney, *Masaniello* 31, 20). The fault rests with policy rather than with the officials appointed to govern. Alphonso, for example, is willing to shoulder the blame for the people's discontent, and Kenney gives him added lines to reflect that "the natives have little cause to love us, and griefs like theirs, it should have been my office rather to have relieved than aggravated" (Kenney, *Masaniello* 8). Kenney's Masaniello strives to organize the protest and objects to the intemperate mob. Omitting Act IV, scene i, in which the vanquished Spaniards beg for mercy, Kenney inserts instead a soliloquy in which Masaniello laments, "Whither have my passions hurried me? Seeking to rouse men to their rights, I have unkennelled bloodhounds to their prey." Kenney also abbreviates Pietro's role, omitting the duet with Masaniello, and curtailing the dialogue. He then has Borella denounce Pietro's poisoning of Masaniello for his presumed betrayal: "The punishment should have waited the offence. 'Tis a black deed—a rash deed—and you'll repent it" (Kenney, *Masaniello* 35, 49–50).

MILNER'S MASANIELLO (2)

On the same night that Kenney's *Masaniello* opened at Drury Lane, Henry Milner once again opened his rival production. *Masaniello; or, The Dumb Girl of Portici* (Royal Coburg, May 4, 1829), followed closely Scribe's version. Milner, however, did not totally abandon his first version, for the lines that he gives to Masaniello still echo the speeches from Midon's *History*. Selections from Auber's score were adapted by Thomas Hughes and Montague Corri, retaining the overture, the choruses, and the barcarole.[30] Even in this new version, Masaniello remains for Milner the prominent advocate of liberty, motivated not merely by the injustice against his sister. When Fenella

is captured at the marketplace, he sees it as an assault on the rights
of all: "Who dares to lay his hand on a free citizen of Naples?" The
struggle for freedom is a defense against ruthless exploitation of the
poor and innocent. Pointing to the children, he calls upon his fellow
Neapolitans, "Is it not your duty, when the tyrant snatches from their
famishing mouths the hard-gained morsel that their hunger asks?
Is't not your duty to step in between, and fell to earth the monster
who would laugh and glory in their sufferings?" Milner emphasizes
the evil outcome of a rebellion without restraint. Shielding Elvira
from the mob, Masaniello is fatally wounded. With his dying breath,
he castigates his followers. Scribe had Elvira relate this moment to
Alphonse rather than actually showing it. By bringing it on stage,
Milner heightened the emotional impact of the *dénouement*. The
concluding scene now moves rapidly as one after another character
joins in the pantomimic tableau: Elvira is rescued; Masaniello is shot;
Fenella rushes in and throws herself on his body; Alphonso enters
with his troops and embraces Elvira. With the tableau thus complete,
Masaniello breaks the silence and utters his death speech: "[I] was
mad enough to think that liberty could take into her ranks those
whose abject souls stamps them eternally base slaves...never can fair
liberty unfold her banner, but where bright virtue stands to uphold
the sacred standard" (Milner, *Masaniello; or, The Dumb Girl of Portici*,
21, 18, 40). When Masaniello's voice is silenced, the thundering voice
of Vesuvius grows louder, and the voiceless Fenella plunges to her
death into the erupting volcanic flow (Milner, *Masaniello; or, The
Dumb Girl of Portici*, 39, 40.).

This finale, a *coup de théâtre*, was the contribution of the house
mechanist, James Burroughs, a master of conflagrations and explo-
sions. As the *deus ex machina* in many melodramatic spectacles of
revolution, the pyrotechnics of Burroughs were frequently featured among the special effects at the Coburg. Many instances of
Burroughs's pyrotechnics are noted in the playbills, such as the "Melo-
Dramatic Spectacle in 4 Acts, from the French Drama, *Salvator; or,
The Invisible Brothers*," which apparently ended "with the Explosion
and Destruction of the Castle and Fortifications of the City of
Regusa." Burroughs was listed as the technician for that spectacle,
and also for the fate of "Gondimar, who becomes the Victim of the
Temple of Death, and Vanishes with the Altar in multiplied Torrents
of Fire," in an adaptation by Milner of the French production of *The
Temple of Death*, "which has [according to the playbill] for months
past excited the Wonder and Admiration of all Paris." Burroughs
is credited with effects possessing "a degree of Magnificence and

an extent of Machinery never before attempted." The technician also staged pyrotechnic effects for *Guy Fawkes; or, The Gunpowder Treason!* (September 22, 1822); the *Siege of Acre; or, Britons in the East* (January 26, 1824); *Miller and his Men* (Covent Garden, October 21, 1813); and the "Grand, Historical, Anecdotic, Local Melo-Drama and Panoramic Spectacle," *The City of the Plague! and the Great Fire of London* (December 26, 1825). Following the great fires at Covent Garden and Drury Lane, theatres installed rooftop-water tanks that also served a double function in providing for storms and waterfalls. Stage pyrotechnics were nevertheless a dangerous risk, and perhaps for that very reason a thrill to audiences, as documented in Giuseppe Antonio Borgnis's *Traité complet de mécanique appliquée aux arts* (1820).[31] The Coburg playbill for *Masaniello* promised a stunning display: "TREMENDOUS IRRUPTION OF THE VOLCANO! *Overflowing of the Lava*...produced by entirely Novel Scenic Contrivances, excelling all former efforts to realize THAT TREMENDOUS PHENOMENON, THE EXPLOSION OF A VOLCANO!"[32]

A week following the opening of Kenney's *Masaniello* at Drury Lane and Milner's *Masaniello* at the Royal Coburg, a third production, this one an equestrian spectacle, opened at the Royal Amphitheatre (May 11, 1829).[33] As Milner's adaptation makes evident, Scribe's *Masaniello* could be presented with heightened emphasis on its revolutionary purport. Certainly, the Italian immigrants in the Coburg audience responded to the play's echoing of events currently unfolding in their native country. And it would soon become clear that the Italians were not the only ones responding to Masaniello's call to freedom.

SCRIBE'S MASANIELLO AND THE BELGIAN REVOLUTION

At a performance of *Masaniello, ou La muette de Portici* at the Théâtre de la Monnaie, Brussels on the August 25, 1830, a riot broke out that rapidly escalated into the revolution that led to Belgian independence. Perhaps it is too much to claim that the Brussels performance of *Masaniello* incited a revolution, but in a situation in which discontent was so rampant it is easy to understand how a drama on the plight of Naples could serve as a match to the powder keg. At issue was the secession of the southern provinces from the United Kingdom of the Netherlands. In the southern region the population was Roman Catholic and French-speaking. There were high levels of unemployment and, for those who were employed, unequal pay among the working classes. The rule of King William I favored the north. As a result of the Belgian Revolution an independent Kingdom of Belgium was established on February 7, 1831 with the ratification of the Belgian Constitution. Not until 1839, however, did the Dutch acknowledge an independent Belgian government (see Logie 21).

Perrot's Undine

Although it might seem only obliquely relevant, the ballet version that was performed at Her Majesty's Theatre, London; June 22, 1843, is in fact crucial to the reception history of Masaniello in Britain. It had an astonishing run, commanding the stage from 1843 to 1848, and was frequently revived in years following. Not at all similar to the earlier ballet version by André-Jean-Jacques Deshayes, which adhered closely to Auber's opera, the ballet by Jules Perrot, *Ondine, ou La naïade*, had a new plot and new music. To be sure, the familiar plot previously underwent significant changes in the "feminine interest," from the jealous Lorina, to the heroic Leona, to the abused and exploited Fenella. But Perrot has taken that change even further by centering his ballet, not on a mute of Portici, but on a mute of the waters. Ondine, a naiade, entices the revolutionary fisherman Mattéo into the sea. With music by Cesare Pugni, Perrot's choreographic tale was inspired by Friedrich de la Motte Fouqué's *Undine*, which had already been staged twenty-seven years earlier as an opera with a score by E. T. A. Hoffmann (Königliches Schauspielhaus, Berlin, August 3, 1816). In merging that plot with the account of the fisherman-become-revolutionary, Perrot appropriately shifted the location from the Danube to the shores of Sicily, and replaced the aristocratic Sir Huldbrand with the fisherman Mattéo.[34] Rather than perish as martyr to a doomed rebellion, Mattéo the fisherman is brought into the aquatic paradise beneath the sea.

Coda: Turner's Undine
Giving the Ring to Masaniello

That moment of apotheosis is the subject of Masaniello as mythic hero in Joseph Mallord William Turner's painting, *Undine giving the Ring to Masaniello* (1846). Turner has dismissed Mattéo and restored his hero's name,[35] perhaps even punning on his name and the Italian word for "ring" (*anello*). Intending the comment only as a snide jest, the critic in the *Art Union* (June 1846) wrote: "We know the Doge of Venice used to marry the Adriatic, and throw a ring into it, but we were not aware that one of these rings had been picked up by Undine, and given to Masaniello" (qtd. in Butlin and Joll 2:269). Turner painted that scene in his *Venice: the Piazzetta with the Ceremony of the Doge marrying the Sea* (1835), and another painting, *The Grand Canal, Venice* (1837), has also been interpreted, perhaps mistakenly, as depicting the annual ritual of "The Marriage of the Adriatic," in which the Doge espouses the sea (Butlin and Joll, plates 373 and 501, 2:219–10, 296). Wherever she has acquired the ring, Undine's purpose is exactly what Perrot celebrated in his ballet. Masaniello has returned home, folded into the ranks of mythic heroes in the same moment he is given his place in the Italian pantheon.

CONCLUSION

Exciting moments in theater history have occurred when an audience is aroused to action by a play. Such a moment occurred at the premier of Luigi Pirandello's *Six Characters in Search of Author* (*Sei personaggi in cerca d'autore*; Teatro Valle, Rome, May 10, 1921), with audience members shouting "Manicomio! [Madhouse!]." Another stunning moment was the response to Victor Hugo's *Hernani* (Comédie-Française, February 25, 1830 place) that set off the battle between the Classicicists and the Romantics. Scribe's *Masaniello*, however, was the play that precipitated the most massive revolution in theater history. A hero was wanted, and it was a stage hero, Masaniello, who sparked the action of the revolutionaries that fought for Belgian independence. A performance of *Masaniello* achieved the unique record of having provoked a national revolution larger than that led by its title hero. A more modest victory was obtained in London, when not once but twice an illegitimate theater on the south side of the Thames triumphed in competition with the venerable Drury Lane. Soane failed completely. Kenney met with modest success. But Milner, with two very different versions of the rise and fall of Masaniello, packed the Royal Coburg, as his own playbills confirm, with cheering crowds. Masaniello's story thus played a role in both the political and cultural lives of the patriots—and expatriots—who crowded the seats in London, as well as Paris and Brussels.

NOTES

1. For example, the burletta *Robin Hood* was performed at New Theatre [Tottenham Street Theatre] on November 27, 1810.
2. George Soane, *Rob Roy, the Gregarach* (Drury Lane, March 25, 1818); Isaac Pocock, *Rob Roy Macgregor; or, Auld Lang Syne!* (Covent Garden,

March 12, 1818); William Henry Murray, *Rob Roy* (Edinburgh, June 10, 1818); Corbett Ryder, *Rob Roy* (Caledonian, Edinburgh, March 29, 1825); and an anonymous *Rob Roy McGregor* (Coburg, July 8, 1828).

3. *Twm John Catty, the Welsh Rob Roy* (Coburg April 14, 1823; The Garrick, January 3, 1831).

4. British Library, mic.c.13137. Playbills 174, dated Monday, February 7, 1825.

5. See Mitchell 25, 77, 89, 102. See also Kershaw and Pearsall's *Immigrants and Aliens*. In 1793, when many refugees were arriving from France, the government introduced a Regulations of Aliens Act (RAA). All foreigners coming to Britain were required to register with officials. A Superintendent of Aliens was appointed as head of the Aliens Office responsible for the registration of migrants. In 1798, a more rigorous law established a system of registration at British ports, where migrants had to sign declarations upon entry into Britain. Migrants already living in Britain, and those arriving after January 1793, had to give their names, ranks, occupations, and addresses to a magistrate. In March 1797, the home secretary distributed forms for providing details on all migrants who had arrived after May 1792. Householders who had taken in migrants as lodgers had to give details to local officials. Passports, issued by the secretary of state, were required for travel outside of London. The wartime regulations regarding aliens were repealed at the peace of 1814, but were renewed with modifications later in the same year, and in 1815 when war broke out again. The RAA 1816 required masters of ships to declare in writing to the Inspector of Aliens or Officer of the Customs, the number of foreigners on board with their names and descriptions. The RAA 1826 required migrants to send to the secretary of state, or to the chief secretary for Ireland, a declaration of their place of residence every six months. Most of the early records of the Aliens Office have been destroyed but Foreign Office Records at The National Archives, reference FO 83/21 contain lists of migrants arriving at British ports for the period August 1810–May 1811. The vast majority of certificates issued under the Aliens Act 1826 were destroyed when the Aliens Office was absorbed in to the Home Office in 1836, but there is an index of certificates from 1826 to 1849 at The National Archives in series HO 5/25–32, and CUST 102/393–396 contains certificates of arrival for the Port of London from July to November 1826, and for the port of Gravesend from October 1826 to August 1837. HO 2 contains original certificates of arrival of individuals arranged under ports of arrival for the period 1836–1852. Each certificate gives the person's name, nationality, profession, date of arrival, and last country visited, together with their signature, and sometimes other details.

6. See A. W. Smith's "Irish Rebels and English Radicals 1798–1820."

7. See Farrell's "The German Community in Nineteenth Century East London" and Panayi's *German Immigrants in Britain during the Nineteenth Century, 1815–1914.* Records of the Old Bailey document a few skirmishes with the law by Spanish and Portugues sailors in London. Another source are the records of the Portuguese and Spanish chapels in London: Spanish/Portuguese communities existed in Thameside, Sardinian chapel in Duke Street, Lincoln's Inn Fields, the Sardinian, Spanish chapel in Manchester Square, and the Portuguese chapel in South Street, Grosvenor Square.

8. See also Taliani, *L'emigrazione italiana in Inghilterra tra Letteratura e Politica, 1820–1860.*

9. The regional origins of most were the valleys around Como and Lucca. The people from Como were skilled artisans, making barometers and other precision instruments. People from Lucca specialized in plaster figure making. The people from Parma were predominately organ grinders, while the Neapolitans from the Liri valley made ice cream.

10. As numbers increased and competition grew fiercer in London, Italians spread to the north of England, Wales, and Scotland, although never in great numbers in the northern cities. The Italian Consul General in Liverpool, in 1891, reports that the majority of the 80–100 Italians in the city were organ grinders and street sellers of ice cream and plaster statues. The 500–600 Italians in Manchester included mostly Terrazzo specialists, plasterers and modelers working on the prestigious, new town hall. In Sheffield 100–150 Italians made cutlery.

11. T. B. [Thomas Belke, or Thomas Bakewell], *The Rebellion of Naples, or The Tragedy of Massenello. Commonly so called: but rightly Tomaso Aniello di Malfa generall of the Neopolitans.* (Printed at London, For J.G. & G.B. at Furnivals-Inne Gate in Holborne, 1649); dedicated "To the right worshipfull his honoured kins-man, John Caesar of Hyde hall, in the county of Hertford, esquire," signed: T. B. "Written by a gentleman who was an eye-witnes where this was really acted upon that bloody stage, the streets of Naples. Anno Domini MDCXLVII."

12. See Genest 2:161: "the author of this piece has dramatized the principal events in a tolerable manner—it concludes with the funeral of Massenello—a Herald proclaims a general pardon Massenello revives and speaks the Epilogue—in the 3d act, Agatha, the 2d wife of Massenello, stabs Flora, the daughter of Massenello by a former wife, in the face—Massenello breaks Agatha's neck between his hands. Antonio, the son of the Viceroy, falls in love with Flora, and means to marry her—in the 5th act, Ursula, Massenello's daughter by Agatha, poisons Flora—as also her Grandmother—the latter unintentionally—Flora dies—Ursula is cut in pieces, and thrown to the dogs—as T. B. professed to write a true account of the story, he

ought not to have introduced circumstances, which not only did not happen, but could not happen—Massenello was too young to have a marriageable daughter."

13. See *Massinello; or, A Satyr against the Association and the Guild-hall-riot.*

14. Genest also provides a commentary on D'Urfey's version and summarizes the historical sources. He also notes that the two parts of Masaniello were reduced to one by Thomas Walker and performed at Lincoln's Inn Fields, July 31, 1724 (2:158–163).

15. I have relied on a later edition of this much-published work (London: Printed for R. Manby , 1756). For a recent history, see Villari, *The Revolt of Naples.*

16. For an account of Scribe's career, see Fuhrmann, "In Enemy Territory? Scribe and Grand Opera in London, 18291833."

17. For a brief account of Soane's career, see Burwick, "George Soane."

18. These interferences are documented in the British Library's copy of G. Soane, *Masaniello,* Plays Submitted to the Lord Chamberlain. British Library Add. Mss. 42870, ff. 1–68.

19. *Theatrical Observer* February 18, 1825.

20. See Genest 2:160: "many and various are the reflections that have been made upon his [Masaniello's] sudden madness—some are of opinion, that that stupendous height of power to which he arrived, as it were in an instant, made him giddy and turn'd his brains—others will have it to be occasioned by the great and continual fatigues he underwent, scarce ever allowing himself time to take the natural refreshments of food or sleep—but, the most probable and received opinion is, that the Viceroy had given him an intoxicating draught, which, by inflaming his blood, should make him commit such extravagancies, as would oblige the people to despise and forsake him.

"On the 16th of July Masaniello was murdered with the approbation of the Viceroy—at the time of his assassination the people seemed stupified and motionless, but on the next day they buried him with great solemnity."

21. If the 1824 date of the imprint is correct, then Milner's play was published before its first performance at the Royal Coburg Theatre, February 7, 1825.

22. Midon, *Remarkable History of the Rise and Fall of Masaniello,* first published in 1729 (London: Printed for C. Davis, and T. Green, 1729), appeared in subsequent editions in 1747 (London: Printed for C. Davis; and L. J. Davis, 1747), 1748 (Oxford: Printed by R. Walker & W. Jackson, 1748); 1756 (London: Printed for R. Manby, 1756), 1768 (London: Printed by J. Browne, 1768), and 1770 (London: H. Fenwick's Wholesale Book Warehouse, 1770).

23. Rant and rhodomontade, according to William Oxenberry, were prominent among H. S. Kemble's shortcomings as an actor (Oxenberry 1:146, 149–155).

24. *The Vampire* (August 21, 1820) was adapted from Charles Nodier's French adaptation of the novel by John Polidori, Lord Byron's sometime physician.

25. Lowenberg states in *Annals of the Opera* that Carafa de Colobrano's play was given at the Opéra-Comique 136 times and was revived in 1882; there were also performances in Ghent in 1828, and Amsterdam 1834.

26. See Marian Smith's "Three Hybrid Works at the Paris Opéra, circa 1830."

27. The barcarole is a Venetian Gondolier's song, often sung to a rhythm reminiscent of rowing. For comparison of Auber's opera and Deshayes's ballet, see commentaries by John Waldie, who witnessed performances in London, Paris, and other theaters. See esp. LVI, 77 (June 27, 1828), LVI, 337 (May 26, 1829), LVI, 370 (June 20, 1829), LVII, 4 (August 1, 1829), tLVII, 42 (September 4, 1829), LX, 53 (September 25, 1832), LX, 94 (November 8, 1832).

28. *Songs from Masaniello ou le Pêcheur de Portici*, Plays Submitted to the Lord Chamberlain, British Library, Add. Ms. 42985, ff. 43–44b. Newspaper reports suggest, however, that only the two numbers mentioned made the final cut for performance.

29. *The New Monthly Magazine and Literary Journal*, May 1, 1829.

30. The score by Hughes and Corri does not survive, but the published play prints the songs and choruses, with notes indicating musical performance.

31. See Giuseppe Antonio Borgnis, *Traité complet de la mécanique appliquée aux arts, Des machines imitatives et de machines théâtrales* (Paris: Bachelier, 1820), 294–298. See also Emaljanow 369–371.

32. British Library, mic.c.13137. Playbills 174, dated Playbill, May 4, 1829.

33. The *Theatrical Observer* notes a production of *Masaniello* (Royal Amphitheatre, May 11, 1829); see also Nicoll 501.

34. Subsequently staged with the title, *La naïade et le pêcheur*, Perrot's ballet also drew from René-Charles Guilbert de Pixerécourt, *Ondine, ou la Nymphe des Eaux* (Théâtre de la Gaîté, Paris, February 17, 1830). See Au, "The Shadow of Herself: Some Sources of Jules Perrot's *Ondine*."

35. See Stuckey, "Turner, Masaniello and the Angel"; Finley, "Turner, the Apocalypse and History: 'The Angel' and 'Undine'"; and Finley, *Angel in the Sun: Turner's Vision of History*, especially notes on page 233.

CHAPTER THIRTEEN

RE-VISIONING RIMINI: DANTE IN THE COCKNEY SCHOOL

Jeffrey N. Cox

It has always been easy to laugh at Leigh Hunt's *Story of Rimini*, a rather unusual item in the history of prison writing. Even a modern critic such as Rodney Stenning Edgecombe, writing one of the few full critical studies of Hunt, speaks of the poem's "structural and linguistic flaws" (52). Romantic era defenders of traditional culture met *Rimini*'s publication with a rousing chorus of jeers. *The Quarterly Review* assailed Hunt's "vanity, vulgarity, ignorance, and coarseness" (14 [January 1816]:481); *Blackwood's Magazine* called *Rimini* "indecent and immoral," and attacked not only its subject but its style:

> Leigh Hunt's chivalrous rhymes are as unlike those of Walter Scott, as is the chivalry of a knighted cheesemonger to that of Archibald the Grim, or, if he would rather have it so, of Sir Philip Sydney. He draws his ideas of courtly splendour from the Lord Mayor's coach, and he dreams of tournaments, after having seen the aldermen on horseback, with their furred gowns and silk stockings. We are indeed altogether incapable of understanding many parts of the description, for a good glossary of the Cockney dialect is yet a desideratum in English literature.... What, for instance, may be the English of *swaling*? (2 [October 1817]:198).

Throughout the nineteenth century, other poets would continue to make fun of Hunt's poem. Henry Ellison, the minor, somewhat spasmodic poet, complains in his sonnet on "Dante's 'Francesca Da

Rimini'" of how "wits more weak [than Dante's] / Play, dally with the passion" of the story and "with freak / Of fancy overlay it" (Ellison, ll. 4–6), presumably complaining of someone like Hunt trying to expand Dante's brief episode. William Edmonstoune Aytoun, husband of John Wilson's daughter, contributor and staff member of *Blackwood's*, and a chief parodist of the Spasmodic School, wrote with Theodore Martin a wonderful satire of Hunt in their Bon Gaultier Ballads, a poem imagining "an impassioned pupil of Leigh Hunt" writing a poem to her beau after a Fancy Ball, where she uses many of the controversial words and phrases from Hunt's Rimini—she has a "clipsome lightness" (Aytoun and Martin 165), for example, and she speaks of the "swaling of a jaunty air" (166)—before closing with a turn from dancing that parallels Paolo and Francesca's turn from reading:

> We pass'd into the great refreshment hall,
> Where the heap'd cheese-cakes and the comfits small
> Lay, like a hive of sunbeams, brought to burn
> Around the margin of the negus urn;
> When my poor quivering hand you finger'd twice,
> And, with enquiring accents, whisper'd "Ice,
> Water, or cream?" I could no more dissemble,
> But dropp'd upon the couch all in a tremble.
> A swimming faintness misted o'er my brain,
> The corks seem'd starting from the brisk champagne,
> The custards fell untouch'd upon the floor,
> Thine eyes met mine. That night we danced no more! (Aytoun and
>   Martin 167)

Such attacks—gentle and violent—have obscured from us, as Jane Stabler's "Leigh Hunt's Aesthetics of Intimacy" points out, the positive reviews from the *Augustan Review*, the *British Lady's Magazine*, and the *Eclectic Review* along with the judicious readings of the *Edinburgh* and *Monthly* reviews (104). For those around Hunt, *Rimini* was a central cultural event, with Charles Lamb writing to indicate that he and his sister "congratulate you most sincerely on the fruit of your prison hours" that they had read "with great delight" (to Hunt, March 23, 1816; *Lamb's Letters* 3:209–210), and with Hazlitt echoing in order to reverse Jeffrey's condemnation of Wordsworth's *Excursion*, "I have read the story of Rimini with extreme satisfaction.... *This will do*" (to Hunt, February 15, 1816; *Hazlitt's Letters* 153.). Charles Cowden Clarke (1816) published a pamphlet defending the poem. Keats, who used a line from *Rimini* as the epigraph to his opening piece to his 1817 *Poems*, wrote a sonnet "On Leigh

Hunt's Poem, The 'Story of Rimini'" in March 1817, with Shelley penning his response in 1816 in his "Lines to Leigh Hunt" and John Hamilton Reynolds publishing a sonnet praising *Rimini* in *The Champion* (December 8, 1816:390). We can find echoes of *Rimini* in such poems as Keats's "Isabella," Shelley's *Epipsychidion*, and the first canto of Byron's *Don Juan*. Hunt taught a generation of poets how to raid the Italian cultural archive in order to remake British poetry, how to use Italian classics to make Cockney poetry in the present.

Perhaps the most famous turn to Italy by Cockneys is the one to Boccaccio taken up by Keats and Reynolds, who planned to collaborate on a volume of versified tales from the *Decameron* as well as by Bryan Waller Proctor writing as Barry Cornwall who like Keats versified the fifth tale from the fourth day in his *Sicilian Story*, but we find a similar engagement with Dante. Through Henry Cary's famous translation of *The Divine Comedy* as *The Vision of Dante* among other adaptations from Gray to Henry Boyd (see Tinkler-Villani), Dante came to be widely read in England after Waterloo, as Ralph Pite has shown; and Diego Saglia explores in particular how second-generation romantics follow Hunt in taking up the Paolo and Francesca episode from the *Inferno*.[1] Cary, Foscolo, Coleridge, and Samuel Rogers all offered important commentary on Dante and *The Divine Comedy*.[2] To glimpse the romantics' wide engagement with Dante, we can think of Blake's illustrations to *The Divine Comedy*, of Coleridge's comments on Dante in *The Friend*, of Shelley's turn to *La Vita Nuova* in *Epipsychidion*, of Keats's use of Dante in "The Fall of Hyperion," or of Byron's evocation of Dante as the voice of national liberation in *The Prophecy of Dante*—or, for that matter, of a sonnet by one of the more notorious Cockneys, Cornelius Webb, where he praises Italy as the "Mother of Dante and Raffaelle" (Sonnet 25, l. 1). Webb would also call Byron "Our England's Dante" in the lines mockingly quoted at the opening of *Blackwood's* Cockney School attacks.

We could trace a similar presence for other Italian writers in "second generation" romantic texts. Having learned Italian as early as 1799, Hunt perused while in prison the fifty-six volumes of the *Parnaso Italiano*. Long an advocate for Italian poetry, he sparked his circle's engagement with Italian pastoral drama, particularly Guarini's *Il Pastor Fido* and Tasso's *Amyntas*, translated by Hunt in 1820 (see Cox 123–145). Tasso would interest Byron, who penned his *Lament of Tasso*, and Shelley, who contemplated a drama on Tasso's life and who used him as one prototype for the figure of the madman in *Julian and Maddalo*. Hunt also worked with Pulci, whose ottava rima would be imitated in very different ways by Shelley and Keats and whose *Morgante Maggiore* Byron would translate, calling it "the best thing I ever did in my life" (to Murray, September 28, 1820, *Byron's Letters and Journals* 7:182), "my grand performance" (to Murray, January 19, 1821, *Byron's Letters and Journals* 8:65). While we might reserve such praise for the Pulci-influenced ottava rima narratives of *Beppo* and *Don Juan*, which are one culmination of the circle's interest in things Italian, the group did devote a considerable amount of effort to translating Italian texts, again lead by Hunt who offered versions of some twenty-three Italian poets and who penned his late prose *Stories from the Italian Poets* (1845). Hunt's *A Jar of Honey from Mount Hybla* (1847) celebrating Sicily and pastoral poetry signals the group's engagement with that tradition. Another Italian prose collection beyond the *Decameron*, the *Florentine Observer*, gave rise to Percy Shelley's "Ginevra" and Hunt's "Florentine Lovers," published in the *Liberal*, and Mary Shelley considered recreating the collection in an abridged English version.[3] Italian history also attracted these writers, as we can see in Mary Shelley's *Valperga; or, the Life and Adventures of Castruccio, Prince of Lucca*, Percy Shelley's *The Cenci*, and Byron's *Marino Faliero* and *The Two Foscari*. One could continue to list poems set in Italy or in an Italianate milieu—*Childe Harold IV*, "Ode to Venice," "The Eve of St. Agnes," *Rosalind and Helen*, and *Lines Written Among the Euganean Hills*. As these links suggest, we need to see this body of work as a collective effort, a group project to recover Italian literature in the name of Cockney culture.

The Cockney project in Italy, like their attempt to create a "Cockney classicism,"[4] was not undertaken simply in the name of abstract literary taste or antiquarian interest but was instead a cultural act with a complex political valence. Italy (not unlike Greece) was constructed by contemporary English observers as possessing a glorious past and an oppressive present; it provided not only artistic inspiration but opportunities (perhaps seen best in the case of Byron's involvement with Teresa Guiccioli family's resistance to Austrian rule) for ideological investment. The central involvement of women writers with Italy— witness beyond Mary Shelley's work, Madame de Staël's *Corinne, or Italy*, Felicia Hemans's *Vespers of Palermo* or *The Recovery of the Works of Art in Italy* and Lady Morgan's *Italy*—suggests that Italy provided a ground from which to contest central cultural assumptions. The widely read Swiss *philosophe* Sismondi linked the late medieval rise of Italian letters to a rebirth of liberty in Italian city states (Butler 119), and, as Thomas Campbell noted in his *Life and Times of Petrarch: With Notice of Boccaccio and His Illustrious Contemporaries*, the supporters of Dante connected "the grand revival of his popularity in our own times to the reawakened spirit of liberty" (qtd in Pite 47). Italian culture could then offer a less controversial ally than that of France for the battle against the "Germanic," "northern" conservative culture that, as Marilyn Butler has argued (112–117), was seen as being embraced by poets such as Coleridge, Scott, and Wordsworth—the Lake School in general—over against the "cult of the South" whose devotees were the younger poets associated with the Cockney School and London radicalism. The turn to Italy is a defining characteristic of what we know as second-generation romanticism.

In the beginning, there was *The Story of Rimini*, which Byron praised in a letter to the imprisoned Hunt as having "2 excellent points... —originality—& Italianism" (to Hunt, October 30, 1815; *Byron's Letters and Journals* 4:326). The epistolary exchange between Byron and Hunt about the poem, recently investigated by Timothy Webb,[5] helps define the power of *The Story of Rimini*, as the two poets discuss their mutual investment in Italian culture. Hunt had cited Italian literature in the notes to his *Feast of Poets* as a source for revivifying "our fancy and versification" and for freeing English poetry from French models (*Selected Works* 5:54). Byron agreed that the Italians are "the *only* poetical *moderns*" (to Hunt, February 9, 1814; *Byron's Letters and Journals* 4:50), as the Italian past becomes a way to move forward in the present. Byron and Hunt were not alone in locating the birth of modern poetry in Dante and his contemporaries. Schelling, in "Über Dante in philosophischer Beziehung" (1803), called *The Divine Comedy* "the archetype of modern poetry" (qtd in Pite 22), and A. W. Schlegel placed Dante on the romantic side of his classic/romantic split. The path to originality, to modernity, lies through an embrace of this literary past that can free the poet from contemporary fashion into true creativity. What Hunt identifies in *The Feast of Poets* as the Italian as opposed to the French School would, when he wrote in *The Examiner* of December 1, 1816 his "Young Poets" review of Shelley, Keats, and Reynolds (with Byron's *Childe Harold III* getting passing praise), become the "new school" of romantic poetry. This school would, of course, be renamed by its enemies as the Cockney School. If Hunt's *The Examiner* is the school's political voice, *The Story of Rimini* was its founding poem, a turn to a foreign cultural past in order to make modern British literature.

Byron's second term of praise for *Rimini*—"Italianism"—is also an interesting one, for the "ism" suggests a self-conscious, distanced relationship to Italian literature itself. Of course, it could point to a kind of negative distance—an ignorance of the Italian language and a dependence upon existing translations for the project of adapting Italian literature. If the Cockneys are famously attacked for having little Latin and less Greek, their turn to Italian sources perhaps received even more extended contempt. In the first Cockney School essay, *Blackwood's* (2 [October 1817]:38) criticizes Hunt's knowledge of Italian literature as "confined to a few of the most popular of Petrarch's sonnets, and an imperfect acquaintance with Ariosto, through the medium of Mr. Hoole," the translator. Z. claims that Hunt is "always desirous of being airy, graceful, easy, courtly, and ITALIAN," but these attempts merely show that "He has gone into a strange delusion about himself" (2:40). The *Honeycomb* makes an even more pointed case against Cockney Italianism:

> What would our *great* poets of England have done without Italy! that rich store-house to which they resorted…and what would our little ones have done—what we may observe would have become of Mr. Leigh Hunt, Mr. John Keats, and Mr. Procter, if Dante, Tasso, and Ariosto, had never written, or been *translated into English*. It is surprising how much Harrington, Fanshaw, Fairfax, and Hoole have done towards facilitating a knowledge of the Tuscan tongue, and supplying our Cit poets with a *spirit of imitation*, and subjects ready cut and dry to their hand. (5 [July 15, 1820]:37–38)

The Cockneys are seen as seeking to acquire an unearned cultural authority; they are trying to translate (in the sense of to transfer) themselves across a cultural (and class) boundary through the use of translations rather than through a true knowledge of the language.

Using the same term as Byron, *Blackwood's* (16 [August 1824]:163), in praising Joanna Baillie, launches into one of its ritual attacks upon the Cockneys, branding them as descendants of the Della Cruscans: "the insect tribe of the *soi disant* della Cruscan school…endeavoured to moan and insinuate themselves into celebrity, by an absurd pretension to *Italianism*, which caricatured refinement, and surpassed Keats in folly, and Shelley in obscurity; and was not inferior to Leigh Hunt himself in vulgarity and affectation." "Italianism" is seen by *Blackwood's* as marked by a false refinement, an attempt to claim a cultural inheritance one does not possess since one is filled with vulgarity; by affectation, a self-consciousness about one's project that might lead to obscurity; and by folly—foolishness, even derangement, but also lewdness, wantonness.

We need to recover from behind such abuse the sense in which Byron could praise Hunt's Italianism. Cockney Italianism should be understood as a self-consciously distanced and ironizing approach to a foreign literature adopted in the hopes of achieving a certain cultural power, a power that arises from a simultaneous linguistic and erotic liberation that helps define the Cockney excursion into Italian as linguistically hybrid and sexually worldly. What *Blackwood's* labels the "vulgarity" of Hunt, the "affectation" and "arrogance" of Keats, the "obscurity" of Shelley are all markers of their resistance to a supposedly classless literacy, grounded in a knowledge of foreign languages, that would in fact leave social distinctions in place; they are signs of their struggle for a liberated language that can in turn image a liberated body.

Francis Jeffrey, in his review of *Rimini*, while also pointing to the "affectation" and "cant phrases" found in Hunt's poem (477), suggests how one might approach this issue differently, locating the "peculiar and original" (476) nature of Hunt's poetry in a turn to early English and Italian poetry that is grounded in a recognition of distance: where earlier poets "described things and actions as they saw them, without expressing...the deep-seated emotions from which the objects derived their interest.... The moderns, on the contrary, have brought these [emotions] most prominently forward, and explained and enlarged upon them perhaps at excessive length" (476). Jeffrey recognizes the impossibility of simply recreating the past, with the drive to do so prohibiting innovation in the present. Byron noted this distance himself in calling his *Prophecy of Dante* a "Harsh Runic copy of the South's sublime" ("Dedication," l. 5), and we find similar comments throughout Cockney poetry, as in Keats's famous apology to Boccaccio in "Isabella." Hunt makes the clearest statement on this self-conscious, ironic turn to a past literary moment in the "Florentine Lovers," by way of an explanation of why a writer, who seeks to revive "the good faith and simplicity in the old romances," must make ironic interjections:

> It is the fault of the "accursed critical spirit," which is the bane of these times, that we are obliged to be conscious of the matter at all. But we cannot help not having been born six hundred years ago, and are obliged to be base and *reviewatory* like the rest. To affect not to be conscious of the critical in these times, would itself be a departure from the natural. (*The Liberal*, 1 [1822]:70)

What has been ridiculed as awkward, affected, or contrived in *Rimini* or for that matter what has been seen as "mawkish" and "smokeable" in Keats's "Isabella" are in fact features natural to the critical, ironic,

self-conscious times in which we live—a point Friedrich Schlegel had
made in Germany. As "sentimental" poets, in Schiller's sense, Hunt
and his circle must remain aware of their distance from "naive" classics such as Boccaccio, but they must also realize that in this difference
lies their ability to approach the natural through a self-conscious or
critical idea or ideal, which as Schiller argues produces modern literature as satiric and elegiac—a good description of the mode of poems
such as "Isabella," with its satiric account of the world of capital and
its elegiac turns to romance, or *Rimini* with its sorrowful account of
entrapped lovers and its critique of patriarchal society (what Jeffrey in
his review sees as a blend of "the voluptuous pathos of Boccaccio with
Ariosto's laughing graces"; 477). Through this modern, reviewatory
turn to a "classic" text, the Cockney use of Italian literature enables
them to locate their literary innovations in a valued foreign precursor
and to discover behind Byron's "Runic copy," behind what Shelley
calls in *The Defence of Poetry* "the mask and mantle" (*Shelley's Poetry
and Prose* 526) of a past ideological moment embodied in the great
works of Italian literature, an argument for cultural and sexual liberation in the present.

Before turning to Hunt's *Story of Rimini*, we can see some of
the key tactics of this Cockney revision of Dante in Byron's and
Keats's engagement with the Paolo and Francesca episode, as Diego
Saglia's "Translation and Cultural Appropriation: Dante, Paolo and
Francesca in British Romanticism" has forcefully shown. Hunt called
this canto of the *Inferno* "the most cordial and refreshing" moment
in Dante's poem (*Selected Works* 165). Byron, who would translate
the passage in 1820, made a similar comment in disputing Schlegel's
claim that Dante demonstrates a "want...of gentle feelings. Of
Gentle feelings! and Francesca of Rimini—and the father's feelings
in Ugolino—...Why, there is gentleness in Dante beyond all gentleness, when he is tender" (*Byron's Letters and Journals* 8:39). Keats
would seem to have agreed. In writing to his brother and sister-in-law
about a sonnet he had recently completed, he explained

> The fifth canto of Dante pleases me more and more—it is that one in
> which he meets with Paulo and Francesca—...I dreamt of being in
> that region of Hell. The dream was one of the most delightful enjoy-
> ments I ever had in my life...o that I could dream it every night.
> (Keats, *Selected Poetry and Prose* 326–327)

Keats, publishing a sonnet based on the dream in Hunt's *Indicator*
(June 28, 1820; Keats, *Selected Poetry and Prose* 336), joins with

Byron and Hunt in seeing the Paolo and Francesca story as consoling. He unites with Hunt in finding an erotic excitement and liberation in Dante's story of unsanctioned sex as a sin subject to punishment. Comparing the "second circle of sad hell" (l. 9) to the Arcadian site of Tempe and Mount Ida, where Paris awarded Venus the prize as the most beautiful goddess, Keats reimagines hell as a kind of paradise. Where Dante's Francesca like other inhabitants of his Inferno compulsively tells her tale, in Keats's hell "lovers need not tell / Their sorrows" (ll. 11–12) but instead enjoy kisses; Byron suggests a similar reading of the episode when he wrote to Augusta, comparing their forbidden relationship to that of Paolo and Francesca, but noting that "Dante is more humane in his 'Hell' for he places his unfortunate loves…in company—and though they suffer—it is at least together" (May 17, 1819; *Byron's Letters and Journals* 6:129). The Dantean parable of admonition about the dangers of lust is converted into a romance of erotic consolation and wish fulfillment.

As Saglia points out, Keats also follows Hunt in interjecting himself into Dante's poem (Saglia, "Translation" 111), for if Hunt (most clearly in the introductory lines of Canto 3) interpolates his imprisoned subjectivity into his poem, Keats becomes in a sense both Dante and Paolo in his reworking of the passage, voyaging to hell like Dante and enjoying Francesca like Paolo. Saglia, following Frederick Beatty's "Byron and the Story of Francesca da Rimini," finds a similar autobiographical investment in Byron's translation, for Byron repeatedly used the Paolo and Francesca episode to comment upon his own situation, whether his incestuous love for Augusta or his love triangle with Teresa Guiccioli. Saglia sees Keats's sonnet as a "rich intersection of poetical reinvention, autobiographical projection and intertextual quotation" (111), as he shows how Keats draws upon his own experiences and how he interweaves key features of Cary's translation. This autobiographical turn and this reliance upon translated texts point, of course, to what Hunt called the "reviewatory" nature of modern creative work, to the "Italianism" of this work in both its positive and negative senses.

Another typically Cockney and Keatsian device used to move from Dante to a quite different vision is the merging of Italianate or medieval or "romantic" material with classical allusions. Keats sets up his sonnet with an elaborate simile involving the story—presumably taken from Ovid's *Metamorphoses*—of Jove's love for the nymph Io: Juno, jealous of her husband, has the hundred-eyed Argus guarding Io; Jove's winged messenger, Hermes, lulls Argus to sleep by playing upon his pipe. Keats argues that just as Hermes causes Argus to swoon and sleep, so does his own spirit play upon "a Delphic reed" (l. 3) in order to charm and conquer the "dragon world of all its hundred eyes" (l. 5) so that he can escape to visit Francesca in her edenic hell. This mingling and shift from classical to medieval/ early modern/ "romantic" material is also found, for example, in the opening of "Lamia" with its displacement of nymphs and satyrs by medieval fairies or in the movement in "Ode to Psyche" from classical materials to echoes of Milton and beyond. These moves work to historicize Keats's borrowings, to place them in a cultural schema in which prior cultural moments are always surpassed: the classical culture of Virgil or Ovid gives way to the Christian culture of Dante, and, by extension, Christianity will be superseded by the romantic culture embraced by Keats. The autobiographical presence noted by Saglia coupled with this historicizing frame enables Keats to follow what Hunt argues is the "natural" critical, ironic bent of modern poetry, creating enough distance from his great precursor so as to be able both to draw upon his cultural cache and to put his metaphysical ideology on its very bodily feet.

Byron, who contemplated a tragedy about Francesca and perhaps began translating (with Hobhouse) Silvio Pellico's play on the same subject, made clear, as Saglia argues, the potential political import of this Italian import. As Saglia puts it, "Byron and other liberal Romantic *literati* transformed Dante into a symbol of libertarian ideals and action against tyranny as well as an emblem of the patriotic poet and exiled voice of truth" (106). Byron undertook his translation at the request of Teresa Guiccioli and to correct Cary's translation. In the headnote he wrote for the poem, he argued, "I have sacrificed all ornament to fidelity" (*Complete Poetical Works* 4:280). Or as he put it in a letter to Murray, "Enclosed you will find *line for line* in *third rhyme* (*terza rime*) of which your British Blackguard reader as yet understands nothing—Fanny of Rimini" (March 20, 1820; *Byron's Letters and Journals* 7:58). The striving for accuracy and erudition combined with the slangy transformation of Francesca into "Fanny of Rimini" allies the noble poet with his Cockney colleagues. Even in seeking to translate the piece exactly, Byron seems to recognize that he can never recapture the immediate terror and tenderness of Dante, that there will always be the ironic distance of modern Italianism. Again, the distance allows an opening for an idea or an ideology, here Byron's portrayal of Dante as a force of liberation: he wanted the translation to be published with his *Prophecy of Dante* where the tale of Paolo and Francesca might, in conjunction with the evocation of

Dante as an opponent of tyranny in the longer piece, have been read, as it was by Hunt, as an assault upon patriarchal oppression.

As *Blackwood's* bitterly complained of *The Story of Rimini*, Hunt remakes Dante's episode of Paolo and Francesca's adulterous, incestuous desire into a luxurious narrative about the growth of an overpowering love. As the poem opens on an often admired description of "a morn of May" (1.1), a procession enters Ravenna, apparently bringing Francesca's intended, Giovanni, lord of Rimini, to wed her. As Francesca learns too late, the party from Rimini in fact brings the groom's brother who marries her as a fraternal proxy. Hoodwinked with desire's faery fancy and the ploys of her father and husband, she has already fallen for the man who will become her lover, famously while they are reading the tale of Guinevere and Lancelot—"That day they read no more" (3. 608). The first canto is given over to the procession and the springing of what Hunt calls "the elaborate snare" (2.49) in which Francesca is caught. The second canto, after a rushed wedding ("Quick were the marriage-rites"; 2.82) and a paltry public celebration, describes the trip to Rimini through a rather ominous landscape, while the third tracks the rise of the love between Paolo and Francesca. When in the autumnal fourth canto the love affair is discovered, the lovers are not murdered by a revengeful husband as in the sources; instead, the brothers fight a duel in which Paolo commits suicide by running upon his brother's sword. Francesca dies of heartbreak and the two lovers are buried "side by side, and hand in hand"—"and on fine nights in May / Young hearts betrothed used to go there to pray" (4.517–520). This ending—often criticized in the reviews (see Eberle-Sinatra 74–78)—is far from the tone and attitude of Dante's poem, where, whatever the appealing attributes of the lovers, a sin is a sin. In Hunt's poem, to the disgust of *Blackwood's* and other conservatives, love—even when it is adulterous and incestuous—conquers all.

This triumph of love arises within a particular context. When the opening procession arrives in Ravenna, we hear of "peace returning" (1.26) and, while the sound of horses and trumpets might suggest that "harnessed war were near," in fact Paolo's troops appear in the "garb of peace" (1.143–144). The text does not indicate what war has just concluded, though, as Hunt notes in his preface (166), the historical Paolo does appear in Tassoni's mock epic, *The Rape of the Bucket*, which parodies a war between Modena and Bologna.[6] While we might recall other scenes of warriors entering a city to pursue love after war such as those that open *Much Ado About Nothing* or Baillie's *Count Basil*, at the moment of the bulk of *Rimini*'s composition in

1814 and its completion and publication in 1816, returning peace must have evoked the recent end of the Napoleonic wars.

The official attempt to define that moment, particularly in 1814 but also again in 1815–1816, was marked by the kind of celebration adumbrated in Hunt's first canto. The festivities following Napoleon's abdication in the spring of 1814 were lavish, with new fêtes greeting each arriving dignitary. On April 20, 1814, for example, there was a triumphal procession for Louis XVIII from Hyde Park to Grillon's Hotel. Alexander I, King William of Prussia, Marshal Blucher, Prince Metternich, and Prince Leopold joined the Regent at Covent Garden on June 11, and the Corporation of London would offer a dinner to the visiting monarchs on June 18. Wellington made his triumphant entry into London on June 28 to be met by the Queen at her Buckingham House. One thousand seven hundred people (including Byron) attended a ball at Burlington House to pay tribute to Wellington on July 1, and another gala would be held at Carlton House on July 21 in his honor. July 7 would witness the Service of General Thanksgiving for the Allied Victory in St. Paul's; while some papers reported that the Regent was cheered all along the route to the Cathedral, Hunt's *The Examiner*, noting the number of troops in place to keep the crowd under control, claims that "the applauses bestowed were mixed with repeated hissings and groans" (July 10, 1814:446).

The government organized elaborate displays in London's parks that were opened to the public and to vendors who supplied them with beer, food, and a variety of goods. One could hear military bands, watch acrobats, and enjoy swings and merry-go-rounds, with the festivities thus "forming," as *The Examiner* put it, "a Vauxhall on the most magnificent scale" (July 24, 1814:475). These daily pleasures were the backdrop for more extravagant displays, including fireworks, admired by Charles Lamb, "rockets in clusters, in trees, and all shapes, spreading about like young stars in the making" (letter to Wordsworth, August 14, 1814; *Letters* 3:97). On the Serpentine in Hyde Park, the battle of Trafalgar was reenacted on June 20 with three-foot long ships maneuvering around the lake until the French fleet went up in flames as the national anthem played. The Battle of the Nile was fought again in St. James Park on August 1 for a joint celebration of its anniversary and the Hanoverian Centenary. Also on that day, in Green Park, James Sadler ascended over the crowd in a balloon from which he dropped favors and programs announcing other events. After dark, the crowds were delighted by a display in which the "Castle of Discord"—about one hundred feet in diameter and one hundred thirty feet high, with transparencies and paintings exhibiting "the devastations of war and the evils of Despotism & Tyranny"—disappeared behind a cloud as fireworks announced its transformation into a "Temple of Concord": the upper part of the temple then revolved to reveal the apotheosis of the Prince Regent and the "Triumph of England."[7]

This is exactly the kind of nationalist propaganda that Hunt echoed in order to reverse in his masque, *The Descent of Liberty*, finished in the midst of these celebrations while he was also at work on *Rimini*. Hunt, who in the preface to his *Foliage* volume called England this "war and money-injured land" (8), clearly allies himself with those reformers within Parliament such as Samuel Romilly and Lord Folkestone who were concerned about the militarization of British social life after the end of the war, with the Prince Regent, for example, opening Parliament in a field-marshal's uniform and with new institutions such as the Royal Military Asylum, the Royal Military College, and the Military Club being created to grace the peace.[8] Hunt wrote in *The Examiner* for May 22, 1814 that the visiting monarchs should not be greeted with military parades and feasts but instead with instances of great British art. In fact, he recommends the performance of a masque, much as he was writing, though Hunt suggests it be written by Wordsworth or Southey with sets designed by Turner (321–322). Hunt also argues that the Emperor Alexander, rather than spending time with the Regent with his "disreputable companions,...effeminate   accommodations,...and   insipidity," should instead travel to the Lake District to visit Wordsworth. In his own dramatic offering, Hunt stages the kind of glorious transformation scene offered in the parks of London, as he images Napoleon as the Enchanter floating on a dark cloud being defeated by an opposing cloud of Liberty, but he uses the spectacle to offer a different reading of the end of the war, As I have argued elsewhere, Hunt in his masque celebrates the victory, but not as a triumph for the Allied Monarchs, but rather for the peoples of Europe; his final "Vision of Real Glory" does not praise, say, the Prince Regent as did Nash's "Temple of Concord" display, but the yeomanry, artists, and lovers who will build a utopia of peace, art, and pleasure (Cox 130).

By the time *The Story of Rimini* was published in 1816, Napoleon had been defeated decisively at Waterloo on June 18, 1815. There were fewer public demonstrations at the time—the battle would not be commemorated with an official Thanksgiving until January 1816— and the country failed to build a Waterloo monument to match its remembrances of Trafalgar: Wellington would have to wait until 1822

for the Achilles statue dedicated to him by the women of Britain with
the Merchants and Bankers of the City of London presenting him
with the Waterloo Shield in that same year. It is not that the government was not concerned about controlling the public images of the
victory. For example the Licenser of Plays blocked the production of
what its anonymous author called "a mere trifle," *The Duke's Coat; or,
The Night After Waterloo*, a play based on a French precursor in which
an innkeeper mistakes an aide-de-camp wearing the Duke's coat for
Wellington himself. In his preface to the published version, the anonymous author speculates that "the Licenser may think the Battle of
Waterloo too grave and tragical a subject for an Interlude" (*Duke's
Coat* vi), a notion in keeping with the Licenser's tendency to ban all
contemporary history from the stage and with conservative concerns
about the nature of tragedy that we will see again in reactions to
Hunt's *Rimini*. While the theater, then, was not felt to be the place
to represent Waterloo, there were, of course, various commemorations
and celebrations. Wellington would host an annual Waterloo dinner,
eventually adding the Waterloo Gallery to Apsley House in order to
seat all his guests. More humbly, in Denby Dale, the second of its
famous gigantic pies—containing two sheep and twenty fowls—was
baked in honor of Waterloo (the first had been created for the recovery
of George III in 1788). There were private expressions of pleasure as
well: after the battle, Wordsworth and Southey danced around a bon-
fire on Skiddaw singing "God Save the King" and eating the standard
British roast beef and plum pudding (Bainbridge 153).

As the Lake Poets' delight might suggest, there was an outpouring
of writing, both poetic and not, on the battle. Hunt's poem is part
of a spate of post-Waterloo literature—we might note Southey's *Poet's
Pilgrimage to Waterloo* and Wordsworth's *Thanksgiving Ode*—that
sought to define the state of British society and culture after twenty
years of revolution and war. Hunt's engagement in *Rimini* with the
contemporary political scene was clearer in the original opening he
penned for the poem but did not publish:

> For not [merely] by contrast lov'd was Guido's heir
> Nor the mere dotage of a realm's despair,
> No pamper'd prodigal, unshamed in waste,
> Whose childishness remains when youth is past,
> No smirking ~~idler~~ ideot, trusting for its throne
> To custom and a worn out race alone,
> Nor aught that makes an old head shake to see
> The fond neglect of sinking royalty[.] (qtd. in Short 209)

Every bit as biting as Shelley's famous 1819 lines on the "old, mad, blind, despised and dying King" with his sons, the "dregs of their dull race" (ll. 1–2), Hunt's draft verses, surely alluding to the king (the "old head" shaking "to see / The fond neglect of sinking royalty") and the Regent ("whose childishness remains when youth is past"), would have opened a poem that, again like Shelley's sonnet, moves on to imagine a rebirth from a tomb; for if in Shelley's poem a "glorious Phantom may / Burst" from the "graves" created by government oppression to "illumine our tempestuous day" (ll. 13–14), so at the close of Hunt's poem the tombs of Paolo and Francesca become a site where lovers gather to celebrate an erotic liberation. While *Rimini* is not explicitly a poem about the end of the war, it does offer its own way of reading the postwar period, and it offers a new style of writing in order to imagine a world of peace.

Hunt plots out two attitudes toward life after war in contrasting the two brothers. Of the two, Giovanni, a model of "manly soldiership" (3:36), had a "countenance [that] was the martialler; and 'twas a soldier's truly" (3:31–32). Absent war, his greatest pleasures are engaging in the jousts and duels of "martial play" (l. 188) and reviewing his troops. Hunt connects Giovanni's outward violence to an inward-turned egotism, an "ill-tempered pride" (l. 68), a "self-love" (4:459); he does not recognize the needs of others, and while he "struck a meaner deference in the many," his nature "Left him, at last, unloveable with any" (ll. 96–97). Giovanni remains so marked by war and violence that he cannot accept the love open to him in a time of peace. It might help to remember that on the very day that peace was declared in November 1815, Austria, Britain, Prussia, and Russia created the Quadruple Alliance, suggesting there was something to be allied against, even in peace, that there was no time to turn to love when one had to maintain an ongoing war on the terror the Jacobins at home and abroad supposedly threatened. Giovanni would have understood the tactics of Castlereagh and Metternich.

Paolo, by contrast, was made for this time of peace: "Not that he saw," Hunt tells us, "beyond / His general age, and could not be as fond / Of wars and creeds as any of his race—/ But most he loved a happy human face" (ll. 107–110). His own face is "No soldier's, for its power was all of mind, / Too true for violence, and too refined" (3:44–45). Where Giovanni is self-enclosed and thus unable to enjoy the infinite variety of pleasures Francesca offers, Paolo finds himself increasingly drawn to her as someone who can open up a realm of peaceful delights, a realm of poetry and passion found in Francesca's pavilion, "Spared from the rage of war" (3:457).

Hunt dreams of a perfect—because mutual—love for Francesca: "To bless and to be blessed—to be heart-bare / To one who found his bettered likeness there" (3:207–208). Celebrating female sexuality, Hunt creates Francesca as a free sexual agent. Described as looking on Paolo with "an eye / Of self-permission" (1:334), Francesca has—in one of the phrases people love to ridicule—"stout notions on the marrying score" (2:28), which Hunt later amended for clarity to "She had a sense of marriage, just and free." She is capable of true companionate marriage, a marriage of true minds and of "double...delight" (3:211). However, she finds herself in a world where such delight is denied through the institution of marriage, here "The holy cheat, the virtue-binding sin" (3:17). While she struggles to meet the demands of her father and husband, "hard it is, she thinks, to have no will" (1.115). As in Byron's *Manfred*—another post-Waterloo take on incestuous desire—love exists only beyond the laws and mores designed to regulate sexuality. While Hunt follows his source in seeing the love of Paolo and Francesca as doomed, he makes it clear that much of the fault lies with a culture that values masculine violence over what is seen as a feminizing pleasure and that seeks to control that pleasure, and particularly feminine sexuality, through a series of oppressive regimes. The world may condemn the lovers, but Hunt proclaims, "Who that feels one godlike spark within, / Shall say that earthly suffering cancels not frail sin!" (4:401–402).

Blackwood's was convinced that Hunt wrote the poem to defend incest, aiming in *Rimini* "a deadly wound...at the dearest confidences of domestic bliss" (2 [October 1817]:40). In the "Letter from Z.," Hunt's adversary vows to defend marriage against men like Hunt who "versify vice into virtue" (3 [May 1818]:199). *Blackwood's* hinted in its attacks that Hunt was perhaps working from his own personal situation, and commentators have continued to find echoes of the complex intimacy between Hunt, his wife Marianne, and her sister, Elizabeth Kent. I think that Z. was not far wrong in his estimation of Hunt's rewriting of Dante, though I find his motivation more ideological than personal. Hunt believes that Dante was of the devil's party without knowing it, that behind the labeling of Paolo and Francesca's love as sin one can recover the erotic as a site of resistance to a society dedicated to repression and violence. Hunt, like Shelley and others in their group, was trying to imagine a sexuality freed from the rules and roles of convention. Roe speaks of the free love ideal Hunt shared with Shelley (195), and Kucich argues that Hunt and his circle created "an important model of progressive gender relations."[9] Hunt, as he himself later put it, wrote against the "depreciators of this world"

in order to celebrate "ourselves as what we really are—creatures made
to enjoy more than to know, to know infinitely nevertheless in proportion as we enjoy kindly" (*Foliage* 15–16). He argues that social
bonds, community, are created through a proper appreciation of sexuality, "all the sentiment and social tenderness which a right sense of
the sexual intercourse is calculated to produce" (28). Hunt joins in
this with Shelley who in *Epipsychidion* argues for the power of erotic
love, which in its infinite mobility and proliferation of desire "differs
from gold and clay" (l. 160), or Byron who in *Don Juan* traces desire's
ability to evade the constraining tentacles of various forms of cant
or Keats who, according to his friend Benjamin Bailey, embraced in
Endymion "that abominable principle of *Shelley's*—that *Sensual Love*
is the principle of *things*."[10]

As Hunt repeatedly makes clear, this liberation of the erotic is
to be accomplished through a revisionary poetics. While Dante was
sometimes praised for the purity of his language (i.e., in Coleridge,
Biographia Literaria 2:30), Hunt may well have turned to Dante as
an early advocate of vernacular language in order to push colloquial
speech as far as he can, as Eberle-Sinatra notes: Hunt "goes further
than Dante in his advocacy of 'vernacular' language by using colloquial language in the *Story of Rimini*, as well as simple, feminine, and
urbane words" (68). Hunt hoped to introduce "a freer spirit of versification" and "a free and idiomatic cast of language" (*Selected Works*
167), that is, to open up the heroic couplet—the very heart of conservative poetics—and to deploy what John Strachan has identified
as a "vibrant use of what might be called reclaimed vulgarisms."[11]
The Italianate "new school" of Cockney poetics works to overturn
the "French" school embraced by conservatives such as Gifford and
Croker. *Blackwood's* and its allies understood that Hunt was drawing
upon an Italian classic in order to complicate any restrictive sense of
the English language, to underwrite the importation of other socio-
lects into a hybridized literacy. They thus attack Hunt for creating
an illiterate, "Cockney" dialect. We have already heard Z. call for
a Cockney glossary, and Croker complained, "In what vernacular
tongue, for instance, does Mr. Hunt find a lady's waist called *clipsome*" (*Quarterly Review* 14 [January 1816]:477). Such coinages
along with various Cockney rhymes—most infamously the lines
"The two divinest things this world has got, / A lovely woman in
a rural spot!" (3:257–258)—infuriated critics but are in fact what,
Strachan again, labels "the avant gardist exploitation of the contrast
between historical narrative and the real language of men" (xvii). A
pseudo-Italian poem, offered in *Blackwood's* (11 [March 1822]:363)

and ascribed to a mock-Foscolo ("a certain great Italian genius, who cuts a figure about the London routs—one Fudgiolo"), suggests that the hybridized texts that arise from Hunt's and Keats's investment in Italian literature result in a kind of mongrelized babble, neither Italian nor English:

> Signor Le Hunto, gloria di Cocagna
> Chi scrive il poema della Rimini
> Che tutta apparenza ha, per Gemini,
> D'esser cantato sopra la montagna
> Di bel Lugato, o nella campagna
> D'Amsted, o sulle marge Serpentimini
> Com'esta Don Giovanni d'Endymini
> Il gran poeta d'Ipecacuanha?
> Tu sei il Re del Cocknio Parnasso
> Ed egli il herede appanente,
> Tu sei un gran Giacasso ciertamente,
> Ed egli ciertamente gran Giacasso!
> Tu sei il Signor del Examinero
> Ed egli soave Signor del Glystero.

The Cockneys are seen—given the references to the emetic ipecacuanha and the enema "Glystero" (for glyster, for clyster)—as engaging in a kind of oral-anal dissolution of the literary into the fecal, of evocative writing into the voiding of the bowels. As the dialogists in *Blackwood's* put it in querying the rhyme between Hunt's journal as the "Examinero" and "Glystero," "Both vehicles of dirt, you know."

Hunt uses his border raid across national literatures to justify a shift across other registers, those within native language use as well as those of class distinction—seen most directly in his dedication of the poem to Byron, a move decried by *Blackwood's* as an attempt by a plebian to link himself to a lord. The turn to an Italian source is revealed as an attempt to gain cultural capital across linguistic lines when it has been denied across the divisions of rank. To take but one example of using an Italian text to give authority to Cockney practice, Hunt's later translation of Redi's *Bacchus in Tuscany* is filled with what would have struck contemporaries as Cockneyisms that turn out to be accurate translations of Redi's original. We seem to get a Cockney coinage when Hunt rhymes "muscular" with "majuscular"—this being the first time the latter word is used in English according to the OED—but we find that this is Redi's word "Majuscolo" and that Hunt supplies Redi's note explaining that the word is used to refer to capital letters (*Bacchus in Tuscany* 2, 69). We come upon an incredible word "goatibeardihornyfooted" and assume we have one of Hunt's infamous compoundings, but he in fact works from "Capribarbicornipede" and notes that the Italians are very proud of such compound words (*Bacchus in Tuscany* 32, 182). As the *Honeycomb* complained in a passage cited above, the Cockneys—or "Cit poets" as they call the Hunt circle—found in Italian literature linguistic material "cut and dry to their hands"; Italian imports justify a redistribution of English cultural capital.

Z. also objected to Hunt's generic moves. In his preface to the poem, Hunt says of the *Inferno* itself that "some call [it] a satire, and some an epic, and which I confess, has always appeared to me a kind of sublime nightmare" (*Selected Works* 165). Hunt later referred to the Paolo and Francesca episode as "a long tragedy in a half-a-dozen lines" (*Stories from the Italian Poets* 1:67), but he wrote a revisionary romance. As one might argue of Keats's "Hyperion" or Byron's *Don Juan*, Hunt's *Rimini* turns most obviously from the epic of war to a romance of love, and if the *Inferno* is, in Hunt's words, a satire "disposing both of friends and enemies" (*Selected Works* 165), then *Rimini*—taking up what Hunt calls "the most cordial and refreshing" episode of Dante's poem (165)—sympathizes with everyone, even the sinners. The poem's relation to tragedy was more controversial. As Z. points out in his attack on the poem, Hunt's subject—incest—had traditionally been thought of as a tragic subject, and Z. talks at length of Sophocles, Euripides, Ford, and more modern tragedians such as Alfieri and Schiller. For Z. following neoclassical notions of poetic justice, tragedy insures that incest will be punished, and he criticizes Hunt for avoiding tragedy, calling *Rimini* "the genteel comedy of incest" (2 [November 1818]:197).

For conservative critics, Hunt's poetic experiment is found wanting in relation to traditional tragedy, here for lacking moral seriousness. One key attack on Romantic writers has centered on their supposed inability to create tragedy, with this complaint particularly being wielded against Romanticism's radical wing, say, Shelley, who has been found to lack a tragic sense of life by denying the central reality of evil. In a sense, the sharp criticism that surrounded Hunt's poem— not to mention the suppression of that dramatic "trifle" *The Duke's Coat*—arises from a contention that writers of the Romantic period did not know how appropriately to deal with the tragedy of their time: the threat of revolutionary France, more broadly the massive violence that marked the Napoleonic wars. While I believe Romantic writers did remake dramatic tragedy in plays from *De Monfort* to *The Cenci*, I also believe that central works of Romanticism such as *Prometheus Unbound* and *Faust* join Hunt's *Rimini* in finding that tragedy's vision of closure and death is not the last judgment on man's condition, that there is a world of love and liberation to be won beyond tragedy (Cox 144–145). It is, of course, true that the years between 1789 and 1815 have a tragic cast defined by the massive violence that marked this era of worldwide war, as Mary Favret and others have recently reminded us.[12] Hunt, faced with serious historical matters that might well have found their way into tragedy, chose to write a romance, but he swerves from tragedy not to escape, to spiritualize, or to displace the painful political realities that faced him, but instead to insist that poetry, that Romantic culture, can preserve the hope for creating a world on the far side of tragedy. Recently released from prison into a world that was still not free, still attacking the government and dreaming of a better future, Hunt, in rewriting Dante, created in *Rimini* innovative, avant garde poetry that sought through the extravagance of its verse to image a world remade by love.

NOTES

1. See Pite's *The Circle of Our Vision: Dante's Presence in English Romantic Poetry*; and see Saglia's "Translation and Cultural Appropriation: Dante, Paolo and Francesca in British Romanticism."
2. See Braida's *Dante and the Romantics* (65–87).
3. See Weinberg's *Shelley's Italian Experience* 139; also *The Journals of Mary Shelley* 360–362; and *The Letters of Mary Wollstonecraft Shelley*: Letter to Hunt April 17, 1821 and letter to Charles Ollier January 16, 1827 [?] (189–97, 539).
4. See Roe's *Keats and the Culture of Dissent*, esp. pp. 51–87, and see Cox 146–186.
5. See Webb's two fine essays, "Leigh Hunt to Lord Byron: Eight Letters from Horsemonger Lane Gaol" and "Leigh Hunt's Letters to Byron from Horsemonger Lane Gaol: A Commentary."
6. See James Atkinson's 1825 translation of *La Secchia Rapita; or, The Rape of the Bucket*, where he notes Dante's account of Paolo and Hunt's expansion of that story (note to Fifth Canto, Stanza xliii).
7. The display was designed by John Nash with the transformation engineered by the munitions expert, Colonel Sir William Congreve. For an account of the display, see Farington's *The Farington Diary* (7:273–274).
8. See Halévy, *A History of the English People in the Nineteenth Century* 1:92.

9. See Kucich's "'The Wit in the Dungeon': Leigh Hunt and the Insolent Politics of Cockney Coteries," published in *Romanticism on the Net* http://www.erudit.org/revue/ron/1999/v/n14/005850ar.html. Accessed on March 22, 2011.
10. See Rollins, *The Keats Circle: Letters and Papers* (1:34–35).
11. See Hunt's *Selected Works* (xvii).
12. See Favret's *War at a Distance*.

Chapter Fourteen

"Syllables of the Sweet South": The Sound of Italian in the Romantic Period

Timothy Webb

Part One

For most people, the experience of traveling abroad, and particularly of engaging with foreign culture, resulted not so much in feelings of superiority as in confusion. Take, for example, the well-travelled William Coxe writing in a book published in 1789:

> I cannot describe how much I am perplexed with a variety of languages. I speak Italian or French with the principal gentry, and sometimes am obliged to hold a conversation in Latin. I talk a smattering of German with my servant, who understands no other language, and, with my guide and the common people, a kind of corrupt Italian, like the Milanese. I write my notes in English.... (from Coxe's *Travels in Switzerland*, qtd. in Brant 139)

This letter catches, more accurately than many accounts, the bewildering linguistic realities of travel in a period long before the influence of forces that were, at least partly, universalizing. Coxe's account draws to our attention the uncomfortable practicalities of making oneself understood in a world of linguistic uncertainty, the crucial connection between the divisions of class and of languages, and the day-to-day difficulties that these awkward conditions often produced. In spite of his linguistic facility, Coxe found himself "perplexed" rather than blessed or enriched by "a variety of languages" and feared that this might result, not in a dimension that was more European and more harmoniously inclusive, but in a "confusion of tongues," a troubling plurality with uncomfortable echoes of the Tower of Babel. As Byron's letters and *Don Juan* demonstrate, it was possible to recognize in such plurality a situation that was both stimulating and creative, but (like William Coxe) most travelers interpreted such confusion as a difficulty rather than a creative opportunity. In this respect, Coxe is representative. His linguistic perplexity is more extreme and more internalized than that of the inquisitive and perceptive Lady Morgan, for example, when she observes the phenomena she encounters on her journey through border country from France into Italy; but she, too, is suffering from a similar complaint to that of Coxe, when she records a "confusion of tongues" and notices that the postilion replies to the traveler's questions "in a jargon composed of bad French, Italian, and Piedmontese" (Morgan 1:23).

A different take on linguistic difficulty, with greater emphasis on listening to a foreign soundscape, was offered by Thomas De Quincey in *Confessions of an English Opium Eater* (1821). Unlike Coxe or Sydney Owenson, De Quincey was not faced by the challenges of traveling abroad, but his five-shilling visits to the opera house in London brought him into contact with a cultural dimension in which he could luxuriate and which reminded him (by way of another traveler's reminiscence) of the powerful and suggestive attractions of ignorance:

> And over and above the music of the stage and the orchestra, I had all around me, in the intervals of the performance, the music of the Italian language talked by Italian women: for the gallery was usually crowded with Italians: and I listened with a pleasure such as that with which Weld the traveller lay and listened, in Canada, to the sweet laughter of Indian women; for the less you understand of a language, the more sensible you are to the melody or harshness of its sounds: for such a purpose, therefore, it was an advantage to me that I was a poor Italian scholar, reading it but little, and not speaking it at all, nor understanding a tenth part of what I heard spoken. (De Quincey 79)

In our turn, De Quincey's suggestive memory reminds us how, for many an English witness, Italian was a language primarily associated with musical performance and how their first consciousness of Italian was inextricably linked to origins specifically musical. Even beyond its immediately musical context, the passage also claims (like many another) that, as a language, Italian is inherently musical (a claim also made by Charles Burney, the adventurous historian of European music and Leigh Hunt, one of the first exponents of opera criticism). For De Quincey, an evening at the opera seems to have been an exercise in multiple musicality, since it included not only the primary experience of the operatic music itself, as expressed by the singers and the orchestra, but also the language of the libretto that was normally Italian, and the "music of the Italian language" spoken by the audience during the interval. The delightful musicality of the occasion was, therefore, happily overdetermined and linked to its Italianness (or "Italianità," as Italians themselves might have said).

De Quincey's response obviously feminizes the language of the opera house by associating it with "the music of the Italian language talked by Italian women" and, later, with Isaac Weld's response to "the sweet laughter of Indian women." In fact, Weld had made a helpfully explicit connection himself, since he had reported that American Indian women "speak with the utmost ease, and the language, as pronounced by them, appears as soft as the Italian" (notice the defining adjective "soft," which occurs frequently in accounts of the Italian language or its dialects) (De Quincey 220). De Quincey, like Weld but with rather a different justification, derives a knowledgeable pleasure from not knowing Italian.

Strikingly enough, it was precisely this ignorance that had once caused such trouble in audiences at the Italian Opera, though a sensible system of practical compromises had gradually evolved. One history offers the following account:

> From the time of Addison critics scoffed at the notion of an entertainment in a language the audience could not understand. They had a point, though the problem was alleviated in various ways. A small minority of the audience knew some Italian, and others probably picked it up.

> Dual-language librettos and a lighted auditorium allowed one to follow along. The conventions of gesture...were designed to assist in understanding both emotion and action. Many librettos were used over and over. The fact remains that subscribers might easily attend half (and some might attend all) of the company's performances, seeing five or ten or fifteen performances of a work they understood no more than hazily, if that. (Price, Milhous, and Hume 1:9)

De Quincey had something in common with these audiences and these subscribers; but his ignorance was willed and included the audience as well as the action on the stage and, as he tells his readers, constituted one of the regular pleasures of opium. Such meaning-ful passivity is entirely characteristic of the English Opium–eater: his negative capability enables him to enjoy the phenomena of the occasion, even the seemingly mundane, with a heightened consciousness and no irritable reaching after fact and reason.

Though De Quincey's experience seems to have been entirely positive, the significance of not knowing the language one hears or encounters can work in a variety of ways and serve many different purposes, not all of them positive. In many cases, unintelligibility can be troubling or isolating rather than delightful. In 1770 Charles Burney was regularly puzzled by the range of Italian dialect, which often proved too much for his flimsy linguistic confidence. For example, he records at Padua: "The people here speak so Venetian, that I can scarce understand a word they say." Or again, he confides to his traveling notes his own incapacity to make sense of what he hears: "Through all the Genoese State, the language the people speak is a jargon wholly unintelligible" (Burney, *Eighteenth-Century* 1:98, 308). Such ignorance can easily have the effect of making the traveler feel excluded or threatened—see, for example, Coleridge on the subversive uses of Erse and the uncomfortable sense that a language not understood can be used to undermine the "innocent" traveler, who cannot interpret what he hears; or see the stories of linguistic impotence narrated by Mary Shelley and Byron (which feature in the next section).[1]

On the other hand, as De Quincey seems to have realized, ignorance can sometimes liberate the imagination and encourage the creation of powerful and happily creative fantasies, which may not always accord with the reality. Consider, for instance, the presentation of the process at work in the Venetian memories of Edmund Malville that feature in Mary Shelley's dialogic story "Recollections of Italy" (published in January 1824). In the face of the skeptical responses of his interlocutor, Malville recreates the world of Venice in evocative detail. One of his memories, which "combined to raise and nourish romantic feeling," concerns the Erse song of the gondoliers on his nightly return from the opera: "The dark canal, shaded by the black houses, the melancholy splash of the oar; the call, or rather chaunt made by the boatmen, 'CaStalì!' (the words themselves delightfully unintelligible)" (Shelley, *Collected Tales* 26). Here the unintelligibility is a climactic contribution to the charm. Or consider Dorothy and William Wordsworth listening to half-articulate Gaelic "hootings" in the Scottish highlands (Dorothy Wordsworth, *Recollections* 114), or William Wordsworth interpreting the song of a solitary reaper (suggestive to a traveler who did not speak Gaelic and its dialects), or Keats asking John Hamilton Reynolds to read him some passages from Homer because of the pleasurable "mistiness" of Greek to his own uninstructed hearing (Keats, *Letters* 1:274).[2] Sometimes the benefits of such not knowing, whether calculated or inevitable, may outweigh a reality that is limited (or unglamorously delimited) by a knowledge of the language.

PART TWO

On May 13, 1818 Mary Shelley wrote from Livorno to Leigh and Marianne Hunt, who had spent the last night in England with the Shelleys only a short time before and with whom they shared a strong preference for Italy. Her letter is full of news and gossip but at its center is a curious anecdote that is not so easily shared or dismissed.

> They told us that whenever you call at an Italian house the servant always puts her head out of window and demands *chi è* [who is it?] whatever time of day or night it may be—The proper answer to this question is *amici* [friends] but those people [who[do no[t] know the proper reply are terribly puzzled to know what to answer to this *chi è* which meets them at every corner—one of their friends visiting a house after having been kept a long time in the street while they were screaming *chi è* to him from the window and he was exhausting all answers to them but the right one—at length he made his way to the stairs which as they always are in Italy, were dark and as he was groping along the mistress of the house called out *chi è* and the poor man quite confounded not recognizing the voice—called out Brut[t]a bestia, andate al dia*volo* [nasty thing (literally), go to the devil]—and rushed out of the house. (Mary Shelley, *Letters* 1:67)

This anecdote is suggestively supplemented by a story told by Byron in a letter written from Albaro to James Wedderburn Webster on October 26, 1822, in which he apologizes for his failure to make contact:

> I called at three precisely, and asked *thrice* for the Cavalier Webster, in much *better Italian* than is spoken at *Genoa* [of which Albaro is a suburb]; but the *name* seemed incomprehensible, tho' not ye. title. The answer was—Do you mean the "nobile Inglese" who came here two days ago? I replied—I mean the Gentleman who called on me yesterday. "He is gone out and returns at 5—to Dinner" was the reply. I left no card, as it was not impossible that they w'd have left it with a

Stranger. It is provoking enough that you should have been detained by their stupidity, for such it was as Count Gamba, who was with me heard my inquiries, but repeated the *name* himself—as well as an Italian can repeat a name with four consonants in it. (*Byron's Letters and Journals* 10:18–19)

With characteristic facility, Byron enjoys both the joke at the expense of the amiable Pietro Gamba (brother to Teresa Guiccioli) and the fact that Italian does not recognize the letter "w," awkward in the circumstances since (even ignoring the teasing possibilities of "Wedderburn") the name "Webster" begins with a "w" and itself includes four teasing consonants. His own relations with the absurd Wedderburn Webster (a name which was ludicrously problematic to Italian speakers) ensured that he would have been maliciously amused by such a situation. And yet, as the parallels between his story and that of Mary Shelley improbably indicate, both narratives may convey more than their authors originally intended about their own attitudes to Italian culture and to the Italian language.

Some initial qualifications are in order. Neither anecdote adequately expresses the mastery of the Italian language ultimately achieved by its author. Mary Shelley became more confident in her own language skills, partly because as the mother of small children she was often in direct contact with Italians; on December 3, 1820 she wrote to Hunt a letter in Italian while only a few months later she transmitted to him a lengthy document, also in Italian. Her letters, particularly those to Maria Gisborne and to Jane Williams both of whom shared her Italian background, frequently make use of Italian words and phrases (Mary Shelley, *Letters* 1:162–164, 190–193, 132). For his part, Byron had been familiar with Italian texts before he left England, but his stay in Venice and his closeness to Margarita Cogni, and later to Teresa Guiccioli, ensured an intimate exposure to oral Italian that informed his considerable correspondence in that language and richly supplemented his more literary encounters with its writers. In a sense, both anecdotes are traveler's tales (though Byron's is ostensibly an excuse), and take advantage of the comical possibilities of cross-purposes and cultural misunderstandings. And yet perhaps they also give expression to a feeling of anxiety at least partly fuelled by an inevitable sense of cultural difference and an awkward consciousness either of linguistic incompetence or of the ultimate uselessness of words to the uninitiated. In both stories, even native speakers of the language are unable to crack the mysterious code. Something there is, it seems, which is resistant to any obvious oral communication. In both cases, the house remains at the heart of the problem, dark, mysterious, impenetrable, bafflingly secret, indifferent to linguistic approaches. The self-confident Byron was "a decent Italian," as he declares in an earlier anecdote in which he is forced to rely on his servant for an explanation of a local idiom (*Byron's Letters and Journals* 8:35), and (by his own account) spoke much better Italian than is usual in Genoa; as he declares in one letter, he even hoped in the fullness of time to write poetry in Italian and anticipated that one day he would meet his daughter and converse with her through the shared medium of Italian (*Byron's Letters and Journals* 6:105, 8:210). Yet even he was forced to recognize that, in spite of his apparent fluency and his genuine linguistic ambitions, he was inevitably excluded and could never be totally familiarized or, in the truest sense, an Italian insider. Like Mary Shelley, Byron eventually discovered that an "apparent" knowledge of the language was sometimes less than adequate, especially when one was faced with the challenge of making oneself understood in a world that was inscrutably foreign.

PART THREE

For visitors to Italy a first encounter with the sound of the Italian language often conveyed a special significance. Sometimes the language had been studied through books, less frequently by means of oral instruction, but to hear Italian spoken by Italians in Italy was a totally different experience and carried a primal charge. The difference is elucidated in some detail by Charles Burney, who visited Italy in 1770, attracted by a professional curiosity about its musical practices and institutions. On July 19 in Milan he recorded the embarrassing reality: "Here I cannot help observing that 20 years study and reading at home are of less use as to speaking a foreign language than 2 months practice abroad, among the natives." Burney was so painfully conscious of his linguistic limitations that he refused an invitation to attend a conversazione: "But to confess the truth, I had had such little experience in speaking Italian, that I found my powers of conversation in that language were insufficient to qualify me for such an honour. So I went a book hunting" (Burney, *Eighteenth-Century* 1:71, 80).

Other travelers had similarly upsetting linguistic experiences. Coleridge, for instance, occupied much of his time on the voyage to Malta in "fagging" Italian; but his first experiences of Sicily brought to his attention the disconcerting difference between the neatly abstract formulations of the grammar and the challenging realities of spoken

Italian: "Difficulty of learning Italian in Sicily—1. from the utter want of distinct Ideas & of Judgment which makes a muddy *stream* of sound, 2. bad It[alian]" (Coleridge, *Notebooks* 2:2179). On another occasion, he confided to his notebook a surprising comparison:

> The Italian a most harmonious at least melodious Language in the mouth of a sensible agreeably voiced Englishman, and the language of Love itself set to the sweet tones of an accomplished, *self-respecting*, and therefore of necessity *reflectionate*, English Lady / but in the mouths of the Italians themselves (at least 99 out of a hundred of all ranks, tho' of course more intensely in the lowest, and in the women worse than in the men) it is beyond all comparison the most ear-insulting chaos of shrill and guttural, up and down, sounds that I have ever heard, tho' familiar with the sounds of the corrupt Maltese Arabic, and the Platt-Deutsch of the Hartz. Rome is perhaps better than Naples, Florence & c, but bad is the best—In the mouths of women of the Middle and lower ranks there are really no *words,* but a fusion of sounds, the voice breaking off, *snapping* as it were, more often in the middle, or after the first Syllable of a word, than at the end of a word...it is all one rough ragged *Scab*-rough, ragged & uneven, yet still but *one.*—How indeed is it possible that persons so entirely unhabituated to reasoning, so wholly the creatures of habit and momentary passions & impulses should talk harmoniously?

Coleridge continued to explore possible reasons for such a paradox and then modulated into another paragraph that, although relatively short, is highly revealing both in its analysis of the sound-effects of Italian and in the intensity of its personal remembering:

> I have often heard a long sentence & without its being repeated found that I had understood it yet for some sounds I have been so ear-poniarded with the physical sound, that it was like seeing a fist that had just struck fire from your Eye—Not so with the French or German. (Coleridge, *Notebooks* 2:2812)

The complete and extraordinary notebook passage—analytical, emotional and, on occasions, inventively metaphorical—clearly takes its origin from a comparison between the Italian of the "right" kind of English ladies and gentlemen and that of the Italians themselves who, according to Coleridge, speak their own language less harmoniously than the harmonious English: while the English are "agreeably voiced" and produce "sweet tones," the Italians (whatever their social background) can only generate an "ear-insulting chaos." In both

cases, an indignantly patriotic Coleridge pays attention to voice production and to sound (or sounds): his analysis of Italian speech clearly
indicates that, with whatever prejudices, he has listened carefully to
the sound of the language. By using the phrase "in the mouth" or "In
the mouths" (which occurs three times in the course of this passage),
he emphasizes that what offends him most is the physical sounding
of the language itself. For Coleridge, as for Burney, but in a different
degree and with critical emphasis on the shortcomings of the Italians
rather than those of Coleridge himself, the reality of Italian speech
was a shock to his carefully organized preconceptions.

Linguistic challenges also faced other visitors to Italy, who had
some previous knowledge of the language. An instructive case is
that of Leigh Hunt, who had been a particularly keen observer of
Italian performers in the opera. Unlike De Quincey, he had listened
to Italian with knowledgeable attention, as is shown, for example, by
his detailed review of Mozart's *Don Giovanni*.[3] Hunt was exquisitely
alert to the characteristics of Italian speech production. His review of
a production of Thomas Arne's *Artaxerses* published in *The Examiner*
on April 16, 1820 provides a striking example of the discriminating
sensitivity of his ear to the sounds of Italian (which, at this point, he
had only encountered in England and mainly, or exclusively, on the
stage, though he was a close friend of the Novello family, which had
its roots in Piedmont):

> In Italy especially, where recitative had its origin..., the speech of the
> inhabitants of some districts is perhaps as nearly allied to recitative as
> to ordinary talking.... There are some Italian words the intonation of
> which are decidedly musical, or what is called *cantabile*. Such are most
> of the last syllables but one, and especially before a double consonant,
> where a very marked suspension takes place, as if the speaker were
> lingering over the beauty of it. When it closes a period, particularly at
> the end of a stanza, it has a great resemblance to the favourite cadence
> of recitative... [Hunt reports that a "celebrated living writer" regards
> recitative] as the fittest mode of expressing tender and lofty passions—
> the only sounds equal to a high sense of humanity.[4]

Charles Burney would have agreed in principle. He had also noticed
that the language of "the common people of Italy" was flavored by an
inherent musicality or, as he once put it, "The language of the Italians
is more favourable to music than that of any other people" (Burney,
Eighteenth-Century 2:78, 244). Burney's emphasis here is different
from that of Hunt but both observers registered an unusual quality
in the spoken language.

Hunt had translated from Italian when he was in England and was regarded as an authority on and a promoter of Italian culture, particularly of opera and literature; his enemies in *Blackwood's Edinburgh Magazine* had even suggested, with the wicked memorability of satire, that he modeled himself on Petrarch whose appearance, they maliciously claimed, he attempted to resemble. He had encouraged Keats and Shelley to read Boccaccio, had involved Byron in the composition of *The Story of Rimini*, and had used the *Parnaso Italiano* as well as his own Italianate poem to make his two-year imprisonment endurable. Yet, in spite of all this expertise, there was a notable deficiency. By his own admission, Hunt's spoken Italian when he first arrived in Italy was still literary rather than vernacular, and sometimes painfully out of date: "I amused her [Teresa Guiccioli] by speaking bad Italian out of Ariosto, and saying *speme* for *speranza*; in which she good-naturedly found something pleasant and *pellegrino* [foreign]; keeping all the while that pleasant countenance, for which a foreigner has so much reason to be grateful." As Hunt notices, Teresa Guiccioli herself had an observable Romagnese dialect, though "to me, at that time, all Italian in a lady's mouth was Tuscan pearl; and she trolled it over her lip, pure or not, with that sort of conscious grace, which seems to belong to the Italian language as a matter of right" (Hunt, *Lord Byron* 1:66–67).[5] Hunt does not say, though the phrase "at that time" clearly suggests, that this innocent early view was revised in the light of later experience; though his sentence seems to imply that with the painful passage of time he learnt to be less trusting in his admiration. Yet, whatever the lessons of experience, it might be argued in Hunt's defense that idealization of the female speaker also characterized a number of his contemporaries (e.g., it marks Coleridge's "reflectionate English ladies," who speak Italian so agreeably). In fact, such an obviously gendered aesthetic belongs recognizably to that period in the history of Italian travel, if not to all travelers.

Leigh Hunt finally sailed to Italy in the early summer of 1822. Unlike Lady Morgan, or the Shelleys, or Byron, he did not reach Italy by traveling through France or other countries where Italian had, at best, a marginal existence. He and his family traveled to Italy by sea and Hunt himself was self-consciously delighted by the apparent conclusion of a happy arrival at the "queen-like" city of Genoa: "The lucid Mediterranean sea washed against our vessel, like amber; a sky, blue indeed, was above our heads: inconveniences and dangers were left behind us; health, hope, and Italy, were before us." This account, which relies on many more telling details and a revealing array of metaphors, was printed in an essay in the second number of

The Liberal, which was published on January 1, 1823.[6] Though much of Hunt's account also appeared in later versions, certain details (such as the sentence about the "lucid Mediterranean") did not. Perhaps the most significant part of his description did not enter the record till 1828 when it appeared in *Lord Byron and his Contemporaries* (to be reprinted many years later as part of Hunt's account in both versions of his autobiography):

> [A]t two o'clock, the waters being as blue as the sky, and all hearts rejoicing, we entered our Italian harbour, and heard Italian words. Luckily for us, these first words were Tuscan. A pilot boat came out. Somebody asked a question, which we did not hear, and the captain replied to it. "VA BENE," said the pilot, in a fine open voice, and turned the head of the boat with a tranquil dignity. "Va bene," thought I, indeed. "All goes well" truly. The words are delicious and the omen good. My family have arrived so far in safety; we have but a little more voyage to make [to Leghorn], a few steps to measure back in this calm Mediterranean; the weather is glorious; Italy looks like what we expected; in a day or two we shall hear of our friends [the Shelleys]; health and peace are before us, pleasure to others and profit to ourselves [with the publication of what was yet to be named *The Liberal*]; and it is hard if we do not enjoy again, before long, the society of all our friends, both abroad and at home. In a day or two we received a letter from Shelley, saying that winds and waves he hoped, would never part us more.[7]

The description may seem innocent and "realistic": the pilot's "fine open voice" is precisely the kind of detail that might strike so observant a critic of opera. Yet research reveals that, even if the detail has a recognizable authenticity, the larger passage is a careful construction (or reconstruction). Hunt was right to think that "Va bene" was Tuscan (a Genoese would probably have said "Va ben"): the surprising formulation works precisely to underline the apparent and unproblematic easiness of Hunt's arrival. But one might query the translation itself since "All goes well" is more inclusive and more portentous than the Italian original, which probably signifies no more than "Fine" or "All right." It is impossible to say whether Hunt deliberately portrays his younger self as sadly guilty of an overinterpretation when he unfortunately reflects "The words are delicious and the omen good"; but, in the light of Shelley's tragic death scarcely three weeks later, the rest of the passage certainly underlines the ironical misappropriateness of the Italian. There is no reason to believe that such words were not spoken at the time; but it is suggestive that they did not enter the written record till 1828, by which stage Hunt had had more than enough time to appreciate to the full the dramatic ironies of his arrival at Genoa.

Yet another example is provided by the writer who was a close friend of Hunt and whose presence in Italy constituted one of the main attractions that drew Hunt to Genoa and Pisa. Percy Bysshe Shelley had first studied the language with a French émigré family in England but, according to a letter to Thomas Love Peacock, his reactions to a direct aural encounter consciously suggest the new beginning he so strongly desired: "With what delight did I hear the woman who conducted us to see the triumphal arch of Augustus at Susa speaking the clear & complete language of Italy, tho' half unintelligible to me, after that nasal & abbreviated cacophany of the French!" (Percy Shelley, *Letters* 2:4). [the misspelling of *cacophony* seems to be Shelley's, contriving to make the sound of French even narrower and less pleasing than the correct spelling]. As the Shelleys moved southward through France, Mary Shelley had already acknowledged a growing sense of liberation, when she recorded in a letter to the Hunts from Lyons that "The sun shines bright & it is a kind of Paradise to which we have arrived at through the valley of the shadow of death" (Mary Shelley, *Letters* 1:62); as she would put it many years later in *Rambles in Germany and Italy* (1844), when she attempted a more mature replication of her youthful experience: "We left the abrupt, gloomy, sublime north, and gently dropped down to truly Italian scenes."[8]

Percy Shelley's epiphany, like that of many others, interprets the sound of the language as part of a larger context. The Shelleys had reached the north of Italy by way of France, and Percy Shelley's delight in the phonic character of the "clear & complete" language was informed by a comparative instinct. For all her excitement at the view from her hotel window in Lyons, Mary Shelley also recognized the intimations of a transforming southern experience and shared her husband's preference for Italy: "Why to be born in such a town [as Douai] is like living out of the circle of human things—an ambitious individual of Douai would almost like Erostratus wish to burn down a fine building or two to let his fellow men know that there was such a place in the world" (Mary Shelley, *Letters* 1:62). Though Lyons had its own dark and secret history, it was "a pleasant city and very republican" but, as she told the Hunts, "In Italy we breathe a different air [from that in France] and every thing is pleasant around us" (Mary Shelley, *Letters*, 1:64). (Here, as so frequently, an Italian experience seems to induce a more relaxed kind of breathing, as if the climate itself were subject to influence.) Her letter of April 6, 1818 directed from Milan to the Hunts in England insists on that comparative element that marks her husband's letter to Peacock, also written in Milan; for instance, she claims that "Italy appears a far more civilized place than France" (Mary Shelley, *Letters*, 1:64). As the Shelleys would have known, French may have been the language of the rights of man (if not that of *The Rights of Man*) but it was still commonly associated with decorum and claustrophobic convention.

The comparison between French and Italian was made in more detail and with different emphasis by other travelers. In Ravenna in March 1821 Byron gave expression to his own views on this subject, which were complicated but clear: "Though I read & comprehend French with far more ease & pleasure than Italian—(which is a heavy language to read in *prose*) yet my foreign speech is Italian—and my way of life very little adapted to the eternal French vivaciousness—& gregarious loquacity" (*Byron's Letters and Journals* 8:91). Byron's preference for Italian (the harder and less obvious choice) is affected by factors that seem to absorb the character of the language in a larger identification of national characteristics. His connection of the French with "eternal...vivaciousness" and "gregarious loquacity" seems hard on a culture that produced Voltaire, Rousseau, and the *philosophes* but is characteristic of the generalizations that shaped his conduct and has much in common with the sweeping dismissals of Charles Burney, Germaine Staël, and the Shelleys. Yet another example is provided by Coleridge, who explored in elaborate detail on more than one occasion the comparative possibilities of language. Although he praised the superior "sweetness" of Italian, Coleridge also noted a delightful superficiality that was unique to French:

> French is at once the most perspicuous & the most pointed language, & therefore the very own language of conversation & colloquial writing, of light passion, and the social Vanity, which finds its main pleasure in pleasing, & attains its end by turns of phrase (that like the painted dust-plumes on the Butterflies wing, or the colours of a Bubble must not be examined by the grasp)....(Coleridge, *Notebooks* 2:2431 [February 4, 1805])

PART FOUR

Perhaps this chapter should have begun with definitions; yet, however the language may have been defined, the experience of speaking "Italian" or its local versions, and of engaging with the varieties of Italian speech undoubtedly played a significant part in the framing of definitions. For that reason, experience has been placed first, in all its baffling complexity, followed by attempts at definition that are culturally significant but necessarily partial (in more than one sense). Many visitors and travelers felt impelled to generalize (in the usual manner of visitors and travelers), but it seems best to concentrate here on two definitions that suggest some of the leading characteristics of Italian or "Italian" as perceived in the "Romantic" period, while clearly indicating that most "definitions" are controversial, far from scientific, and strongly inflected by personal concerns.

Both definitions are fictions within fictions written by sympathetic non-Italians. The first is made by Germaine Staël in her hugely influential *Corinne, ou l'Italie* (1807) that allocates its opening chapters to a description of aspects of contemporary Italy and its culture, and then devotes the whole of Book VII to a detailed account of Italian literature. Paradoxically but significantly, this description (like the whole novel) was written in French and delivered by Corinne herself, who embodies the spirit of Italy with which she identifies, but is half-English in origin and has even lived in Northumberland. In an important passage in this chapter, Corinne defines Italian literature (which she characterizes as "our") by way of contrast with English; this contrast exemplifies that difference between the north and the south that is the most enduring feature of Staël's controversial definition of Romanticism.

> Doubtless there is not in our poets this profound melancholy, this knowledge of the human heart which characterizes yours; but this kind of superiority belongs rather, does it not, to philosophical writers than to poets? The brilliant melody of Italian [La mélodie brillante de l'Italien] is more suitable to [the] lustre [l'éclat] of exterior objects than to meditation. Our language would be more appropriate for depicting furor [la fureur] than sadness, because reflected feelings require more metaphysical expressions, while the desire for vengeance animates the imagination and turns sorrow outward. Cesarotti[9] has made the best and the most elegant translation of Ossian which exists; but it seems, in reading it, that the words themselves have a festive air [un air de fête] which contrasts with the somber ideas which they recall.[10]

Corinne (or *Corinne*) goes further. Charles Burney had expressed the opinion that "the language is more musical than in any other country in Europe," contrasting it on another occasion with the unfavorable raw material of German (Burney, *Eighteenth-Century* 2:78; see also 2:244). Other travelers were in agreement with this verdict, though less precisely and with less technical authority. *Corinne* offers an equation, or a connection, which is subtly but significantly different when it (or its central figure) connects Italian with music and with nature: "One lets oneself be charmed by our sweet words...as by the murmur of waters and the variety of colors." Like De Quincey in the opera house, acknowledging "the music of the Italian language," this submission to the effects of charm abandons analytical intellect or irritable searching after fact and reason. Once again, there is a special pleasure in passive ignorance and in not knowing; Italian ministers to that special requirement. Why, queries Corinne (speaking also perhaps for Staël?), should one ask the nightingale the meaning of its song? One can only "understand" it by going along with the impression which it produces. Italian poetry can achieve a variety of effects: "The measure of the lines, the harmonious rhymes, these rapid endings...imitate sometimes the light steps of dance; sometimes more serious tones recall the noise of the storm or clatter of weapons." The emphasis here may seem to fall on the imitative potential of verse (including, one might observe, "the light steps of dance" which suggests that, within its repertoire, Italian verse may include the superficially pleasurable, not unlike French, according to Byron and Coleridge); but, more significantly, Corinne (or Staël) actually claims that, although Italian poetry and its gliding soundscape is beyond interpretation, it is "a marvel of the imagination" (une merveille de l'imagination) and produces a special kind of harmony that properly defies analysis.

A second "definition" is offered by a stanza 44 in Byron's *Beppo*, written when Byron was in Venice in latish 1817; the poem first appeared in print, in England, in 1818. The narrator, who bears some resemblance to Byron but who is also, recognizably, a literary persona, a "broken dandy on his travels," is calculating in traditional fashion the rival merits of Italy and England. To this equation, the language makes a significant contribution:

> I love the language, that soft bastard Latin,
>   Which melts like kisses from a female mouth,
> And sounds as if it should be writ on satin,
>   With syllables which breathe of the sweet South,
> And gentle liquids gliding all so pat in,
>   That not a single accent seems uncouth,
> Like our harsh northern whistling, grunting guttural,
> Which we're oblig'd to hiss, and spit, and sputter all.

Written in an Italian verse-form which was new to most English readers, the whole stanza is predicated on a contrast between the pleasing phonetic effects of Italian and the gruff languages of the north, such as English and German. It celebrates "the language," though traveling and experience must have suggested (as alert readers were perhaps expected to recognize) that such generalizations were dangerous, not least because the language varied greatly from locality to locality. The narrator's admired Italian has much in common with the "beautiful language" celebrated in the dedicatory essay to the fourth Canto of *Childe Harold's Pilgrimage* that also pays tribute to the "paese tutto poetico, che vanta la lingua la più nobile ed insieme la più dolce" (Byron, *Complete Poetical Works* 2:123). But, as Byron was well aware even when he wrote *Beppo*, "Italian" is not the same as Venetian. Venetian (or Veneziano) was, as Byron said, "soft & peculiar" or, as he told John Murray, "something like the Somersetshire version of English."[11] The emphasis on softness was part of a long interpretative tradition. For example, Metastasio had even defended the translations of Hoole by claiming that "the language itself is so soft and musical, that no other can furnish words equivalent in sweetness."

Charles Burney, who reported this, had listened attentively to the speech of the Venetians and observed: "The Venetians seem to try, in pronouncing good words, to make the language already soft, still more soft" (Burney, *Eighteenth-Century* 2:102, 1:103). Nearly forty years later though only about a year after the publication of Byron's poem, Mary Shelley reported to Leigh Hunt: "The Romans speak better Italian & have softer voices than their country men" (Mary Shelley, *Letters* 1:92), clearly suggesting that softness is not a universal quality of spoken Italian and shifting the centre of softness as far south as Rome. Hunt himself was sensitive to the dialectal manifestations of softness. Not long after he had arrived in Italy, he felt able to inform readers of *The Liberal* that, in spite of their reputation for speaking "pure Italian," "The Pisans in general...seem to have corrupted their pronunciation, and the Florentines too, if report is to be believed. They use a soft aspirate instead of the C, as if their language was not genteel and tender enough already."[12] And Isaac Weld's Indian women (as remembered by De Quincey) spoke a language that appeared "as soft as the Italian."

Yet, in spite of all these testaments, softness is a characteristic that does not feature in all versions of Italian, and it is highly controversial. Consequently, the narrator's claim is not the simple endorsement it may appear. According to the narrator, the language sounds "as if it should be writ on satin"; it provides an unbroken harmonious flow ("gentle liquids gliding"). In contrast to this easy progress, which is partly mimed by the gentle fluency of Byron's own verse, the stanza sets the heavily accented soundscape of the northern languages, whose awkward utterances are simulated by the difficult movements of the verse itself ("our harsh northern whistling, grunting guttural,/ Which we're oblig'd to hiss, and spit, and sputter all"). As so frequently, the separate identity of the text is difficult to distinguish from the facts of Byron's own life and opinions.[13] In his own person, Byron distanced himself in one letter from the inhuman "eructation of sound" that he claimed as a characteristic of German, while in another he admitted that his knowledge of German was limited and that he used the language mainly for purposes of swearing (to some extent, Byron may have been reflecting the confusing linguistic situation lamented by Coxe, though here, as elsewhere, he was taking calculated pleasure in the simplifications of stereotyping) (*Byron's Letters and Journals* 8:26). Italian, the narrator of *Beppo* argues, is attractive partly because it seems to be liberated from such uncomfortable linguistic constraints. If "not a single accent seems uncouth," the primary implication concerns the ways in which individuals speak Italian (and the ways in which it is received by a hearer); yet avoidance of effects which are too obviously "uncouth" may also be facilitated by the nature of the language, because, in Italian, accentuation is only minimally evident. According to this account: "the stanza concentrates on language as a combination of sounds rather than a system of signs or a conveyor of precise meanings" (Webb, "'Soft Bastard Latin'" 75). This version of "Italian" has much in common with that of Staël in its concentration on musicality and the pleasing sound-pattern of the language, and in its focus on sensually gratified reception at the expense of exact interpretation. Strangely enough, too, its emphasis on communication that transcends or avoids the restrictions of conventional "meaning" even comes close to Staël's controversial characterization of Italian.

These lines in *Beppo* are also based on an overt geographical contrast between the guttural speech of the north and the "syllables which breathe of the sweet South"; both polarities are underlined by Byron's use of characterizing alliteration, while the South's animating relaxation ("breathes"—compare Leigh Hunt's "breathing passion") is set against the grotesque activities of the northern verbs, with their ugly concentration of "s" and "t" sounds ("hiss, and spit, and sputter"). All of these contrasts are enforced by the structure of the verse and the fact that the final two lines, which clinch the presentation with their forced comic rhyme, are longer than the other lines in the stanza. Where Pope would have signaled the contrast through the force of antithesis, Byron employs the structure of ottava rima, which establishes a different kind of equation but allows him much the same kind of mimetic indulgences as his master. Here, too, the poem seems to be in accord with Staël and to offer that kind of contrast between north and south that was common to travelers and to which *Corinne* had accorded the most influential expression.

Yet, just as softness turns out to be a feature that is less than reliable, this attribution of the guttural to the unpleasing north, as opposed to the mellifluous south, can be contradicted by the facts of autopsy (or personal observation). Dante, who provided a pioneering account of Italian dialects in *De Vulgari Eloquentia*, noticed that the language could be either soft or harsh. He observed that there was a dialect which, because of "the softness of its words and pronunciation, seems so feminine that it causes a man, even when speaking like a man, to be believed to be a woman." There was also, another type of dialect that worked in the opposite way: this language was "so bristling and shaggy in its words and accents that, owing to its rough harshness, it not only distorts a woman's speech, but makes one doubt whether she is not a man" (Dante, *Translation of the Latin Works* 46–47). Dante may have established the importance of the subject; many later travelers continued to confirm his basic findings. For example, Tobias Smollett, who visited Italy in 1766, recorded examples of the "bristling and shaggy" that would have come as no surprise to Dante. His offended sourness justifies Laurence Sterne's nickname "Smelfungus" for Smollett, but this does not negate Smollett's accuracy of observation:

> You have often heard it said, that the purity of the Italian is to be found in the *lingua Toscana*, and *bocca Romana*. Certain it is, the pronunciation of the Tuscans is disagreeably guttural: the letters C and X they pronounce with an aspiration, which hurts the ear of an Englishman; and is, I think, rather rougher than that of the X, in Spanish. It sounds as if the speaker had lost his palate. I really imagined the first man I heard speak in Pisa, had met with that misfortune in the course of his amours. (Smollett 231)

Charles Burney, whose visit took place only four years later, also noticed this feature: "It is astonishing how gutturally the Florentines speak particularly words with a hard C or Q" (Burney, *Music* 108). In the next century, Coleridge characterized Italian (as we have seen) as "beyond all comparison the most ear-insulting chaos of shrill and guttural, up and down, sounds that I have ever heard." He described its effects with forceful disillusionment: "for some sounds I have been so ear-poniarded with the physical sound, that it was like seeing a fist that had just struck fire from your Eye." The awkward compound word "ear-poniarded" gives expression to Coleridge's search for the most appropriate word and strikingly embodies the uncomfortable physicality of his linguistic experience. Like Smollett and Burney before him, Coleridge also registered Florentine pronunciation with that mixture of shock and exasperation that often accompanies the loss of an ideal:

> After the being used to the sweet Roman Pronunciation, the Florentines appear to have lost the roof of the mouth & so to *substitute* the throat, that the person who speaks most distinctly, quite *gargles*/ and of those who speak least unpleasantly, the sounds to a foreigner's ear seem wandering about in the roofless Hollow of the mouth seeking in vain for a something necessary to make them words. (Coleridge, *Notebooks* 2:2862)

In contrast, *Beppo*'s Italian language is conspicuously feminized. This emphasis not only underlines the contrast between the "sweet South" and the north, but also makes its mark on suggestive descriptions such as "melt like kisses from a female mouth," where the seductive impact of Italian can hardly be separated from other factors that were part of Byron's own linguistic education. Much the same might be claimed for the celebration of liquids. As Tony Tanner puts it: "Everything is made to seem to contribute to the unashamed arousal and satisfaction of desire, including the language, indeed particularly the language, with its 'gentle liquids gliding all so pat in'— which could hardly be more frankly lubricious" (Tanner 53). What *Beppo* begins to provide here is an erotics of language, or perhaps an account of language inflected by a strikingly personal dimension. Through the narrator, Byron seems to be profiting from his own initiation into Italian; his "female mouth" makes an interesting contrast to Coleridge's "In the mouth," which punctuates an account of the language dictated by Coleridge's own concerns and is much less comfortable with its soundscape. Here, as elsewhere, sound is an essential part of a full cultural immersion; but here, too, the representation of sound is even more subjective, a product of psyche and informing context rather than of scientific observation or objective aural attention.

NOTES

1. See Coleridge on "The Facilities of Concealment Afforded by the Erse Language" in *Essays on His Times* 2:414.
2. In spite of its appearance of immediacy ("Behold her, single in the field...."), William Wordsworth's "The Solitary Reaper" was essentially inspired by a reading of the manuscript of Thomas Wilkinson's *Tour to the British Mountains.* See William Wordsworth, *The Poems.* Ed. John O. Hayden, 2 vols. (New Haven and London: Yale UP and Penguin Books, 1997), 1:659–660, 1013. Stanzas 3 and 4 are devoted to the problem of interpreting an unfamiliar language.
3. *The Examiner*, No. 501 (August 3, 1817), 489–490.
4. *The Examiner*, No. 642 (April 16, 1820), 251.
5. For "trolling," see Hunt's account of the Pisans, especially: "But they speak well out, trolling the words clearly over the tongue." For Italian linguistic tolerance, see Hunt's description of Pietro Gamba, to whom he had to apologize for "running on in my bad Italian," and his admiration for Luigi Gianetti of Pisa, to whom, during a walk from Florence to Maiano, he "must have uttered a thousand malapropisms, not one of which did he give me a sense of by a smile" (Hunt, *Lord Byron* 1:38–39).
6. "Letters from Abroad. Letter 2.—GENOA," *The Liberal*, 2nd ed., 2 vols. (1822), 1:269.
7. Hunt's *Autobiography* adds a further detail to the irony: "—Alas! for that saying." The time of arrival (14.00 on June 15) is confirmed by the essay in *The Liberal*, 1:270 (see preceding note). For Shelley's letter of June 19, 1822 to Hunt, see Percy Shelley, *Letters* 2: 437–439, esp. 438.
8. Mary Shelley, *Rambles in Germany and Italy* (1844), in *The Novels and Selected Works* 8:265.
9. Melchior Cesarotti (1730–1808) also translated the *Iliad* and the tragedies of Voltaire.
10. See Hogsett 128–129. Hogsett's versions are the source of this and subsequent translations, which have been tested against the original French.
11. For Byron on Venetian, see *Byron's Letters and Journals* 5:133, 138; for a detailed account of Byron and the Italian language (including Venetian), see Webb, " 'Soft Bastard Latin.' "
12. "Letters from Abroad. Letter 1.—PISA," *The Liberal*, 1 (October 15, 1822): 118–119.
13. This problem is discussed in Webb, " 'Soft Bastard Latin' " 75–79.

WORKS CITED

[Anonymous]. *The Duke's Coat; or, The Night After Waterloo.* London: J. Miller, 1815.

———. *Massinello; or, A Satyr against the Association and the Guild-Hall-Riot: Entered According to Order.* London: Printed for James Norris, 1683.

Alfieri, Vittorio. *Memoirs,* 1810. Trans. rev. E. R.Vincent. Oxford: Oxford UP, 1961.

———. *Opere I.* Int. Mario Fubini. Ed. Arnaldo di Benedetto. Vol. 50 / 1 of *La Letteratura Italiana.* Milano, Napoli: Riccardo Ricciardi, n.d.

Alighieri, Dante. *See* Dante.

Altick, Richard D. *The Shows of London.* Cambridge, MA: Harvard UP, 1978.

Archenholtz, Johann Wilhelm von. *A Picture of Italy.* Trans. Joseph Trapp. 2 vols. London: C. C. J. & J. Robinson, 1791.

Ariosto, Ludovico. *Orlando furioso e cinque canti.* Ed Remo Ceserani and Sergio Zetti. 2 vols. 1997. Turin: UTET, 2006.

———. *Satira. Opere minori.* Ed. Cesare Segre. Milan: Ricciardi, 1954. 497–579.

Armstrong, Isobel. *Victorian Poetry: Poetry, Poetics, and Politics.* London and New York: Routledge, 1993.

Atkinson, James. *La Secchia Rapita; or, The Rape of the Bucket.* 2 vols. London: J. M. Richardson, 1825.

Au, Susan. "The Shadow of Herself: Some Sources of Jules Perrot's Ondine." *Dance Chronicle,* 2.3 (1978): 159–171.

Auber, Daniel-François-Esprit. *La muette de Portici: opéra en cinq actes: représenté pour la première fois, sur le theâtre de l'Académie royale de musique, le 29 février 1828.* Libretto by Eugène Scribe and Germain Delavigne. Paris: Chez les éditeurs du Theâtre de M. Scribe, Bezou...Aimé André...et chez Roullet, libraire de l'Académie royale de musique, 1828.

Aytoun, William Edmonstoune, and Theodore Martin. *The Book of Ballads. Edited by Bon Gaultier.* New York: W. J. Widdleton, 1862.

Bainbridge, Simon. *Napoleon and British Romanticism.* Cambridge: Cambridge UP, 1995.

Balayé, Simone. "Corinne en Spectacle." *Littératures* 41 (1999): 97–109.

———. *Les Carnets de voyage de Madame de Staël: Contribution a la genèse de ses oevres.* Geneva: Droz, 1971.

Bandiera, Laura, and Diego Saglia, eds. *British Romanticism and Italian Literature: Translating, Reviewing, Rewriting*. New York: Rodopi, 2005.

Bataille, Georges. "The Psychological Structure of Fascism." *Visions of Excess: Selected Writings, 1927–1939*. Trans. Allan Stoekl et. al. Minneapolis: U of Minnesota P, 1985. 137–160.

Beattie, William, ed. *Life and Letters of Thomas Campbell*. 3 vols. London: Moxon, 1849.

Beatty, Frederick L. "Byron and the Story of Francesca da Rimini." *PMLA* 74 (1960): 395–401.

La Belle Assemblée; or, Bell's Court and Fashionable Magazine. London. Vol. 29 (January–June 1824).

Bindman, David, et al. *Dante Rediscovered: From Blake to Rodin* [Catalogue of an Exhibition]. Grasmere: Wordsworth Trust, 2007.

Bauman, Richard. *Verbal Art as Performance*. Rowley, MA: Newbury House Publishers, 1978.

Black, John. *The Life of Torquato Tasso; with an Historical and Critical Account of His Writings*. 2 vols. London, 1810.

Blessington, Marguerite Gardiner, Countess of. *Conversations of Lord Byron with the Countess of Blessington*. London: Routledge, 1834.

Blix, Göran. *From Paris to Pompeii: French Romanticism and the Cultural Politics of Archaeology*. Philadelphia: U of Pennsylvania P, 2009.

Bolter, Jay David, and Richard Grusin. *Remediation: Understanding New Media*. Cambridge, MA: MIT P, 1999.

Boyle, Nicholas. *Goethe: The Poet and the Age*. 2 vols. to date. Oxford: Clarendon, 1991.

Braida, Antonella. *Dante and the Romantics*. Basingstoke: Palgrave Macmillan, 2004.

Brand, C. P. *Italy and the English Romantics: The Italianate Fashion in Early Nineteenth-century England*. Cambridge: Cambridge UP, 1957.

———. *Ludovico Ariosto: A Preface to the 'Orlando Furioso'*. Edinburgh: Edinburgh UP, 1974.

———. *Torquato Tasso: A Study of the Poet and His Contribution to English Literature*. Cambridge: Cambridge UP, 1965.

Brant, Clare. "Climates of Gender." *Romantic Geographies: Discourses of Travel 1775–1844*. Manchester and New York: Manchester UP, 2000.

Brooke, Stopford, introduction to *Epipsychidion*, Shelley Society Facsimile. London: Reeves and Turner, 1887.

Brooks, Peter. *The Melodramatic Imagination: Balzac, Henry James, Melodrama, and the Mode of Excess*. New Haven: Yale UP, 1976.

Browning, Robert, and Elizabeth Barrett Browninig. *The Brownings's Correspondence*. Vols. 1–8 ed. Philip Kelley and Ronald Hudson; vols. 9–14 ed. Philip Kelley and Scott Lewis. Winfield, Kansas: Wedgestone P, 1984–1998.

Burckhardt, Jacob. *The Civilization of the Renaissance in Italy* (1860). Trans. S. G. C. Middlemore. London: Penguin, 1990.

———. *The Letters of Jacob Burckhardt.* Ed. Alexander Dru. Indianapolis: Liberty Fund, 2001.

———. *Reflections on History.* Trans. M. D. Hottinger. 1943. Rpt. Indianapolis: Liberty Fund, 1979.

Burney, Charles. *An Eighteenth-Century Musical Tour in Central Europe and the Netherlands.* Ed. Percy A. Scholes. 2 vols. London, New York, Toronto: Oxford UP, 1959.

———. *Music, Men, and Manners in France and Italy 1770.* Ed. H. Edmund Poole. London: Eulenberg Books, [1969] 1974.

Burwick, Frederick. "George Soane." *Faustus: From the German of Goethe, Translated by Samuel Taylor Coleridge.* Ed. Frederick Burwick and James McKusick. Oxford: Oxford UP, 2007. 139–144.

———. *Poetic Madness and the Romantic Imagination.* University Park, PA: Pennsylvania State UP, 1996.

———. *Romantic Drama: Acting and Reacting.* Cambridge: Cambridge UP, 2009.

Butler, Marilyn. *Romantics, Rebels, and Reactionaries.* Oxford: Oxford UP, 1982.

Butlin, Martin, and Evelyn Joll. *The Paintings of J.M.W. Turner.* Revised Edition. 2 vols. Published for The Paul Mellon Centre for Studies in British Art and The Tate Gallery. New Haven: Tale UP, 1984.

Byron, George Gordon, Lord. *Byron's Letters and Journals.* Ed. Leslie Marchand. 13 vols. London: Murray, 1973–1994.

———. *The Complete Poetical Works.* Ed. Jerome McGann and Barry Weller. 7 vols. Oxford: Clarendon, 1980–1993.

———. *The Complete Miscellaneous Prose.* Ed. Andrew Nicholson. Oxford: Clarendon, 1991.

———. *A Selection of Hebrew Melodies, Ancient and Modern, by Isaac Nathan and Lord Byron,* a facsimile edited and with an introduction and notes by Frederick Burwick and Paul Douglass. Tuscaloosa: U of Alabama P, 1988.

Cameron, Kenneth Neill, "The Planet-Tempest Passage in *Epipsychidion.*" *PMLA* 63 (1948): 950–972; incorporated into *Shelley: The Golden Years.* Cambridge, MA: Harvard UP, 1974. 275–288.

Cameron, Kenneth Neill, and Donald Reiman eds. *Shelley and His Circle 1773–1822.* 10 vols. to date Cambridge, MA: Harvard UP, 1960–.

Carafa de Colobrano, Michele. *Masaniello ou le Pêcheur napolitain.* Libretto by Charles François Jean Baptiste Moreau de Commagny and A. M. Lafortelle. Paris: Chez l'auteur, 1827.

Cary, Henry Francis. *The Vision of Dante: Cary's Translation of The Divine Comedy.* Ed. Edoardo Crisafulli. Market Harborough, England: Troubador, 2003.

Cavaliero, Roderick. *Italia Romantica: English Romantics and Italian Freedom.* London: I. B. Tauris, 2005.

Chambers, Iain. *Mediterranean Crossings: The Politics of an Interrupted Modernity.* Durham, NC: Duke UP, 2008.

Chaney, Edward. *The Evolution of the Grand Tour*. London: Routledge, 2000.

Cheeke, Stephen. *Byron and Place: History, Translation, Nostalgia*. Basingstoke: Palgrave, 2003.

Clarke, Charles Cowden. *Address to that Quarterly Reviewer who Touched upon Mr Leigh Hunt's Story of Rimini*. London: R. Jennings, 1816.

Coleridge, Samuel Taylor. *Biographia Literaria*. Ed. James Engell and W. Jackson Bate. 2 vols. Vol. 7 of *The Collected Works of Samuel Taylor Coleridge*. Princeton: Princeton UP, 1983.

———. *Collected Letters of Samuel Taylor Coleridge*. 6 vols. Ed. Earl Leslie Griggs. Oxford: Clarendon, 1956–1971.

———. *Essays on His Times in the Morning Post and the Courier*. 3 vols. Ed. David V. Erdman. Princeton and London: Princeton UP and Routledge & Kegan Paul, 1978.

———. *The Friend*. Ed. Barbara E. Rooke. Vol. 4 of *The Collected Works of Samuel Taylor Coleridge*. Princeton: Princeton UP, 1969.

———. *Lectures 1809–1819: On Literature*. Ed. R. A. Foakes. 2 vols. Princeton: Princeton UP, 1987.

———. *Lectures 1818–1819 on the History of Philosophy*. Ed. J.R. de J. Jackson. 2 vols. Princeton: Princeton UP, 2000.

———. *The Notebooks of Samuel Taylor Coleridge*. Ed. Kathleen Coburn. 5 vols. London: Routledge and Kegan Paul, 1962–2000.

———. *Poetical Works*. Ed. J. C. C. Mays. Vol. 16 of *The Collected Works of Samuel Taylor Coleridge*. Princeton: Princeton UP, 2001.

Cox, Jeffrey N. *Poetry and Politics in the Cockney School: Keats, Shelley, Hunt and their Circle*. Cambridge: Cambridge UP, 1998.

Crisafulli, Edoardo. "The Translator as Textual Critic and the Potential of Transparent Discourse." *Translator: Studies in Intercultural Communication* 5.1 (April 1999): 83–107.

Cronin, Richard. "Asleep in Italy: Byron and Shelley in 1819." *Keats-Shelley Review* 10 (April 1996): 151–180.

Curran, Stuart. "Figurando il Paradiso: Shelley e Dante." *Shelley e L'Italia*. Ed. Lilla Maria Crisafulli Jones. Napoli: Liguori, 1998, 43–53. Trans. "Figuration in Shelley and Dante."

———. "Figuration in Shelley and Dante." *Dante's Modern Afterlife: Reception and Response from Blake to Heaney*. Ed. Nick Havely. New York: St Martin's P, 1998. 49–59.

———. "Romanticism Displaced and Placeless." *European Romantic Review* 20 (2009), 637–650.

———. *Shelley's Annus Mirabilis: The Maturing of an Epic Vision*. San Marino, CA: The Huntington Library P, 1975.

Curry, Kenneth. "Uncollected Translations of Michael Angelo by Wordsworth and Southey." *Review of English Studies* 14 (1938):193–199.

Dante [Alighieri]. *Dante in English*. Ed. Eric Griffiths and Matthew Reynolds. London: Penguin, 2005.

———. *The Vision, or Hell, Purgatory, and Paradise of Dante Alighieri*. Trans. Henry Francis Cary. London: Oxford UP, 1916.

————. *Translation of the Latin Works of Dante Alighieri.* Trans. A. G. Ferrers Howell and Philip H. Wicksteed. London: Dent, 1929 [1904].

————. *Vita Nuova, Italian Text with Facing English Translation.* Trans. Dino S. Cervigni and Edward Vasta. Notre Dame, IN: U of Notre Dame, 1995.

DeJean, Joan. "Staël's Corinne: The Novel's Other Dilemma." *The Novel's Seductions: Staël's Corinne in Critical Inquiry.* Ed. Karyna Szmurlo. Lewisburg, PA: Bucknell UP, 1999. 117–126.

Deleuze, Gilles and Felix Guattari. *Kafka: Toward a Minor Literature* (1975). Trans. Dana Polan. Minneapolis: U of Minnesota P, 1986.

De Quincey, Thomas. *Confessions of an English Opium Eater.* Ed. Alethea Hayter. Harmondsworth: Penguin Books, 1971 [1821].

Douglass, Paul. "Lord Byron's Feminist Canon: Notes Toward Its Construction." *Romanticism on the Net* #43 (August 2006) http://www.erudit.org/revue/ron/2006/v/n43/013588ar.html

Draper, Anthony. "Cesare Beccaria's Influence on English Discussions of Punishment, 1764–1789." *History of European Ideas* 26 (2000): 177–199.

D'Urfey, Thomas. *The Famous History of the Rise and Fall of* Masaniello. London: Printed for John Nutt, 1700.

Eberle-Sinatra, Michael. *Leigh Hunt and the London Literary Scene: A Reception History of his Major Works, 1805–1828.* London: Routledge, 2005.

Edgecombe, Rodney Stenning. *Leigh Hunt and the Poetry of Fancy.* Madison: Fairleigh Dickinson UP, 1994.

Eliot, T. S. "Tradition and the Individual Talent." *Selected Essays.* 3rd ed. London: Faber, 1951. 13–22.

Ellison, Henry. *Stones from the Quarry; or, Moods of Mind.* London: Provost and Co., 1875. [Electronic.]

Emaljanow, Victor. *Romantic and Revolutionary Theatre, 1789–1860* Cambridge: Cambridge UP, 2003).

Esterhammer, Angela. "The Cosmopolitan *Improvvisatore*: Spontaneity and Performance in Romantic Poetics." *European Romantic Review* 16 (2005): 153–165.

————. "The Improvisatrice's Fame: Landon, Staël, and Female Performers in Italy." *British and European Romanticisms.* Ed. Christoph Bode and Sebastian Domsch. Trier: Wissenschaftlicher Verlag Trier, 2007. 227–237.

————. *The Romantic Performative: Language and Action in British and German Romanticism.* Stanford: Stanford UP, 2000.

————. *Romanticism and Improvisation, 1750–1850.* Cambridge: Cambridge UP, 2008.

The European Magazine, and London Review. London. Vols. 83 (January–June 1823) and 84 (July–December 1823).

Farington, James. *The Farington Diary.* Ed. James Greig. 8 vols. New York: George H. Doran, 1923–1928.

Farrell, Jerome. "The German Community in Nineteenth Century East London." *East London Record* 13 (1990): 2–8.

Fassmann, David. *Wilhelm Tell und Masaniello. Gesprächen in dem Reiche derer Todten.* Leipzig: Körner, 1732.

Favret, Mary. *War at a Distance: Romanticism and the Making of Modern Wartime.* Princeton: Princeton UP, 2009.

Fernow, Carl Ludwig. *Über die Improvisatoren. Römische Studien.* 2 vols. Zürich: Gessner, 1806. 2: 298–416.

Finden, William. *The Gallery of Byron Beauties; or, Portraits of the Principal Female Characters in Lord Byron's Poems, from Original Paintings by Eminent Artists.* London: W. Kent, n.d. [1836]. [Unpaginated.]

———, and William Brockedon. *Landscape and Portrait Illustrations to the Life of Lord Byron: with...information on the subjects of the engravings.* 3 vols. London: John Murray, 1833–1834. [Unpaginated.]

Finley, Gerald. *Angel in the Sun: Turner's Vision of History.* Montreal: McGill-Queen's UP, 1999.

———. "Turner, the Apocalypse and History: 'The Angel' and 'Undine'." *The Burlington Magazine* 121, no. 920 (November 1979): 685–696.

Fletcher, Eliza. *Autobiography of Mrs. Fletcher.* Edinburgh: Edmonston and Douglas, 1875.

Flinn, Michael Walter. *The European Demographic System, 1500–1820.* Baltimore: Johns Hopkins UP, 1981.

Foscolo, Ugo. Review of G. Baglioli's *Dante: With a New Italian Commentary* and of H. F. Cary's *The Vision of Dante. Edinburgh Review* 29 (February 1818).

Foucault, Michel. *The Archaeology of Knowledge and The Discourse on Language.* Trans. A. M. Sheridan-Smith. New York: Pantheon, 1972.

———. "Nietzsche, Genealogy, History." (1971). *Language, Counter-Memory, Practice.* Ed. Donald F. Bouchard. Trans. Sherry Simon and Donald F. Bouchard. Ithaca: Cornell UP, 1977. 139–164.

Frye, Northrop. *Anatomy of Criticism.* Princeton: Princeton UP, 1957.

Fuhrmann, Christina. "In Enemy Territory? Scribe and Grand Opera in London, 1829–1833." *Eugène Scribe und das europäische Musiktheater.* Ed. Sebastian Werr. Münster: Lit Verlag, 2007. 89–106.

Furst, Lillian R. *The Contours of European Romanticism.* Lincoln: U of Nebraska P, 1979.

Genest, John. *Some Account of the English Stage from the Restoration in 1660 to 1830.* 10 vols. Bath: Printed by H. E. Carrington, 1832.

Genette, Gérard. *Paratexts: Thresholds of Interpretation.* Trans. Jane E. Lewin. Cambridge: Cambridge UP, 1997.

Gibson, Mary. "Romanticism and Crime." *The Wordsworth Circle* 19 (Spring 1988): 82–83.

Godwin, William. *An Enquiry Concerning Political Justice.* London: Robinson, 1793.

———. *History of the Commonwealth From Its Commencement to the Restoration of Charles the Second.* 4 vols. London: Henry Colburn.1824–1828.

————. "Of History and Romance." *Things As They Are; or, The Adventures of Caleb Williams*. Ed. Maurice Hindle. London: Penguin, 1988. 359–1973.

Goethe, Johann Wolfgang. *Gedenkausgabe der Werke, Briefe und Gespräche*. Gen. ed. Ernst Beutler. 27 vols. Zürich: Artemis, 1948–1971.

Goldberger, Avriel H., ed. *Woman as Mediatrix: Essays on Nineteenth-Century European Women Writers*. New York: Greenwood, 1987.

Gombrich, Ernst. *In Search of Cultural History*. Oxford: Oxford UP, 1969.

Gonda, Caroline. "The Rise and Fall of the Improvisatore, 1753–1845." *Romanticism* 6 (2000): 195–210.

Gutwirth, Madelyn. *Madame de Staël, Novelist: The Emergence of the Artist as Woman*. Urbana: U of Illinois P, 1978.

————, Avriel Goldberger, and Karyna Szmurlo, eds. *Germaine de Staël: Crossing the Borders*. New Brunswick: Rutgers UP, 1991.

Halévy, Elie. *A History of the English People in the Nineteenth Century*. Trans. E. I. Watkin. 6 vols. New York: Barnes & Noble, 1961.

Halmi, Nicholas. "The Very Model of a Modern Epic Poem." *European Romantic Review* 21 (2010): 589–600.

Hazlitt, William. *Complete Works of William Hazlitt*. Ed. by P. P. Howe after the edition of A.R. Waller and Arnold Glover. 21 vols. London, Toronto: J. M. Dent and Sons, Ltd., [1930–1934].

————. *The Letters of William Hazlitt*. Ed. H. Moeland Sikes. New York: New York UP, 1978.

Hegel, G. W. F. *Aesthetics: Lectures on Fine Art*. (1823–1829). Trans. T.M. Knox. 2 vols. Oxford: Clarendon, 1975.

————. *Philosophy of Mind* (1830). Trans. William Wallace. Oxford: Clarendon, 1971.

————. *Philosophy of Nature* (1830). Trans. A.V. Miller. Oxford: Clarendon, 1970.

————. *Vorlesungen über die Ästhetik*. Vols. 13–15 of *Werke in zwanzig Bänden*. Ed. Eva Moldenhauer and Karl Markus Michel. Frankfurt a.M.: Suhrkamp, 1986.

Hemans, Felicia. "The Maremma." *The Edinburgh Magazine and Literary Miscellany* 7 (November 1820): 396.

————. "Scenes and Passages from Goethe." *Poems*. Edinburgh, 1849. 611–617.

————. *Selected Poems, Letters, Reception Materials*. Ed. Susan J. Wolfson. Princeton and Oxford: Princeton UP, 2000.

————. *Selected Poems, Prose, and Letters*. Ed. Gary Kelly. Peterborough, ON: Broadview, 2002.

————. *The Works of Mrs. Hemans; with a Memoir of her Life, by her Sister*. 7 vols. Edinburgh: William Blackwood; London: Thomas Cadell, 1839.

Hibberd, Sarah. "La Muette and Her Context." *The Cambridge Companion to Grand Opera*. Ed. David Charlton. Cambridge, New York: Cambridge UP, 2003. 152.

Hill, Alan G. "Wordsworth and the Two Faces of Machiavelli." *Review of English Studies* 31 (August 1980): 285–304.

Hill, Alan G. "The Triumph of Memory: Petrarch, Augustine, and Wordsworth's Ascent of Snowden." *Review of English Studies* 57 (2006): 247–258.

———. "Wordsworth and Italy." *Journal of Anglo-Italian Studies* 1 (1991): 115.

Hill-Miller, Katherine C. *"My Hideous Progeny": Mary Shelley, William Godwin, and the Father-Daughter Relationship.* Newark, NJ: U of Delaware P, 1995.

Hogsett, Charlotte. *The Literary Existence of Germaine de Staël.* Carbondale and Edwardsville: Southern Illinois UP, 1987.

Holt, Edgar. *The Making of Italy: 1815–1870.* New York: Murray Printing Company, 1971.

Hughes, D. J. "Kindling and Dwindling: The Poetic Process in Shelley." *Keats-Shelley Journal* 13 (1964): 13–28.

Hunt, Leigh. *Bacchus in Tuscany.* London: John and H. L. Hunt, 1825.

———. *Foliage; or, Poems Original and Translated.* London: C. and J. Ollier, 1818.

———. *Lord Byron and Some of his Contemporaries.* 2nd ed. 2 vols. London: Colburn, 1828.

———. *The Selected Works of Leigh Hunt.* Ed. Robert Morrison, Michael Eberle-Sinatra, et al. London: Pickering and Chatto, 2003.

———. *Stories from the Italian Poets, and Lives of the Writers.* 2 vols. London: Chapman and Hall, 1846.

Isabella, Maurizio. *Risorgimento in Exile: Italian Emigres and the Liberal International in the Post-Napoleonic Era.* Oxford: Oxford UP, 2009.

Isbell, John Claiborne. "Introduction." *Corinne.* Vii–xx.

Jeffrey, Francis. Review of *Rimini. Edinburgh Review* 26 [1816]:476–491.

Jewsbury, Maria Jane. "The History of a Nonchalant" and "Literary Sketches No. 1: Felicia Hemans." In Hemans, *Selected Poems.*

Johnston, Kenneth. *The Hidden Wordsworth: Poet, Lover, Rebel, Spy.* New York: W. W. Norton, 1998.

Jones, Emrys. *Welsh in London in the Seventeenth and Eighteenth Centuries.* Cardiff: U of Wales P, 2001.

Kadish, Doris Y. "Narrating the French Revolution: The Example of *Corinne.*" *Germaine de Staël: Crossing the Borders.* Ed. Madelyn Gutiwrth, Avriel Goldberger, and Karyna Szmurlo. New Brunswick: Rutgers UP, 1991. 113–121.

Keats, John. *The Letters of John Keats 1814–1821.* Ed. Hyder E. Rollins. 2 vols. Cambridge, MA: Harvard UP, 1958.

———. *Selected Poetry and Prose.* New York: W. W. Norton, 2008.

Keiser, Reinhard. *Masagniello furioso.* Libretto by Barthold Feind. [Hamburg 1706] Mainz: Schott, 1986.

Kenney, James. *Masaniello: A Grand Opera in Three Acts.* London: Edward Moxon, 1831.

Kershaw, Roger, and Mark Pearsall. *Immigrants and Aliens: A Guide to Sources on UK Immigration and Citizenship.* Kew, Richmond, Surrey: The National Archives, 2004.

Kucich, Greg. "'The Wit in the Dungeon': Leigh Hunt and the Insolent Politics of Cockney Coteries." *Romanticism on the Net* 14(1999): http://www.erudit.org/revue/ron/1999/v/n14/005850ar.html

Lamb, Charles. *The Letters of Charles and Mary Lamb*. Ed. E. W. Marrs, Jr. 3 vols. Ithaca: Cornell UP, 1975–1978.

Leighton, Angela. *Victorian Women Poets: Writing against the Heart*. New York, London: Harvester Wheatsheaf, 1992.

Lessenich, Rolf. "Italy as a Romantic Location in the Poetry of the Original Della Cruscan Poets." *Romantic Localities: Europe Writes Place*. Ed. Christoph Bode and Jacqueline Labbe. London: Pickering and Chatto, 2010.

Levius, Barham. *Masaniello; or, The Dumb Girl of Portici; a Grand Opera*. London: I. Willis, 1829.

Lewis, Linda M. *Germaine de Staël, George Sand, and the Victorian Woman Artist*. Columbia: U of Missouri P, 2003.

The Literary Gazette, and Journal of Belles Lettres, Arts, Sciences. London. No. 490 (10 June 1826).

Liu, Alan. *Wordsworth: The Sense of History*. Stanford, CA: Stanford UP, 1989.

Lobban, Robin. "Population Movements: Emigration." *Scottish Population History from the Seventeenth Century to the 1930s*. Ed. M. Flinn. Cambridge: Cambridge UP, 1977. 448–462.

Logie, Jacques. *1830 [Mille huit cent trente]: de la régionalisation à l'indépendance*. Paris: Duculot, 1980.

Lokke, Kari. "'Children of Liberty': Idealist Historiography in Staël, Shelley, and Sand." *PMLA* 118 (2003): 502–520.

The London Magazine. London. Vol. 10 (July–December 1824).

Lovejoy, A. O. "On the Discrimination of Romanticisms." *PMLA* 39 (1924): 229–253.

Lowenberg, Alfred. *Annals of the Opera, 1597–1940, compiled from the original sources*. 2nd ed. rev. and corr. Genève: Societas Bibliographica [1955].

Lupton, Julia Reinhard. *Afterlives of the Saints: Hagiography, Typology, and Renaissance Literature*. Stanford: Stanford UP, 1996.

Luzzi, Joseph. *Romantic Europe and the Ghost of Italy*. New Haven: Yale UP, 2008.

Matthews, G. M. "A Volcano's Voice in Shelley." In Percy Shelley, *Shelley: Selected Poems and Prose*. 550–568.

Midon, Francis. *The History of the Rise and Fall of Masaniello, the Fisherman of Naples: Containing An Exact and Impartial Relation of the Tumults and Popular Insurrections, That Happened in That Kingdom, (in the Year 1647) on Account of the Tax upon Fruits. Collected from Authentick Memoirs and Manuscripts*. London: Printed for C. Davis and T. Green, 1729; subsequent editions: London: Printed for C. Davis; and L. J. Davis, 1747; Oxford: Printed by R. Walker and W. Jackson, 1748; London: Printed for R. Manby, 1756; London: Printed by J. Browne, 1768; London: at H. Fenwick's Wholesale Book Warehouse, 1770.

Milner, Henry M. *Masaniello, the Fisherman of Naples. A Historical Drama in Three Acts; as Performed at the Royal Coburg Theatre.* London: John Lowndes, 1824.

———. *Masaniello; or, The Dumb Girl of Portici. A Musical Drama, in Three Acts* Printed from the acting copy, with remarks, biographical, and critical, by D—G. [=George Daniel]... as performed at the Theatres Royal, London. Embellished with a fine engraving, by Mr. Bonner, from a drawing taken in the theatre, by R. Cruikshank. London: Davidson, 1829.

Mitchell, Brian R. *British Historical Statistics.* Cambridge and New York: Cambridge UP, 1988.

Moers, Ellen. "Performing Heroinism: The Myth of *Corinne.*" *Literary Women: The Great Writers.* Garden City, NY: Doubleday, 1976.

Moody, Jane. *Illegitimate Theatre in London, 1770–1840.* Cambridge: Cambridge UP, 2000.

Morgan, Lady [Sidney Owenson]. *Italy.* 3 vols. Paris: Galignani, 1821.

Mortimer, Anthony. "Wordsworth as Translator from Italian." *From Wordsworth to Stevens: Essays in Honor of Robert Rehder.* Ed. Robert Rehder and Anthony Mortimer. Peter Lange: Bern, 2005. 71–81.

Morton, Timothy. "Nature and Culture." *The Cambridge Companion to Shelley.* Ed. Timothy Morton. Cambridge: Cambridge UP, 2006. 185–207.

Naginski, Isabelle. "Germaine de Staël among the Romantics." *The Novel's Seductions: Staël's Corinne in Critical Inquiry.* Ed. Karyna Szmurlo. Lewisburg, PA: Bucknell UP, 1999. 177–186.

The New Monthly Magazine and Literary Journal. London. Vols. 10–15 (1824–1825).

Nicoll, Allardyce. *Early Nineteenth Century Drama, 1800–1850.* Vol. 4 of *A History of English Drama, 1660–1900.* 2nd ed. Cambridge: Cambridge UP, 1955.

Nietzsche, Friedrich. *The Antichrist* (1888). *Twilight of the Idols, The Antichrist.* Trans. R.J. Hollingdale. Harmondsworth: Penguin, 1968. 113–187.

O'Neill, Michael. "'My Vision Quickening': Dante and Romantic Poetry." In David Bindman, Stephen Hebron and Michael O'Neill, *Dante Rediscovered: from Blake to Rodin.* Grasmere: The Wordsworth Trust, 2007.

Origo, Iris. *Leopardi: A Study in Solitude.* London: H. Hamilton, 1953.

Oxenberry, William. *Oxenberry's Drama Biography and Green Room Spy.* New series. London: George Virtue, 1827.

Panayi, Panikos. *German Immigrants in Britain during the Nineteenth Century, 1815–1914.* Oxford: Berg Publishers Ltd., 1995.

Piozzi, Hester Lynch. *Observations and Reflections Made in the Course of a Journey through France, Italy, and Germany.* Ed. Herbert Barrows. Ann Arbor: U of Michigan P, 1967.

Pite, Ralph. *The Circle of Our Vision: Dante's Presence in English Romantic Poetry* Oxford: Clarendon P, 1994.

Pizzamiglio, Gilberto. "Vittorio Alfieri." *A History of Italian Theatre*. Ed. Farrell and Puppa. Cambridge: Cambridge UP, 2006.

"Plagiarisms of Lord Byron Detected." *The Monthly Magazine, or, British Register* 52.357 (August 1821): 19–22, and 52.358 (September 1821): 105–109.

Price, Curtis, Judith Milhous, and Robert D. Hume. *Italian Opera in Late Eighteenth-Century London.* 2 vols. Oxford: Oxford UP, 1995–2001.

Pudbres, Anna. *Lord Byron, the Admirer and Imitator of Alfieri. Englische Studien* 33, 1903.

Quint, David. *Epic and Empire: Politics and Generic Form from Virgil to Milton.* Princeton: Princeton UP, 1993.

Rafferty, Terrence. Review of *The Cook, the Thief, the Wife and Her Lover*, Dir. Peter Greenaway. "The Film File." *The New Yorker* <www.newyorker.com>. Accessed July 2, 2010.

Rajan, Tilottama. "The Dis-Figuration of Enlightenment: War, Trauma, and the Historical Novel in Godwin's *Mandeville*." *Godwinian Moments: From Enlightenment to Romanticism.* Ed. Robert Maniquis and Victoria Myers. U of Toronto P, 2010.

Redfield, Marc. *The Politics of Aesthetics: Nationalism, Gender, Romanticism.* Stanford: Stanford UP, 2003.

Redford, Bruce. *Venice and the Grand Tour.* New Haven: Yale UP, 1996.

Rice, H. A. L. "Wordsworth in Easedale." *Ariel* 1.2 (1970): 31–38.

Robertson, Alexander Cuningham. Translator's Preface to *The Jerusalem Delivered of Torquato Tasso.* Edinburgh, 1853.

Robinson, Henry Crabb. *Diary, Reminiscences, and Correspondence of Henry Crabb Robinson, Barrister-at-Law, F.S.A.* Sel. and ed. by Thomas Sadler. 3 vols. London: Macmillan, 1869.

———. *Diary, Reminiscences and Correspondence of Henry Crabb Robinson.* Sel. and ed. by Thomas Sadler. 2 vols. New York: Hurd, and Houghton; Cambridge, MA: The Riverside P, 1877.

———. *Henry Crabb Robinson on Books and their Writers.* Ed. Edith J. Morley. 3 vols. London: J. M. Dent and Sons Limited, 1938.

———. *The Correspondence of Henry Crabb Robinson with the Wordsworth Circle (1808–1866).* Ed. Edith J. Morley. 2 vols. Oxford: At the Clarendon P, 1927.

Robinson, Jeffrey C. "Romantic Poetry: The Possibilities for Improvisation." *The Wordsworth Circle* 38 (2007): 94–100.

Roe, Nicholas. *Keats and the Culture of Dissent.* Oxford: Clarendon P, 1997.

Rollins, Hyder Edward, ed. *The Keats Circle: Letters and Papers.* 2 vols. Cambridge, MA: Harvard UP, 1948.

Rose, Jacqueline. *Why War?-Psychoanalysis, Politics, and the Return to Melanie Klein.* Oxford: Blackwell 1993. 16–18.

Rossetti, William Michael, trans. and ed. *Gabriele Rossetti: A Versified Autobiography.* London: Sands, 1901.

Rossington, Michael. "Theorizing a Republican Poetics: P. B. Shelley and Alfieri." *European Romantic Review* 20 (2009): 619–628.

Rousseau, Jean-Jacques. *Les Confessions. Œuvres complètes.* Ed. Bernard Gagnebin and Marcel Raymond. 5 vols. Paris: Gallimard, 1959–1995. 1:1–656.

Rudwick, Martin. *Bursting the Limits of Time: The Reconstruction of Geohistory in the Age of Revolution.* Chicago: U of Chicago P, 2006.

Ruskin, John. *Unto This Last and Other Writings.* Ed. Clive Wilmer. London: Penguin, 1997.

Saglia, Diego. "Ending the Romance: Women Poets and the Romantic Verse Tale." *Romantic Women Poets: Genre and Gender.* Ed. Lilla Maria Crisafulli and Cecilia Pietropoli. Amsterdam, New York: Rodopi (2007): 153–167.

———. "Translation and Cultural Appropriation: Dante, Paolo and Francesca in British Romanticism." *Quaderns. Revista de Traducció* 7 (2002): 95–119.

Schelling, Friedrich. *The Philosophy of Art* (1804–1805). Trans. Douglas W. Stott. Minneapolis: U of Minnesota P, 1989.

Schlegel, Friedrich. *Philosophical Fragments.* Trans. Peter Firchow. Minneapolis: U of Minnesota P, 1991.

Schor, Esther. " 'The 'arm South'." *The Cambridge History of English Romantic Literature.* Ed. James Chandler. Cambridge: Cambridge UP, 2009.

Schoina, Maria. *Romantic "Anglo-Italians": Configurations of Identity in Byron, the Shelleys, and the Pisan Circle.* Aldershot, UK: Ashgate, 2009.

Schulze, Earl. "The Dantean Quest of *Epipsychidion.*" *Studies in Romanticism* 21 (1983): 191–216.

Shackford, Martha Hale. "Wordsworth's Italy." *PMLA* 38.2 (1923): 236–252.

Shelley, Lady Jane. *Shelley and Mary.* 4 vols. Privately printed, 1882.

Shelley, Mary Wollstonecraft. *Collected Tales and Stories.* Ed. Charles E. Robinson. Baltimore and London: Johns Hopkins UP, 1976.

———. *The Journals of Mary Shelley.* Ed. Paula R. Feldman and Diana Scott-Kilvert. Oxford: Clarendon P, 1987.

———. *The Letters of Mary Wollstonecraft Shelley.* Ed. Betty T. Bennet, Vol. 1. Baltimore: Johns Hopkins UP, 1980.

———. *The Novels and Selected Works of Mary Shelley.* 8 vols. London: Pickering and Chatto, 1996.

———. *Valperga; or, The Life and Adventures of Castruccio, Prince of Lucca.* Ed. Tilottama Rajan. Peterborough, ON: Broadview P, 1998.

Shelley, Percy Bysshe. *Bodleian Shelley Manuscripts,* VI: *Shelley's Pisan Winter Notebook.* Ed. Carlene A. Adamson. New York: Garland, 1992.

———. *Complete Poems.* Baltimore: Johns Hopkins UP, 1999.

———. *Complete Works of Percy Bysshe Shelley.* 10 vols. Ed. Roger Ingpen and Walter E. Peck London: Ernest Benn; and New York: Charles Scribner, 1926–1930.

———. *Letters of Percy Bysshe Shelley.* Ed. Frederick L. Jones. 2 vols. Oxford: Clarendon P, 1964.

———. *Poetical Works.* Ed. Thomas Hutchinson and G. M Matthews. London and New York: Oxford UP, 1970 [1905].

———. *Poetry and Prose.* Ed. Donald H. Reiman and Neil Fraistat. New York: Norton, 2002.

———. *Shelley's Poetry and Prose.* Ed. Donald H. Reiman and Neil Fraistat. 2nd ed. New York: W. W. Norton, 2002.

———. *Shelley: Selected Poems and Prose.* Ed. G. M. Matthews. Oxford: Oxford UP, 1964.

Short, Clarice. "The composition of Hunt's *The Story of Rimini.*" *Keats-Shelley Journal* 21–22(1972): 207–218.

Simpson, Erik. *Literary Minstrelsy, 1770–1830: Minstrels and Improvisers in British, Irish, and American Literature.* Houndsmill, Basingstoke: Palgrave Macmillan, 2008.

———. " 'The Minstrels of Modern Italy': Improvisation Comes to Britain." *European Romantic Review* 14 (2003): 345–367.

Sismondi, J.C.L. Simonde de. *Histoire des Républiques Italiennes du Moyen Age* (1809–1818). 3rd ed. 12 vols. Paris: Furne et Ce, 1840.

Smith, A. W. "Irish Rebels and English Radicals 1798–1820." *Past & Present* 7.1(1955): 78–85.

Smith, Denis Mack. *The Making of Italy: 1796–1870.* New York: Walker, 1968.

———. *Mazzini.* New Haven: Yale UP, 1996.

Smith, Marian. "Three Hybrid Works at the Paris Opéra, circa 1830." *Dance Chronicle* 24.1 (2001): 7–53.

Smollett, Tobias. *Travels through France and Italy.* Ed. Frank Felsenstein. Oxford, New York, Toronto: Oxford UP, 1979.

Soane, George. *Masaniello, the Fisherman of Naples: an Historical Play, in Five Acts.* London: John Miller, 1825.

———. *Rob Roy, the Gregarach.* London: R. White, 1818.

Sourian, Eve. "Germaine de Stael and the Position of Women in France, England, and Germany." *Goldberger.* 31–38.

Sponza, Lucio. *Italian Immigrants in Nineteenth Century Britain: Reality and Images.* Leicester: Leicester UP, 1988.

Stabler, Jane. *Byron, Poetics and History.* Cambridge: Cambridge UP, 2002.

———. "Leigh Hunt's Aesthetics of Intimacy." *Leigh Hunt: Life, Poetics, Politics.* Ed. Nicholas Roe. London: Routledge, 2003. 95–117.

Staël, Madame Germaine de. *Corinne or Italy.* Intro. by George Saintsbury. 2 vols. London: Dent, 1894. Project Gutenberg Ebook.

———. *Corinne, or Italy.* Trans. Sylvia Raphael. Introduction by John Claiborne Isbell. Oxford: Oxford UP, 1998.

Starobinski, Jean. "Suicide et mélancolie chez Mme de Staël." *Madame de Staël et l'Europe: Colloque de Coppet (18–24 juillet 1966) organisé pour la célébration du deuxième centenaire de la naissance de Madame de Staël (1766–1966).* Paris: Klincksieck, 1970. 242–252.

Stuckey, Charles F. "Turner, Masaniello and the Angel." *Jahrbuch der Berliner Museen* 18 (1976): 155–175.

Sturrock, Jane. "Wordsworth's Italian Teacher." *Bulletin of the John Rylands University Library* 67 (1984–1985): 797–812.

Sullivan, Alvin, ed. *British Literary Magazines.* Vol 2: *The Romantic Age, 1789–1836.* Westport, CT: Greenwood P, 1983.

Sultana, David. *Samuel Taylor Coleridge in Malta and Italy.* New York: Barnes and Noble, 1969.

Sweet, Nanora. "History, Imperialism, and the Aesthetics of the Beautiful: Hemans and the Post-Napoleonic Moment." *At the Limits of Romanticism: Essays in Cultural, Feminist, and Materialist Criticism.* Ed. Mary A. Favret and Nicola J. Watson. Bloomington and Indianapolis: Indiana UP, 1994.

Szmurlo, Karyna, ed. *The Novel's Seductions: Staël's Corinne in Critical Inquiry.* Lewisburg, PA: Bucknell UP, 1999.

Taliani, Elisabetta. *L'emigrazione italiana in Inghilterra tra Letteratura e Politica, 1820–1860* [Italian Immigration in England between Literature and Politics, 1820–1860]. Università degli Studi di Pisa, 1998–1999.

Tanner, Tony. *Venice Desired.* Oxford and Cambridge, MA: Blackwell, 1992.

Tasso, Torquato. *Discorsi sul poema eroico. Prose.* Ed. Ettore Mazzali. Milan: Ricciardi, 1959. 487–729.

———. *Gerusalemme liberata. Opere.* 3rd ed. 1976. Turin: UTET, 1980. 1:95–653.

Taylor, Anya. "Romantic *Improvvisatori*: Coleridge, L. E. L., and the Difficulties of Loving." *Philological Quarterly* 79 (2002): 501–522.

Taylor, Diana. *The Archive and the Repertoire: Performing Cultural Memory in the Americas.* Durham: Duke UP, 2003.

Tenenbaum, Susan. "*Corinne*: Political Polemics and the Theory of the Novel." *The Novel's Seductions: Staël's Corinne in Critical Inquiry.* Ed. Karyna Szmurlo. Lewisburg, PA: Bucknell UP, 1999. 154–164.

Tinkler-Villani, V. *Visions of Dante in English Poetry: Translation of the Commedia from Jonathan Richardson to William Blake.* Costerus n.s. 72. Amsterdam: Rodopi, 1989.

Tomlinson, Charles. *Selected Poems 1951–1974.* Oxford: Oxford UP, 1978.

Vallois, Marie-Claire. "Voice as Fossil: Germaine de Staël's *Corrine, or Italy*: An Archeology of Feminine Discourse." *Germaine de Staël: Crossing the Borders.* Ed. Madelyn Gutwirth, Avriel Goldberger, and Karyna Szmurlo. New Brunswick: Rutgers UP, 1991. 127–138.

Vargo, Lisa. "Mary Shelley, *Corinne*, and 'the mantle of enthusiasm'." *European Romantic Review* 19 (2008): 171–177.

Vassallo, Peter. *Byron: The Italian Literary Influence.* London: Macmillan, 1984.

Villari, Rosario. *The Revolt of Naples.* Cambridge, UK; Cambridge, MA: Polity P, 1993.

Waldie, John. *The Journal of John Waldie: Theatre Commentaries 1798–1830.* Ed. Frederick Burwick. Los Angles: eScholarship Repository, California Digital Library, 2008. http://repositories.cdlib.org/uclalib/dsc/waldie/.

Wasserman, Earl R., *Shelley's: A Critical Reading.* Baltimore: Johns Hopkins UP, 1971.

Webb[e], Cornelius. *Sonnets: Amatory, Incidental, and Descriptive; with Other Poems.* London, 1820. [Electronic.]

Webb, Timothy. "Leigh Hunt to Lord Byron: Eight Letters from Horsemonger Lane Gaol." *Byron Journal* 36 (2008):131–142.

———. "Leigh Hunt's Letters to Byron from Horsemonger Lane Gaol: A Commentary." *Byron Journal* 37 (2009): 21–32.

———. "'Soft Bastard Latin.': Byron and the Attractions of Italian." *Journal of Anglo-Italian Studies* 10 (2009): 73–100.

———. "The Unascended Heaven: Negatives in *Prometheus Unbound.*" In Shelley, *Poetry and Prose* (2002) 694–711.

———. *The Violet in the Crucible: Shelley and Translation.* Oxford: Clarendon P, 1976.

Weinberg, Alan. M. *Shelley's Italian Experience.* New York: St. Martin's P, 1991.

Weintraub, Wictor. "The Problem of Improvisation in Romantic Literature." *Comparative Literature* 16 (1964): 119–137.

Weise, Christian. *Christian Weisens Zittauisches Theatrum Wie solches Anno M DC LXXXII. præsentiret worden: Bestehende in drey unterschiedenen Spielen. I. Von Jacobs doppelter Heyrath. 2. Von dem Neapolitanischen Rebellen Masaniello. 3. In einer Parodie eines neuen Peter Sqvenzes von lautern Absurdis Comicis.* Zittau: Hartmann, 1683.

Wilkie, Brian. "Byron and the Epic of Negation." *Romantic Poets and Epic Tradition.* Madison: U of Wisconsin P, 1965. 188–226.

Wolfson Susan. "'Domestic Affections' and 'the spear of Minerva': Felicia Hemans and the Dilemma of Gender." *Re-Visioning Romanticism: British Women Writers, 1776–1837.* Ed. Carol Shiner Wilson and Joel Haefner. Philadelphia: U of Pennsylvania P, 1994.

Wood, Gillen. "The Castrato's Tale." *The Wordsworth Circle* 38 (2008): 74–79.

———. "Crying Game: Operatic Strains in Wordsworth's *Lyrical Ballads.*" *English Literary History* 71 (Winter 2004): 969–1000.

———. *Romanticism and Music Culture in Britain, 1770–1840: Virtue and Virtuosity.* Cambridge: Cambridge UP, 2010.

Wordsworth, Christopher. *Memoirs of William Wordsworth, Poet-Laureate, D. C. L.* Ed. Henry Reed. 2 vols. Boston: Ticknor, Reed, and Fields, 1851.

Wordsworth, Dorothy. *Recollections of a Tour Made in Scotland, A.D. 1803.* New Haven and London: Yale UP, 1997.

Wordsworth, Jonathan. *William Wordsworth: The Borders of Vision.* Oxford: Clarendon P, 1982.

Wordsworth, William. *The Major Works*. Ed. with introduction and notes by Stephen Gill. Oxford: Oxford UP, 2000.

———. *Poems, in Two Volumes, and Other Poems, 1800–1807.* Ed. Jared Curtis. Ithaca, NY: Cornell UP, 1983.

———. *The Prose Works of William Wordsworth.* Ed. W. J. B. Owen and Jane Worthington Smyser. 3 vols. London: Oxford UP, 1974.

———. *The Prelude 1799, 1805, 1850.* Ed. Jonathan Wordsworth, M. H. Abrams, and Stephen Gill. New York: W. W. Norton & Company, 1979.

———. *Sonnet Series and Itinerary Poems, 1820–1845.* Ed. Geoffrey Jackson. Ithaca, NY: Cornell UP, 2004.

Wordsworth, William and Dorothy. *The Letters of William and Dorothy Wordsworth: The Early Years: 1787–1805.* Ed. Ernest de Selincourt. Revised by Chester L. Shaver. Vol. 1. Oxford: Oxford UP, 1967.

———. *The Letters of William and Dorothy Wordsworth: The Later Years, Part 1: 1821–1828.* Vol. 3, Part 1. Ed. Alan G. Hill from the first edition by Ernest de Selincourt. Oxford: Oxford UP, 1982.

———. *The Letters of William and Dorothy Wordsworth: The Later Years, Part III: 1835–1839.* Vol. 3, Part 3. Ed. Alan G. Hill from the first edition by Ernest de Selincourt. Oxford: Oxford UP, 1982.

Wrigley, Richard. "Infectious Enthusiasms: Influence, Contagion, and the Experience of Rome." *Transports: Travel, Pleasure and Imaginative Geography.* Ed. Chloe Chard and Helen Langdon. New Haven and London: Yale UP, 1996. 75–116.

———. "Pathological Topographies and Cultural Itineraries: Mapping 'Mal'aria.' in Eighteenth- and Nineteenth- Century Rome." *Pathologies of Travel.* Ed. Richard Wrigley and George Revill. Amsterdam and Atlanta: Rodopi, 2000. 203–228.

Wu, Duncan. *Wordsworth's Reading 1770–1799.* Cambridge: Cambridge UP, 1993.

———. *Wordsworth's Reading, 1800–1815.* Cambridge: Cambridge UP, 2007.

Wyatt, John. *Wordsworth's Poems of Travel, 1819–1842.* London: Palgrave Macmillan: 1999.

Wynn, Frances Williams. *Diaries of a Lady of Quality, from 1797 to 1844.* 2nd ed. Ed. A. Hayward. London, 1864. http://diariesofaladyofquality.blogspot.com/

Zuccato, Edoardo. *Coleridge in Italy.* New York: St. Martin's P, 1996.

———. *Petrarch in Romantic England.* Basingstoke and New York: Palgrave Macmillan, 2008.

CONTRIBUTORS

Frederick Burwick, Professor Emeritus at UCLA, has taught courses on Romantic drama and directed student performances of a dozen plays. Author and editor of twenty-six books and over a hundred articles, his research is dedicated to problems of perception, illusion, and delusion in literary representation and theatrical performance. His book, *Illusion and the Drama* (Penn State, 1991), analyzes affective theories of the drama from the Enlightenment through the Romantic period. His *Poetic Madness and the Romantic Imagination* (Penn State, 1996) won the Book of the Year Award of the International Conference on Romanticism. He has been named Distinguished Scholar by both the British Academy (1992) and the Keats-Shelley Association (1998). Recent publications include his electronic edition of *The Theatre Journal of John Waldie* (California Digital Library, 2008), *Romantic Drama: Acting and Reacting* (Cambridge UP, 2009), and *Playing to the Crowd: London Popular Theatre, 1780–1830* (Palgrave Macmillan, 2011).

Peter Cochran read English at Cambridge, where he was President of the Marlowe Society and Secretary of the Footlights, and sat at the feet of F. R. Leavis. He then acted professionally for nine years, his finest roles being Inspector Truscott in *Loot*, Ed in *Entertaining Mr. Sloane*, and Jonathan Brewster in *Arsenic and Old Lace*. While teaching English and Drama in Bishop's Stortford, he did a PhD at Glasgow, where he sat at the feet of Drummond Bone. His thesis was an edition of Byron's *The Vision of Judgement*. He is now an independent scholar living in Cambridge. He has lectured on Byron in many places worldwide, and is responsible for the editions of Byron's works and correspondence on the website of the International Byron Society. His books include *Byron and Bob, Byron and Hobby-O*, and *"Romanticism"—and Byron*.

Jeffrey N. Cox is Professor of English and Humanities and Associate Vice Chancellor for Faculty Affairs at the University of Colorado, Boulder. He is the author of *Poetry and Politics in the Cockney School:*

Shelley, Keats, Hunt, and Their Circle (Cambridge 1998), and the editor of *Seven Gothic Dramas 1789–1825* (Ohio UP 1992), *Slavery, Abolition, and Emancipation in the British Romantic Period* Volume 5: *The Drama* (Pickering & Chatto 1999), *Keats's Poetry and Prose* (Norton 2008), and (with Greg Kucich) *Collected Works of Leigh Hunt*, Vols. 1 and 2: *Periodical Essays 1805–1821* (Pickering & Chatto 2003), and (with Michael Gamer), *The Broadview Anthology of Romantic Drama* (2003), and (with Larry Reynolds) *New Historical Literary Study* (Princeton 1993).

Stuart Curran, Vartan Gregorian Emeritus Professor of English at the University of Pennsylvania, holds a Laurea Honoris Causa from the University of Bologna. He is President of the Keats-Shelley Association of America and author of several books, including *Annus Mirabilis: The Maturing of an Epic Vision* (Huntington Library, 1975), *Poetic Form and British Romanticism* (Oxford 1986), and editor of *The Cambridge Companion to British Romanticism* (1993).

Paul Douglass is Professor of English and American Literature at San Jose State University, where he also directs the Martha Heasley Cox Center for Steinbeck Studies and the Steinbeck Fellows Program in Creative Writing. He is author of *Lady Caroline Lamb: A Biography* (Palgrave Macmillan, 2004) and *The Whole Disgraceful Truth: Selected Letters of Lady Caroline Lamb* (Palgrave Macmillan, 2006), and the editor (with Leigh Wetherall Dickson) of *The Collected Works of Lady Caroline Lamb* (Pickering and Chatto, 2008). He is also an editor, with Frederick Burwick, of *The Crisis in Modernism* (Cambridge University Press, 1992) and *A Selection of Hebrew Melodies, Ancient and Modern, by Isaac Nathan and Lord Byron*, a facsimile edition (Alabama 1988). His essays and reviews have appeared in *Keats-Shelley Journal, European Romantic Review, The Byron Journal,* and *Newstead Abbey Byron Society Review.* In 2009 he was selected as San Jose State University's "President's Scholar," and in 2007 was named as one of the recipients of the Elma Dangerfield Award of the International Byron Society for publication of new and original work related to the life, works, and times Lord Byron.

Angela Esterhammer holds a Chair in English Literature at the University of Zürich. She works in the areas of English and German Romanticism; performativity, performance, and improvisation; and philosophy of language. Her publications include *Creating States: Studies in the Performative Language of John Milton and William Blake* (1994), *R. M. Rilke's Two Stories of Prague* (1994), *The*

Romantic Performative: Language and Action in British and German Romanticism (2000), *Romanticism and Improvisation, 1750–1850* (2008), and the edited volumes *Romantic Poetry* (2002) and *Spheres of Action: Speech and Performance in Romantic Culture* (2009). Recently published articles are on Romantic sincerity, Byron and cosmopolitanism, Coleridge's journalism, and the fiction of John Galt, and her current research examines interrelations among performative media, print culture, periodicals, and fiction during the early nineteenth century.

Marilyn Gaull is Research Professor at the Editorial Institute at Boston University. She has taught at William and Mary, Temple University, and New York University, and is the founding editor of *The Wordsworth Circle* as well as the editor of book series including *Nineteenth-Century Major Lives and Letters* (Palgrave). Her publications include *English Romanticism: The Human Context* (1988), editions such as the Longman edition of *Northanger Abbey* (2005), and articles, introductions, reviews, and public lectures in British and American literature, intellectual history, folklore and oral performance, and the history of science.

Bruce Graver is Professor of English at Providence College. He is the editor of Wordsworth's *Translations of Chaucer and Virgil* for the Cornell Wordsworth series, an electronic edition of *Lyrical Ballads* for Cambridge University Press, and essays in journals such as *European Romantic Review, Romanticism, Studies in Philology*, and *The Wordsworth Circle*. His recent publications include "Classical Inheritances," in *Romanticism: an Oxford Guide*, edited by Nicholas Roe, and "Romanticism and the Classical Tradition," in *Blackwell's Companion to the Classical Tradition*, edited by Craig Kallendorf. His book-in-progress is called "The Stereographic Picturesque." It will examine stereo photographs of British and American landscape scenery, especially scenes connected with the life and works of major Romantic writers.

Nicholas Halmi is University Lecturer in English Literature of the Romantic Period at the University of Oxford and Margaret Candfield Fellow of University College. He is author of *The Genealogy of the Romantic Symbol* (2007), coeditor of the Norton Critical Edition of *Coleridge's Poetry and Prose* (2003), and editor of the forthcoming Norton Critical Edition of *Wordsworth's Poetry and Prose*.

Diane Long Hoeveler is Professor of English at Marquette University, where she specializes in teaching courses on the Gothic,

British Romanticism, and women's literature. She is author of *Romantic Androgyny: The Women Within* (1990); *Gothic Feminism: The Professionalization of Gender from Charlotte Smith to the Brontës* (1998); and *Gothic Riffs: Secularizing the Uncanny in the European Imaginary, 1780–1820* (2010). In addition to publishing some sixty-five articles on a variety of literary topics, she coauthored with Lisa Jadwin a critical study of *Charlotte Bronte*, and edited the Houghton Mifflin volume of *Wuthering Heights*. Her ten coedited volumes of essays include *Approaches to Teaching Jane Eyre*; *Approaches to Teaching the Gothic* (both for the MLA); *Interrogating Orientalisms*; *Comparative Romanticisms*; *Romanticism and its other discourses*; *Romantic Drama*; *Romanticism and the Law* (both for *European Romantic Review*); *Women of Color*; *Women's Literary Creativity and the Female Body*; and the *Historical Dictionary of Feminism*. More recently, she has coedited a new Broadview edition of Edgar Allan Poe's *Narrative of Arthur Gordon Pym*. She served as President of the International Conference of Romanticism from 2001–2003, and is now coeditor of the *European Romantic Review*.

Michael O'Neill is a Professor of English at Durham University, UK. Recent books include *Wheel* (Arc, 2008), a collection of poems, and, as editor, *The Cambridge History of English Poetry* (2010). He is coeditor (with Madeleine Callaghan) of *Twentieth-Century British and Irish Poetry: Hardy to Mahon* (Wiley-Blackwell 2011). He is a contributing editor on the multivolume Johns Hopkins edition of Shelley's poetry (the third volume is due out in 2011) and coediting (with Timothy Webb) *The Prose of Percy Bysshe Shelley 1818–1822* for Oxford University Press.

Tilottama Rajan is Canada Research Chair and Distinguished University Professor at the University of Western Ontario. She is the author of four books, most recently *Romantic Narrative: Shelley, Hays, Godwin, Wollstonecraft* (Johns Hopkins, 2010) and *Deconstruction and the Remainders of Phenomenology: Sartre, Derrida. Foucault, Baudrillard* (Stanford, 1001). She has edited Mary Shelley's *Valperga* (Broadview, 1998) and coedited four other volumes, most recently *Idealism Without Absolutes: Philosophy and Romantic Culture* (SUNY, 2004). She is working on a book entitled *Entangled Knowledge: Encyclopedics from Romanticism to Deconstruction*.

Diego Saglia teaches English Literature at the University of Parma (Italy) and his research interests focus mainly on Romantic-period literature and culture, particularly their contacts and exchanges with other European traditions. He is the author of a study on the Spanish imaginary in British poetry of the Romantic period, *Poetic Castles in Spain: British Romanticism and Figurations of Iberia* (2000), has edited a special issue on "Romanticism and Cultural Geography" for the *European Journal of English Studies* (2002), and coedited *British Romanticism and Italian Literature: Translating, Reviewing, Rewriting* (with Laura Bandiera, 2005). His essays have appeared in *Textual Practice, Studies in Romanticism, The Keats-Shelley Journal, Romanticism, Nineteenth-Century Contexts, ELH, Studies in the Novel, Gothic Studies, SEL* and other international journals. He is currently completing the first critical edition of Robert Southey's *Roderick, the Last of the Goths* and working on a book-length study of the European dimension in British Romantic-period literature.

Timothy Webb is Senior Research Fellow and Emeritus Professor at Bristol University. He is the author of *Shelley: A Voice Not Understood* (1977), *English Romantic Hellenism: 1700–1824* (1982), and *The Violet in the Crucible: Shelley and Translation* (1976). He was editor of *Keats-Shelley Review* from 1998 to 1992 and a founding editor of *Romanticism*. Webb is the editor of *Shelley: Poems and Prose* (1995; originally published in 1977 in a shorter version as *Shelley: Selected Poems*). He has also edited *Yeats: Selected Poetry* (1991), and, with Alan Weinberg, *The Unfamiliar Shelley* (2008). He has served as an editor for The Bodleian Shelley Manuscripts series published by Garland, and has also published numerous articles and book chapters, mainly on Romantic or Irish topics. His fully annotated edition of Leigh Hunt's *Autobiography*, in two volumes, is scheduled for release by Oxford University Press in late 2011 or early 2012. He is currently hard at work on a book on Ireland and the English Romantics.

INDEX

CPSIA information can be obtained at www.ICGtesting.com
Printed in the USA
LVOW080915020512

280023LV00005B/1/P

9 780230 114487